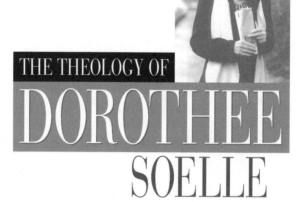

THE THEOLOGY OF

DOROTHEE

SOELLE

THE THEOLOGY OF

DOROTHEE

SOELLE

Sarah K. Pinnock
EDITOR

TRINITY PRESS INTERNATIONAL
A Continuum imprint
HARRISBURG • LONDON • NEW YORK

In memory of Dorothee Soelle
September 30, 1929 – April 27, 2003

Trinity Press International, P.O. Box 1321, Harrisburg, PA 17105
Trinity Press International is a member of the Continuum International Publishing Group.

Scripture quotations are taken from the New Revised Standard Version of the Bible, copyright 1989 by the Division of Christian Education of the National Council of the Churches of Christ in the USA. Used by permission.

Cover photo courtesy of Dorothee Soelle

Cover design: Tom Castanzo

Library of Congress Cataloging-in-Publication Data

The theology of Dorothee Soelle / Sarah K. Pinnock, editor.
    p. cm.
  ISBN 1-56338-404-3 (pbk.)
  1. Soelle, Dorothee. I. Soelle, Dorothee. II. Pinnock, Sarah Katherine.
  BX4827.S65 T53 2003
  230'.044'092—dc21

                2003010214

Printed in the United States of America

03 04 05 06 07 08   10 9 8 7 6 5 4 3 2 1

Contents

Part 3: Suffering and Redemption

Part 4: Mysticism

Part 5: Theological Liberation

Funeral Sermon

Delivered at the Worship Service of Mourning and Thanksgiving for the Life of Dorothee Soelle

by
The Right Reverend Baerbel von Wartenberg-Potter,
Bishop of Nordelbien

St. Catherine's Church, Hamburg, Germany, 5 May 2003[1]

The text of the sermon is from Rev 21:1–5a:

Then I saw a new heaven and a new earth; for the first heaven and the first earth had passed away, and the sea was no more. And I saw the holy city, the new Jerusalem, coming down out of heaven from God, prepared as a bride adorned for her husband. And I heard a loud voice from the throne saying, "See, the home of God is among mortals. He will dwell with them; they will be his peoples, and God himself will be with them; he will wipe away every tear from their eyes. Death will be no more; mourning and crying and pain will be no more, for the first things have passed away." And the one who was seated on the throne said, "See, I am making all things new."

Dear Fulbert, dear family, dear sisters and brothers,
Two great words mark this hour: *death* and *love*. Death has taken away one of the great women of our time, Dorothee Soelle. In a swift move, death has made many of us orphans. We will sorely miss the living, prophetic, and poetic voice of this woman. Death and love: these two words have brought together this large congregation from many parts of Germany and the globe. Love for Dorothee has brought us here, and love for what she wanted to bring close to

us, in ever new ways: the liberating gospel of Jesus Christ—the humble God and poor human being from Nazareth—as well as the living experience of God who had become for her, in a mystical sense, more and more "*ohn' Warum,*" without why or wherefore. Her profound longing for authentic encounter with God spoke in a strong voice to our self-centered and merciless time.

Dorothee Soelle died in the midst of Eastertide. What a contradiction! Easter is a joyous time. Birds build their nests, and trees are in foliage. That first Easter morning, women visited the tomb and found it empty. "Death," we ask in outrage, "what are you doing here today?" We had just become accustomed to the idea that, after her first heart attack, Dorothee had once again recovered. She wanted to finish her book on death and mysticism. Everywhere new life begins—and she dies! No liturgical season in the church calendar could be more inappropriate for this sudden parting.

Dear family, this death touches your personal life deeply, as it does the lives of the broad community that Dorothee gathered around her. People cry on the telephone as if they suffered personally. Countless e-mails bearing the sad news crisscross the World Wide Web from New York to Soweto and from Seoul to La Paz. One voice says: "My theological existence is unthinkable without her." Another voice says: "Hearing her speak was one of the great moments of my life. She gave me such infinite comfort." People read Dorothee's poems to each other and it is always the same: Light shines into their lives. Her words are like bread—texts full of clarity and concrete life experience, honest, nourishing, and illuminating. In her texts, she tried and tested much of life, and lived it in an exemplary fashion. She also stumbled and fell. But her message is: "Such is life. Live!" I learned that from her long ago.

We shall experience what she herself came to realize, namely, that there is "no measure that can fathom how utterly we miss you."

A new heaven and a new earth is what the seer John, exiled on Patmos, describes in the great vision of the book of Revelation. It is a new earth, differently constituted than the one we are accustomed to, with a different way of living and thinking, a new way of loving, acting, and sharing. It is the newness of life in accordance with Christ that will make the earth into a new creation for all living beings. Dorothee's thinking was shaped fundamentally by this vision, and she tirelessly guided us along this path. That is why we will especially miss her in the church and in society.

Our old earth is terribly drenched in blood, torn by war, and damaged by dying forests and withering fields, as Dorothee observed bluntly and incisively. On our old earth, child soldiers in Africa learn to kill with easy-to-use and easily available guns made in Europe. Here wars are waged with fantastic precision, as happened just recently (in Iraq), wars that feed the imperialistic myth of the omnipotence of weapons and hasten the breakdown of international law.

On this earth, the unheeded cries of children, whose mothers have no bread to give them, die inaudibly.

How eloquently she also spoke of the new heaven which we need because—as she stated in her unforgetable and hotly debated address to the general assembly of the World Council of Churches in Vancouver, 1983—"Our country (Germany) has soiled history with the smell of gas."[2]

She did not only work for a new heaven and a new earth. She also sang, wrote poetry, loved and laughed, and assembled people together. What she strove for was not some *fata morgana*, some mirage from the beyond; rather, it was to concretely embed this vision in our hearts and hands. Such vision must reach beyond one's own death, because our efforts are always piecemeal, and because too many hope-filled projects fail. A new Jesrusalem is part of this hope and vision, rising up from the ashes of all that is called hate, violence, greed, and godlessness.

The new heaven and the new earth were major themes during her life. Another theme was finding a new language for speaking about, and with, God.

On this subject, John the Apocalyptist observes: "Behold, the home of God is among mortals." God leaves the heavenly throne in order to live closely and in solidarity with humans. Theologically, Dorothee Soelle rediscovered this new home, the abode and tent of God. She articulated it anew and gave it a language that is once again capable of meaning. "God doesn't want to be alone," she would say in her casual manner. In order to establish this new language and these new images, the old language and images had to be demolished. The new could not be had without the demise of the old. This bold move generated much scolding, and even open hatred. Not one theological faculty in Germany offered her a professorial position, something I regard as one of the most remarkable blunders in post-World War II church history.

Yet like no one else, Dorothee Soelle shed theological light on the godforsaken darkness of the twentieth century. After Auschwitz, and after the "death of God," she enabled people in our churches and congregations with honesty to say God, think God, and believe in God. She cleared a path from the darkness of history into light for herself, and for us women, thereby actively preventing her own and our exodus from the churches. Dorothee was a church woman, despite all assertions to the contrary. When I asked her whether I should take up the office of bishop of Nordelbien, she replied, "Yes! Of course you should."

She was all ears and an attentive learner when it came to her grandchildren's theology. There she learned amazement. She loved to tell the children about God using the image of a baker's oven full of love.

Both the new heaven and the new earth, and finding new language for God, were at the heart of her life. The arduous road she traveled held many contradictions, which you, Fulbert, named in the controversial dialogues you two had about how one can believe in God atheistically.[3] But her journey was sustained by the certainty that we also may know today: "God will wipe away every tear from their eyes." God offers comfort to those who weep. How many tears Dorothee Soelle herself shed! How many of us weep over painful events, or over life's joys accompanied by suffering. "Give me the gift of tears / Give me the gift of speech / Give me the water of life," she wrote in a poem.[4] With all of these gifts, she comforts us even today. For all this, we can only thank God.

There is just one sentence in the wonderful Revelation of John that Dorothee would not have read gladly. John prophesies that "the sea will be no more." (In Near Eastern thought, the sea is a place of menacing evil.) Nothing was as much her element as water. When Dorothee arrived at a lake, she would immediately kick off her shoes, undress, and plunge into the waters. There she received a strength that only the elements are able to provide. I once said to her, "You know, some day you are going to grow gills."

In death, she wanted to become a droplet in the sea of God's love. She said that would be all she wanted, that was her mystical image of death. For every droplet increases the power of the immeasurable ocean, just as every droplet also enters into the depth of being. If she has become such a droplet, then—as I said to Fulbert—she certainly is a golden droplet in the sea of God's love and justice. But perhaps we may also grasp this image as a way of naming the wish that is in all of us: to return to where we come from. Our life begins in a small sack filled with water, in the womb. The Hebrew word for womb is *rechem,* which is embedded in the word for mercy or compassion, *rachamim.* The divine, motherly water of life is the origin of all the mercy God himself gives us. To return there is our wish.

Today, with deep gratitude, we give back into God's hands the rich, grace-filled, and great life of Dorothee Soelle. She was one of the Easter morning women. She knew about graves. In solidarity with all the Easter people of every century, she experienced and endured the personal and collective darkness of our country's history, at times with a shrill and hurtful voice. She wrestled with painful questions, such as when someone from the third world asked her, "Mrs. Soelle, why do you begin your reflections only with Auschwitz and ignore the fact that the Germans first exterminated the Hereros in Namibia?"

Near the end of our text from Revelation there is this promise: "Death shall be no more, mourning and crying and pain will be no more." In all of of life's brokenness, Dorothee's life demonstrated that mourning can be transformed into strength. Her life confirmed the Easter structure of human existence, which transforms the mourning of abandonment into a cry of indignation, and the mourning of death into the quietness and certainty of nearness to God.

When I hosted an Easter discussion group two weeks ago at my home in Lübeck, Dorothee remarked, "Everything carries on; that's what death is about."

Her word to us is: Everything carries on. Love carries on, praying and doing justice carry on. Bread is still baked. Children are conceived and born. The grain of wheat will fall into the soil and grow in the field, and in the heart of humans. We shall carry on reading Dorothee's books and she will carry on speaking to us. She has passed the torch to us: We must love and work for the reign of God and its justice. We shall find our own ways of keeping that word.

Her mortal body is still here in our midst. But by now she will be in the bosom of Abraham or Sarah, or perhaps be a droplet in the sea of God's love, or perhaps be seated with all the impoverished of the world at the heavenly banquet table. All in all, she is close to God. Her name—unmistakable and ineradicable—will be written in the book of life.

Therefore, there is no more appropriate time to die than Easter time, when everything continues near God, and with God. "The beauteous day of Easter! You people, come to the light. Today Christ who has been buried emerges out of his cell."[5]

All of you, wherever you come from, you dear Fulbert, dear children and grandchildren, dear relatives, come to the light!

We thank God for the wonderful, rich, difficult, conflict-filled, and beautiful life of Dorothee Soelle, a true prophet of our time. We thank God for the love and dependability that graced her marriage, and for the joy that she experienced with her children and grandchildren. The name Dorothee means "God's gift." That indeed she was and that she remains. We shall certainly not bury her great hopes with her in the grave. That is a promise. We trust in the word of Revelation, "Behold, I make all things new." Amen.

Notes

1. At the age of seventy-three, Dorothee Soelle suffered a heart attack during the night and died the next morning, on Sunday, April 27, 2003. At the time, she was leading a weekend conference in southern Germany on the theme of *"Gott und das Glück"* ("God and Felicity") with her husband Fulbert Steffensky. She had recovered from a previous heart attack only a few months earlier. The collected essays in this volume were submitted to the press before her death. Many thanks go to Martin Rumscheidt for translating the text of the funeral sermon at short notice for inclusion in this volume.

2. Dorothee Soelle, *Against the Wind: Memoir of a Radical Christian* (trans. Barbara and Martin Rumscheidt; Minneapolis: Fortress, 1999), 93.

3. Dorothee Soelle and Fulbert Steffensky, *Zwietracht in Eintracht. Ein Religionsgespräch* (Zurich: Pendo Verlag, 1996).

4. Dorothee Soelle, *Ich will nicht auf tausend Messern gehen* (Munich: Deutscher Taschenbuch Verlag, 1987), 103.

5. "Der schöne Ostertag! Ihr Menschen kommt ins Helle. Christ, der gegraben lag, geht heut aus seiner Zelle." *Evangelisches Gesangbuch,* no. 117.

Introduction

Sarah K. Pinnock

Dorothee Soelle is a pioneering figure. She is a leader among German Christians in grappling with the collective shame of Auschwitz. She is a poet expressing utopian longings for a better world and the beauty of the here and now. She is a political activist and a socialist, an admirer of Karl Marx, and a liberation theologian who challenges doctrinal orthodoxy and institutional complacency. She is a mystic offering a vision of faith for people disillusioned with bourgeois Christianity.

Born in 1929 in Cologne, Germany, Soelle lived through the Nazi era and the bombings of World War II. Her parents were strongly opposed to the Nazi government in private, although they told young Dorothee to keep quiet about their political views—or else they warned that she would end up in a concentration camp. Her parents had some Jewish friends, and in 1943 they agreed to hide a Jewish woman in their attic for six weeks, an act that emphasized to Dorothee the dangers of Nazi prejudice. As a teenager during the war, Dorothee avidly kept a diary in which she found refuge from the military conflict and a creative outlet for her thoughts. Admiration for literary classicism and romanticism allowed her to construct a positive German identity apart from Nazi politics and ideology. She fell in love with the poetry of Goethe, Rilke, and Hölderlin, and the music of Bach and Beethoven.

Decades later, in a talk entitled "To Love Bach in a World of Torture," Soelle ponders the connections between high German culture and Nazi culture. She

1

asks, How could SS officials gas Auschwitz prisoners by day and enjoy Bach in the evenings? In posing such a question, she approaches the issue of her own teenage complicity in the Nazi cultural paradigm. In response, she differentiates between various receptions of German classics. She argues that for Nazi officials Bach signified security, order, and piety toward authority, not to mention pride in German achievement. For her, Bach expresses worship and aesthetic self-transcendence. Especially Bach's choral works, such as "St. Matthew's Passion," convey Lutheran theology and piety in a way that is emotionally and imaginatively accessible. She asserts that Bach's music is liberating and life changing if it is not privatized or compartmentalized but opened outwards toward inclusive love and community.[1]

Looking back at her teenage war years, Soelle observes that her stance was apolitical and tinged with poetic romanticism. Yet she was not entirely innocent of Nazi influence. When she discovered that her father was one-quarter Jewish, shortly after the end of the war, she was initially upset and embarrassed, and tried to keep the news secret. Not long after, she unlearned the implicit dichotomy between Jew and German that she had absorbed while growing up. Gradually, she began to affirm her distant Jewish connection.

After the Second World War, Soelle's education focused on philosophy and literary studies. As a young adult, she avidly absorbed the works of Kierkegaard, Nietzsche, Heidegger, Sartre, Camus, Freud, and Marcuse. In the late 1940s and the 1950s, the main intellectual option for middle-class members of her generation was existentialist nihilism, which expressed disillusionment with social institutions and humanity in general. During this era, under the guidance of her high school teacher, Marie Veit, she was introduced to existentialist Christianity. She also discovered the writings of Dietrich Bonhoeffer, a truly "political" Christian who became a leading exemplar of faith for post-Holocaust German Christians. As a budding theologian, Soelle was greatly influenced by Rudolf Bultmann, Friedrich Gogarten, and Martin Buber through their writings and personal communications.

Moving deeper into theological studies, Soelle completed her doctoral dissertation in literary criticism in 1954 on the vigils of the medieval theologian Bonaventure. Later, in 1971, she received her Habilitation in philosophy after struggling to gain approval and promotion from her superiors. Her career illustrates a number of negative factors operating within the German universities of her time: patriarchal hierarchy, denigration of women's academic abilities, the dichotomization of passionate activism and scholarly objectivity, and the unacceptability of childrearing as a career interruption. Just a year before passing her Habilitation, she gave birth to her fourth child, which was perceived in university circles as rather unseemly and inappropriate conduct for an academic. When Union Theological Seminary offered her a professorial position in 1975,

Soelle relocated to New York City and quickly discovered politically active Christian allies as well as a receptive audience for her theology. By the 1980s, she ceased to call her work "political" theology and preferred the label "liberation," in solidarity with liberation movements in Latin America and other developing countries. She developed a "first world" liberation theology in conversation with "third world" struggles.[2] From early on, her political orientation was geared toward global economic justice, rather than solely German or European socialist concerns. Until 1987, she taught at Union but lived for part of each year with her husband Fulbert Steffensky in Hamburg.

Today she has a prominent reputation as the foremost feminist German Protestant Christian theologian. Her academic recognition is arguably greatest in North America, whereas in Germany, her popular reputation is most significant among nonacademic church readers and audiences. In North America her writings are canonical within the Christian post-Holocaust, feminist, and liberation movements, signaling pivotal developments in twentieth-century theology. The same is true in Germany to the extent that these fields are taken seriously in university theology faculties. Given her success, it is striking that she is not uniformly well known in theological circles. Among German departments of theology, there is a disdain for her *unwissenschaftliche*, "unscientific" or "unacademic" theology. Her work is studied in seminars on women's theology or liberation theology but is less likely to be covered in seminars on systematic theology or modern Protestant theology. This distancing from status quo German theology is not entirely unwelcome or unprovoked. Soelle deliberately eschews a traditional academic format with copious footnotes and painstaking historical justification. She considers such a style remote from lived faith and contemporary praxis: both the praxis of faith and mysticism, and the political praxis of resistance. She is not overly cautious about doctrinal innovation. In contrast, so-called "scientific" theology tends to conserve and consolidate orthodox positions. Whereas most scholars write for an academic audience, Soelle does not, nor does she necessarily care to defend her method in ivory tower debates. Her theology is pervasively practical, although she employs innovative methodological approaches worthy of academic study. Her writing style suits her priorities, which are social and political, and her audience, which extends far beyond the academy.

Although Soelle is categorized as a feminist theologian, it was only after leaving Germany for New York that she became involved directly with the women's movement. She gradually began to admit the need for feminist consciousness alongside her already well-developed consciousness of social class and nationality. It is interesting and surprising, from an American perspective, that she associated her difficulties in advancing through the German university system more with her politics than her gender, since the German promotion system is so evidently patriarchal. The transition to feminist involved some tension and discomfort. Soelle objected to the exclusion of men from women's spaces, and to militant feminists who labeled homemaking and motherhood as oppressive. She resisted separatist and secularist forms of feminism.[3] Ironically, her theology was implicitly feminist even prior to her engagement with the feminist movement. However, she often reached feminist conclusions driven by nongendered concerns. For instance, her rejection of divine omnipotence and orthodox theism did not begin with opposition to patriarchy or the use of masculine pronouns for God. It was reflection on Auschwitz that spurred her to reject the notion of a God who allows suffering for good reasons and a God who has the power to intervene but stands aloof and merely watches the annihilation of life. Her mystical orientation led her to conceive God as more immanent than transcendent, articulated using nongendered symbols for God, rather than appealing to feminine attributes of the divine or the notion of Goddess. She also found fuel for her critique of authoritarian theism in German philosophy—in Kant's critique of religious heteronomy, Nietzsche's critique of herd morality, and Lessing's biblical historicism. In seeking to create a political German theology after the moral failure of Christianity tragically demonstrated by the Holocaust, Soelle's work was inspired as much or more by philosophy, literature, and the social sciences as by traditional Christian thought.

Living in America gave Soelle many new theological opportunities. She found New York dynamic and frenetic, overflowing with creativity and cultural diversity. The poverty of the streets affected her greatly as she pondered the immense wealth and global power of America. She experienced deep loneliness when separated from her husband and children, but also great encouragement from her Christian community. The openness of the university setting at Union Theological Seminary was refreshing, demonstrating the potential for nonhierarchical and liberalized academic structures. Already while living in Germany, she had been highly critical of U.S. capitalism and militarism. Her trip to Vietnam in 1972 had exposed her to the brutality of U.S. imperialism, anticommunism, and military violence against civilians. But until moving to New York, she was unaware that her critical views were shared by certain groups of American Christians, who were part of an activist counterculture that for the most part was hidden from the mass media.[4] In the 1980s, Soelle traveled to Nicaragua, where she met Ernesto Cardenal and observed the Sandinista liberation movement directly. With America on the wrong side, against liberation, Soelle nevertheless found solidarity with American and Nicaraguan Christians working for the rights of the poor. In the German peace movement, she had felt apologetic for being a Christian, given the conservative profile of the church. However, she encountered many Christians active in resistance while living in the United States.

Since resigning from her position at Union Theological Seminary in 1987, Soelle held a number of guest professorships at German universities and traveled widely. She was tremendously involved in the ecumenical movement, locally in Hamburg and nationally as a member of the *Evangelische Kirche in Deutschland* (EKD). She was also active in the biannual *Kirchentag*, an assembly of Protestant clergy and laypeople held in the former East and West Germany. At these church meetings, discussion of theology and the Bible is applied to current issues such as justice, free trade, unemployment, immigration, and poverty. Her causes as an activist ranged from anti-war and anti-nuclear protests to promotion of "fair trade" consumer goods as a way to ameliorate the injustices of capitalism toward workers. Her marriage to Fulbert Steffensky and her relationships with her four children and grandchildren provided continual sources of deep meaning and joy. It is not contradictory to observe that Soelle has a deep sense of rootedness in home and family but also an international network that often took her away from home.

On April 27, 2003, Soelle died at the age of seventy-three in Bad Boll, southern Germany, while leading a workshop at the *Evangelische Akademie* with her husband Fulbert. She gave a talk on *"Gott und das Glück"* ("God and Felicity") and on the night before she died, she read aloud from her poetry at a musical celebration entitled *"Vergiss das Beste nicht!"* While some poems dealt with war and peace in protest of the war in Iraq, the evening ended with a message of hope as she read her published letter to her grandchildren, "Don't Forget the Best!" with tears in her eyes.[5] During the night she suffered a heart attack and was taken to the hospital. She died with her husband sitting beside her singing her favorite hymns. Her last writing project, left unfinished, was a book manuscript on the mysticism of death.

The Structure of the Book

This collection is the first English-language volume of essays on Dorothee Soelle's life and work. It brings together three recent pieces by Soelle, newly translated into English by Barbara and Martin Rumscheidt, as well as twelve essays giving detailed analysis of her corpus. In part 1, the opening selection is a lecture entitled "The World Can Be Different" delivered at the University of Hamburg one month after the September 11, 2001, terrorist attacks in the United States. Soelle mourns the victims but moves beyond shock and grief to situate the event as a symptom of global conflict and injustice. She deplores the militaristic response to terrorism that seeks revenge and regime change in the interest of security while exacerbating hatred, violence, and political instability. The second text, "The Guarantor of Poor Peoples's Rights," is a speech given at the 2002 annual *Brecht Tage*. Inspired by Brecht's unflinching social critique,

Soelle meditates on the connections between protest, prayer, and injustice. She contrasts the perspective of faith with the reigning scientific discourse of contemporary society. The scientific languages of militarism, science, and medicine will increasingly dehumanize and destroy. However, faith language that admits to divine power beyond our own can be a saving antidote in a world governed by the values of profit, efficiency, and success. These two unpublished talks give readers a sense of her political perspective on the current international situation, in which terrorism has upstaged issues of economic justice and human rights. The third translated selection, "Breaking the Ice of the Soul," is taken from the collection of essays called *Mutanfälle (Attacks of Courage)* first published in 1993.[6] Inspired by Hölderlin's phrase *"Dichterisch wohnet der Mensch"* ("Poetically lives the human being"), Soelle reflects on the close relationship between poetry and prayer, and explicates the role of literature for theology, spanning the genres of myth, narrative, poetry, drama, and dialogue. While she has always integrated these diverse genres in her writing, this essay takes on the meta-level task of explicating their functions in shaping a distinctive theological method.

The twelve commissioned essays are by authors who approach Soelle's writings with diverse interests and backgrounds. Three contributors are German scholars and associates of Soelle currently living in North America: Andrea Bieler, Martin Rumscheidt, and Luise Schottroff. Others are colleagues who have known Soelle since her time at Union Theological Seminary: Anne Llewellyn Barstow, Christine E. Gudorf, Beverly Wildung Harrison, Carter Heyward, and Rosemary Radford Ruether. The remaining contributors know Soelle primarily through the study of her writings: Flora A. Keshgegian, Nancy Hawkins, Dianne L. Oliver, and myself. My inspiration for this edited project began with library research followed by personal meetings with Soelle in Hamburg in 1997 through 1998, and ultimately it was catalyzed by the need to enlarge secondary scholarship investigating her contribution to contemporary theology. Together these essays cover Soelle's work in the areas of biblical, poetic, postmodern, literary, liturgical, feminist, political, and liberatory theological reflection—although even this lengthy list of adjectives does not exhaust the scope of Soelle's interests and influence. As the first collection of its kind, this book analyzes the development, depth, plausibility, and contemporary relevance of her ideas. It covers all eras of her career and all major themes in her writing, shedding fresh light on her biography as well as her publications.

The twelve contributors' essays are divided under four thematic headings. "New Forms of Theological Language" (part 2) explores how Soelle's work escapes the moribund strictures of orthodox and modern theology by experimenting with literary forms. Luise Schottroff, a feminist New Testament scholar and close collaborator with Dorothee Soelle, traces the emergence of

Soelle's theology starting with the political awakenings that occurred in the German churches in the late 1960s. Schottroff reflects on her unique approach to theology as a biblical hermeneutic of liberation, in contradistinction to the dominant theology of the churches and universities. Soelle rejects traditional Lutheran notions of sin as individual powerlessness and bondage. According to Schottroff, Soelle's work is deliberately formulated in opposition to hegemonic German theology, which is alternately indifferent or antagonistic toward such innovations. Schottroff recounts how the political implications of Soelle's words have at times led to exclusion by German Protestant church authorities. For instance, Soelle was not invited to appear on the program of the biannual *Kirchentag* conference in 1985 and 1987, although the governing board later relented. Yet Soelle is not a post-Christian thinker who dismisses the church. Her theology is a biblical hermeneutic of hunger arising from a personal, social, and political context. She employs prayer and poetry to translate Scripture into living words for today's language. In Soelle's hands, the Bible teaches contemporary men and women the languages of lament and despair, hope and resurrection, and profound searching for God.

Andrea Bieler explores Soelle's theology of prayer from the perspective of liturgical studies and Christian worship. She notes an evolution away from a "crisis" approach to prayer in the 1960s, found in the Political Night Prayers held in Cologne. This political liturgical emphasis suppressed nonpedagogical aspects of prayer such as worship and intersession. The crisis perspective is a-theistic and historical, influenced by the "death of God" movement and Bonhoeffer's "religionless" Christianity. Bieler argues that it loses the capacity of prayer to express the fragmentation of experience, and overemphasizes the positive utopian content of prayer. However, in Soelle's later writings on mysticism, she moves past the functionalist, political-crisis orientation of prayer and finds resources for supplication and imagination in negative theology. The mystical resources of language bridge the paradox of intimacy and ultimacy and meet the needs of contemporary Christians for meaningful worship. God is neither privatized, as in bourgeois faith, nor distanced, as in orthodox theism. Rather, God becomes both a comfort in danger and a challenge to complacency. After September 11, argues Bieler, both dimensions of prayer are essential in order to balance American fear of terrorism with moral sensitivity to the suffering of victims of anti-terrorist retaliation.

Martin Rumscheidt maintains that Soelle's theology bridges the abyss that has existed since the Enlightenment between academic theology and aesthetic language. In modern German culture, theology's function is subsumed and displaced by poets such as Hölderlin or Rilke who convey the search for the transcendent in more compelling terms than academic theologians. Rumscheidt agrees with Soelle that poetry is the key to contemporary God language in view of the Holocaust and the disillusionment with Western institutions and values. Entering into dialogue with Soelle's close contemporaries—Luise Schottroff, Heinrich Böll, Johannes Bobrowski, and other German thinkers—he defines the function of theology as democratic poetry that serves the process of humanization, expressing mourning, love, and transitoriness. Although some poetry and theology may be apolitical, these genres have immense potential to draw the listener into critical dialogue with the Word of God, recognized by Soelle. Poetic theological language embodies a rhythm of call and response that reflects social and religious ambiguities standing in tension. Soelle's aesthetic literary expression inspires ordinary people to affirm their creativity and become poets through prayer. Rumscheidt concludes that Soelle has a "calling in a higher sense"—a calling to enter into conversation with God and to point others toward visions of justice.

Part 3, entitled "Suffering and Redemption," explores themes prominent in Soelle's theology since its inception. Her approach to suffering operates on doctrinal, pastoral, psychological, and mystical levels that make it a highly influential aspect of her thought. Flora A. Keshgegian engages the field of trauma theory from a theological perspective in order to shed critical light on Soelle's phenomenology of suffering and her prescriptive conclusions about the meaning of suffering. Trauma theory is based on the work of social theorists, philosophers, psychologists, and other scholars involved with victims of persecution, sexual abuse, torture, or genocide. These scholars observe that trauma is an experience of loss that eludes conscious presentation; in fact, the traumatic past may be experienced as absence. Keshgegian points out that Soelle's disapproval of silent suffering and her encouragement of active resistance miss the legitimate role of silence as a survival strategy, and her persistence in finding active meaning in suffering does not acknowledge dimensions of suffering that are unredeemable. In her mystical approach, Soelle seeks divine presence and memory while disregarding how divine absence and dissociation may persist through trauma. Her insights may indeed relate to certain cases of suffering involving Christian subjects, but her mystical resistance framework has limited application.

Suffering is fundamental to Soelle's Christology developed in her early book, *Christ the Representative*. Dianne L. Oliver reflects on the pervasive importance of Christology that remains consistent despite key shifts in emphasis during Soelle's theological career. Soelle begins with a Christology centered on the singular figure of Jesus as "representative" of humanity before God, and of God to humanity. She then moves toward liberation theology, finally turning her attention to the ongoing suffering in the world and political understandings of Jesus' death. When divine power is envisioned as empowerment of persons, rather than intervention that occurs with no role for human beings, the cross becomes not the objective locus of salvation but a symbol of situations of oppression and resistance throughout history. In Soelle's post-theism, the power of God's love in the world is dependent on human actions and not only on Christ's intervention. Interestingly, while Jesus the Christ does not play a large role in recent writings such as *The Silent Cry*, Oliver notes that incarnation undergirds her claims about God's human presence. In the end, Soelle's Christology is fundamental to her mystical understanding of radicalized divine immanence and human responsibility for enacting redemption.

The question of whether Soelle is a postmodern thinker is related to her theological innovations in dealing with poetics and mysticism and her rejection of modern approaches to theism. My essay, "A Postmodern Response to Suffering after Auschwitz," explores the connections between postmodernism and the rejection of theodicy, tracing responses to suffering through the post-Holocaust, liberation, and mystical arenas of Soelle's theology. Consideration of Holocaust suffering is formative to her critique of theodicy as a sadistic affirmation of divine cruelty. Her response appeals to divine suffering as a sustaining, but not justificatory, support for Christian faith. Addressing victims, Soelle counsels a response to suffering that involves "love of reality" making no demands on God's favor. Addressing Holocaust bystanders, she seeks to demonstrate that true faith is not apathetic but political. In contrast with other post-Holocaust theologians, she does not focus on the evils of perpetrators who cause suffering, or the place of Israel in church history. By eschewing theodicy, Soelle relocates discussion of evil and suffering to the level of narrative discourse at which responses are judged by their liberating potential. Her practical approach has influenced later generations of feminist liberation theologians, who formulate spiritualities of suffering and resistance that focus on action instead of explanation.

Part 4, "Mysticism," deals with Soelle's appropriation of historical and contemporary mystics to create her own synthetic mystical vision. Christine E. Gudorf explores how Soelle shares life patterns and insights with medieval women mystics, such as Teresa of Avila, who are intensely socially active while deeply engaged in seeking God. Like her mystical predecessors, Soelle claims authority independent of hierarchical institutions and has been perceived as being a threat to the German church establishment. Gudorf compares Soelle with thirteenth-century Beguine mystic Marguerite Porete who claimed authority from God to take her mystical vision and message to the common people and who was eventually condemned to death by the Inquisition for her audacity. Gudorf argues that "feminine" forms of spirituality articulated by medieval women are affirmed by Soelle and also echoed by "second wave" feminist liberation theologians from developing countries who accept differences between men and women ignored by the liberal feminism of the 1960s. Where medieval mystics might instruct Soelle concerns the painful dimensions of mystical life. Gudorf observes that the agony of distance from God modeled by Beguine mystic Mechthild of Magdeburg appears infrequently in *The Silent Cry,* in comparison with mystical jubilation. To reflect the full range of mystical reality, Gudorf counsels that Soelle would do well to pay more attention to articulating longing, emptiness, and unfulfillment alongside joy and ecstasy.

Meister Eckhart is the mystic most often cited in Soelle's writings from her earlier works, notably *Suffering,* to her most recent book. Nancy Hawkins points out that Meister Eckhart is a political mystic, from Soelle's viewpoint, because he affirms the ability of the laity to be empowered by God through religious devotion. Also, he challenges the hierarchy of the church on matters of institutional authority and theological orthodoxy, as did the Beguines. To advance individual inspiration by God as Eckhart did is what Soelle refers to as "democratizing" mysticism, giving religious authority to ordinary people. Eckhart disputes the orthodox Catholic position on God's omnipotence and aseity, rejecting "theism" as Soelle does. To imprison God in language not only creates dangerous ideologies but diminishes God's greatness. She often cites Eckhart's phrase "without why" to refer to a faith that relinquishes intentions, material objects, and goals in order to become united with the ground of being, God. For Soelle, Eckhart's mysticism fosters participation in nonviolent resistance without frustration or disillusionment. In contrast, although Eckhart emphasizes withdrawal from the world and mystical union with God, Soelle concentrates on the inward journey as fuel for outward movement into activism. She is controversial both for reading a worldly political message into Eckhart's writings and for insisting that all true mysticism involves resistance.

Exploring Soelle's hypotheses that mysticism is political and that political activists are mystics, Anne Llewellyn Barstow details concrete instances of Soelle's involvement in the peace movement. Two pivotal events that sparked Soelle's activism were NATO's placement of Intercontinental Ballistic Missiles in Germany, and the Sandinista Revolution in Nicaragua in 1979. Anti-war and anti-nuclear protests have been central components of Soelle's political Christian response to Germany's militaristic history culminating in World War II, although her stance is a minority viewpoint among German (and American) churches. Soelle accompanied Barstow to Nicaragua, where they witnessed Christian churches striving to make a socialist political order true to the biblical ideas of justice and love. Having together monitored the elections in 1990 in which the socialist Sandinistas were voted out of office, Barstow can relate her own frustration and discouragement to Soelle's insistence that activists must rely on mystical faith to sustain hope. However, Barstow observes that despite the obvious autobiographical tone of Soelle's reflections on mysticism and resistance, Soelle does not actually reveal many details or incidents of her own mystical encounters with God. Is modesty the reason? Or privacy? Or reliance on the collective testimony of other mystics? Rather than describe personal mystical experiences, Soelle primarily discusses her activism and cites narratives of mysticism and resistance that inspire her.

Part 5, "Theological Liberation," contains essays by American contemporaries of Soelle who advocate feminism and liberation in their own theological writings and who view Soelle as a fellow traveler on the journey. Rosemary Radford Ruether surveys features of Soelle's theology that are distinctively feminist in departure from twentieth-century German theology. She recounts participating in a conference with Soelle at which they agreed on many issues, such as condemning U.S. neo-colonialist manipulation of international affairs, but disagreed sharply on the state of Israel. German memory of the Holocaust makes it difficult for Soelle to condemn Israeli use of force, according to Ruether. She situates Soelle's theology as a refutation of Barthian neo-orthodoxy and liberal existentialist theology—both are impotent regarding social oppression, harmful effects of a market economy, and militarism. Ruether agrees with Soelle's antipathy towards "Christofacism" of the New Christian Right in the United States. She asserts that Soelle's liberation vision is even more urgent after September 11, which has increased the self-righteousness of the "good guys" and polarization of "bad guys," while the peace movement faces even greater obstacles in light of public fears about terrorism. Despite the fact that *The Silent Cry* focuses on individual examples of mystical resistance, Ruether argues that Soelle does not make mystical inspiration an end in itself but a basis for creating prophetic communities of peace and justice.

Carter Heyward interweaves reflection on her personal and intellectual relations with Soelle with investigation of tensions and "crossing over" in Soelle's work. To Heyward, Soelle is a theological mentor and a contemporary in formulating new visions of God rejecting transcendent theism. When they first met, Soelle abruptly asked, "Why are you a priest?"—a question that not only was unsettling but also betrayed a concern that affects Soelle deeply: How can I remain a Christian despite disappointments with the theology and politics of institutional churches, particularly, the lack of action for social justice? As feminist Christians, both Heyward and Soelle are untroubled about blurring the boundaries between God and humanity—as divine love, God is vulnerable and limited, yet God's love is a sacred power, efficacious and totally different from the social and political forces in the world. Being made in God's image means that God is like us, even to the point of suffering. Heyward observes that gradually Soelle's theological writings have become more narrative and poetic as she moves beyond critical reactions to orthodox and liberal forms of modern theology. Whereas in her earlier writings her poetic and theological writings were parallel but often separate venues of expression, Soelle has gradually developed a poetic-political theology. This literary theological voice allows Soelle to cross over standard dichotomies between suffering and acceptance, mysticism and resistance, creativity and justice.

Beverly Wildung Harrison argues that Soelle's poetic liberation approach is distinctively postmodernist. Her work overcomes the divide between Christian ethics and systematic theology that has chronically thwarted the potential social relevance of the latter field. Reading Soelle earlier in her career gave Harrison hope not only for causes of peace and justice but also for the potential of Christian theology to speak to a contemporary audience. To fill its highest purpose, theology should not be primarily explanatory but evocative, using poetic communication to fuel visions of wholeness and struggles against social wrongs. Comparing Soelle with the Jewish lesbian poet Adrienne Rich, Harrison explores how both writers use poetic imagination to reclaim their religious traditions and find spiritual resources to challenge imperialism and injustice. Soelle is part of the "first wave" of postmodern Christian theologians, both in ruling out the possibility of noetically privileged truth claims and in using critical literary discourses to expose hegemonic power structures. But while many postmodernists employ obscure technical styles of rhetorical critique that are largely relativistic and apolitical, Soelle appropriates the tradition of German critical theory to construct a moral response that is neither privatized nor cynical. With poetic conviction, her theology effectively indicts neo-liberal "free" market capitalism, exposing it as an ideology promoting the political interests of the powerful. Soelle exposes the collective social amnesia blocking critical insight into such ideologies of domination, using creative theological expression to inspire the quest for justice and the flourishing of all creation.

Scholars best acquainted with Soelle's theology tend to be admirers, sympathetic with her conclusions. This collection of secondary scholarship on her work displays this correlation without dissimulation or apology. Together these essays communicate the vibrancy of Soelle's contribution to theology in Germany and America. They also reveal important temporal and conceptual parallels among authors engaged in feminist and liberation thought. Just as Soelle rejects the separations between the academic, personal, and political, this book also embodies the necessity of integrating these areas to situate Christian reflection. The authors of these chapters substantially agree with Soelle's critique of modern Christian thought, her linkage of theology with current social issues, and her understanding of faith as essentially concerned with liberation. But agreement aside, various critical observations are raised in the essays that are worthy of further investigation. Three probing questions emerge that weave together the appreciative evaluations of her work. As issues that deserve further attention, I shall conclude by formulating these important concerns with parenthetical references to the contributing authors who address them.

Does Soelle portray an overly "positive" vision of faith? Arguably, her depiction of mysticism underestimates the mysticism of divine absence, especially in comparison with certain medieval women mystics such as Marguerite Porete (Gudorf). Soelle concludes that God is found in suffering and that accepting suffering makes it redemptive. In contrast, scholars who address the "trauma" of suffering suggest that barriers of silence and repression are not always overcome. In response to trauma, God may seem silent rather than present (Keshgegian). Additionally, Soelle responds to the Holocaust with the cross as divine participation in brutal human suffering. She does not deal much with suffering that is nonredemptive, nor does she attend to the evils of the perpetrators as a challenge to her estimation of the human capacity to embody God (Pinnock). Unlike other feminist thinkers responding to evil and suffering, Soelle focuses on liberation from these conditions rather than studying the barriers to release found in oppressive social situations. Nevertheless, her indebtedness to Eckhart highlights the role of negative theology in her thinking (Hawkins). In *The Silent Cry,* Soelle explores the tensions found in speech about a God who cannot be named, but this theological negation seems mainly conceptual. Especially in her political forms of prayer, Soelle leans more toward expressions of wholeness than toward expressions of the pain of absence (Bieler). Even in her mysticism, the apophatic approach to God does not necessarily encompass the utter bereavement endured by those suffering persons who feel abandoned.

A second question concerns the originality and indebtedness of Soelle's thought. What connections exist between Soelle and other thinkers, especially contemporary theologians and philosophers? In many ways, she is original, following her own muse and working independently. She does not expend much ink responding to the recent publications of others, unless they directly support and advance her own writing agenda. Moreover, she may appropriate an author for her purposes without examining how her reading might skew the intent and context of that author. Meister Eckhart is an obvious example of her selectively political reading (Hawkins). On the other hand, she is conversant with a wide range of literature, and she makes profuse references to those thinkers to whom she is indebted. Most often they are historical Christian figures or else modern German writers who are poets, philosophers, or political thinkers. Aside from Martin Buber and Dietrich Bonhoeffer, both unconventional thinkers in their own right, relatively few of her constructive influences are theologians. This demonstrates Soelle's departure from accepted norms of academic theology and her discomfort with "theo-logy" as a label that seems reductive and scholastic (Rumscheidt, Schottroff). Essays on Soelle's feminism uncover that fact that her writings rarely reference fellow feminist writers. She more often refers to male theological predecessors and draws on liberatory ideas found in medieval mysticism, poetry, Marxism, or critical theory (Gudorf, Harrison, Ruether). Given this range of reading and interest, Soelle may not recognize or respond to parallels between her ideas and those of other Christian thinkers whose proposals may be congruent with her own (Heyward). Soelle's work is unique, yet closely aligned with larger movements in contemporary Christian thought.

A final question involves the apparently spontaneous and fragmentary character of her writings. Does incomplete development in areas of Soelle's theology indicate inconsistency? Are there problematic gaps in her thought? For instance, her Christology that was so very important in her early books recedes into the background later on, even though her mysticism itself presumes a framework of divine incarnation that is implicitly, if not explicitly, christological (Oliver). It is also notable that Soelle's treatment of eros and sexuality in *The Silent Cry* is intriguing but unsatisfactorily brief. For Soelle, the erotic remains on a spiritual level referring to the eros for God (such as expressed by Marguerite Porete), which she opposes to the instrumentalism of sexual love as a form of consumerism in contemporary society.[7] Working with this dichotomy, sexual love is not explored as a gateway to sacred presence or God (Barstow). Nevertheless, Soelle's theological emphasis on divine immanence is consistent with the affirmation of embodied love (Heyward). Other topics, such as theo-poetics, suffering, feminism, the Holocaust, or the plurality of religions, also could be addressed more fully in her publications. To some scholars, this incompleteness diminishes Soelle's importance as an outstanding postwar German theologian. But to observe that Soelle could have written more may be too easy and glib. She has certainly written a great deal during her lifetime. Moreover, the postmodern character of her writings rules out appeals to the criteria of systematic completeness, epistemic privilege, or normative justification (Harrison). Her rejection of established patterns of theological writing make it problematic, if not impossible, to judge her work by conventional standards.

Dorothee Soelle's writing is driven by an urgent need to respond to her concrete situation socially, politically, and religiously. She presents a prophetic vision of faith in response to Christian moral apathy, secular indifference to the church, and the many injustices of history. Consistent with her priority on contextual thinking, Soelle's style of theology is poetic and topical. It enacts a unique form of engaged liberation theology, anchored in particular debates and political struggles. And it undoubtedly makes a major contribution to contemporary Christian thought with rich potential for future investigation, as the subsequent chapters illustrate.

Notes

1. Dorothee Soelle, *Against the Wind: Memoir of a Radical Christian* (trans. Barbara and Martin Rumscheidt; Minneapolis: Fortress, 1999), 54–56.

2. Ibid., 98–105. See also Soelle's biographical statement in Jürgen Moltmann, ed., *How I Have Changed: Reflections on Thirty Years of Theology* (trans. John Bowden; Harrisburg, Pa.: Trinity Press International, 1997), 22–28.

3. Ibid., 65–72. See also Dorothee Soelle, *The Strength of the Weak: Toward a Christian Feminist Identity* (trans. Rita and Robert Kimber; Philadelphia: Westminster Press, 1984).

4. Dorothee Soelle, *New Yorker Tagebuch* (Zurich: Pendo Verlag, 1987).

5. Soelle, "Don't Forget the Best," in *Against the Wind*, 165–68.

6. The title is a compound of the word "courage" *(Mut)* and the plural of "attack" *(Anfall)*, a word commonly used in a medical context to describe a heart attack, epileptic attack, spasm of pain, or fit of coughing. Dorothee Soelle, "Das Eis der Seele spalten: Theologie und Literatur auf der Suche nach einer neuen Sprache," in *Mutanfälle: Texte zum Umdenken* (Munich: Deutscher Taschenbuch Verlag, 1996), 187–200.

7. Dorothee Soelle, *The Silent Cry: Mysticism and Resistance* (trans. Barbara and Martin Rumscheidt; Minneapolis: Fortress, 2001), 118–21.

PART 1

RECENT WRITINGS
OF DOROTHEE SOELLE

1. The World Can Be Different[1]

An address delivered at the University of Hamburg on October 3, 2001

The attack of September 11 struck at the heart of Western civilization. That is how many people, including myself, perceived it. It was a mass murder, killing, suffocating, and burying civilians alive. Some of my friends compared the assassins to the Nazi mass murderers. I could not concur since the latter only pushed buttons to release gas without sacrificing themselves. But that does not alter the pain, or the horror. I heard of someone who took half an hour to walk down the stairs from the ninety-fourth floor and, having reached the street level, remembered that he had left behind a flight ticket. He went back up and the building collapsed. I think of this dead man whom I don't even know.

But we must think further. Mourning does not rule out analysis; it rather demands it so that we may live differently. We have been struck at the heart of civilization. What kind of heart is it? It is the financial center of Manhattan whose symbol was the World Trade Center, the symbol that stands above any other representing the modern world of business.

Is it not a heart of stone? And the Pentagon, the center of the military imposition of that very economic power, of this world's power, is it not a heart of steel? In our mourning for the many people who lost their lives that day, in our suffering with those affected and their loved ones, and also as those involved ourselves, belonging as we do to this Western civilization, we feel yet another heart beating within us, another culture next to that of stone and steel, a heart vulnerable and wounded. Now and today, it is essential that we listen to that throbbing heart.

The heart of stone and, consistent with it, the military power's heart of steel, is void of feeling for the misery of human beings, for their needs. For at least ten years now, the world's population is polarized into two groups: winners and losers. Twenty percent of humanity make up the winners; they have the right to live well and long, to buy new hearts, kidneys, livers, etc. when the old ones no longer function. Eighty percent of humanity comprise the losers; they produce little that is useful and scarcely adhere to the proper mode of consumerism. What are those people there for anyway? That is how the heart of stone thinks and feels. The economy we live in becomes ever more totalitarian. It is fundamentally different from the two totalitarian systems we know from the last century: It is more intelligent, more efficient, and above all, it is softer. It does not bellow commands but woos with a soft voice. It dictates the beat of our accelerated lives and coerces those who bear political responsibility into decisions that match its outlook. Business is more important than politics, after all! Having no feeling for the miseries and real needs of human beings, the heart of stone and the heart of steel fix the beat the world lives by, how time is to be apportioned, and what is to be considered relevant. Managers and hospital administrators simply have to work sixty hours a week, and as everyone knows, mass layoffs pump up the value of shares. In the last few years, the most important question of life has been reduced to this one: Is it economical?

Chancellor Schroeder of Germany spoke of a "declaration of war on the civilized world." His choice of words derived from Samuel Huntington's *The Clash of Civilizations?* But is it really possible to call the rich, with the heart of stone, "civilized" and the destitute "uncivilized"? Or, using George W. Bush's language directly, is there now a "monumental struggle of the good against evil"? Which heart is speaking here?

The heart of flesh knows, at least sometimes, of the reality of the destitute world. And we may perhaps have a foreboding of what is demanded in face of this barbaric catastrophe of September 11. Not military retaliation but a redirection of our way of living, an examination of the values that determine our actions. A frank acknowledgment is required of our complicity in the suffering, misery, and humiliation of those who see their enemy in us. There is talk these days of the twenty-first century's first war. As barbaric as the murder of six thousand civilians is, we ought not to shut our eyes to the fact that there already is war: the economic war of the strong and most powerful against the weak and utterly powerless. That war must finally end. It produces nothing but the hatred and destructive will of the strong, technologically perfect who can see no hope at all in the world of the destitute and their misery. A new and gruesome term has been coined: suicide assassins. This principle of revenge, in less violent form, is found in our past: Kill what kills you. (*Macht kaputt, was euch kaputt macht*) Superiority is of no help here, be it technological, economic, or military. As human beings and as an open society, we are vulnerable, and as long as the economic war goes on we will increasingly be under threat. The window of vulnerability cannot be shut! It is a fundamental mistake, widely held and transmogrified in the Reagan-Bush tradition, that it can be shut.

Noam Chomsky, one of the sharpest critics of the United States since the Vietnam War, said that the attack on the Twin Towers was "a shattering blow to the Palestinians, the poor and the oppressed . . . because it pushed their legitimate fears and complaints off the table. . . . If the American government listens to bin Laden's prayers [what a wonderfully ironic remark!] and launches a massive assault on Afghanistan or any other Muslim society, the result will be exactly what bin Laden and his associates desire: a mobilization against the West."[2] Sometimes I ask myself who is the real terrorist.

There are other voices, from the "other America," that I want to make heard now because the American opposition against Bush and Company is so little known here. This opposition took up the term *terrorist*, asking itself who the terrorists are who do the murdering in Columbia, Palestine, Kosovo, Rwanda, Bosnia, the Congo; what financiers and interests are behind those murders? And it asks who it is who has taken up the fight against the terror of the economy: who but the landless peasants of Brazil, the women in India who stand up against the biopiracy of Monsanto, those faithful Christians who still know that we, too, are to forgive our debtors. The great and growing movement against globalization from above is nonviolent; conversely, it is the lords of this world who let themselves be protected by the police-terrorists of Genoa.

An American friend, theology professor Tom Driver, wrote about "our beloved America" in response to September 11. Our nation is "a violent one, both at home and abroad. We are the world's foremost maker and seller of armaments. We have supported some of the world's most oppressive regimes, some of whom we have assisted in acts of terror against their own people. We have cultivated for ourselves a way of life that requires the impoverishment of others."[3]

The terror of the economy is clearly named here. Tim Robbins, the American film director and activist, spoke last August about the new movement of opposition to globalization in the United States. "There is a new, broad coalition of students, environmentalists, labor unions, farmers, scientists and other citizens who understand themselves as the forefront of the struggle for the future of this planet."[4] He compares this movement to the earlier struggles for the abolition of slavery in the eighteenth century. That had been essentially a nonviolent movement, initiated by Quakers and other Christians. Something similar is coming into being before our very eyes also among us here. We all can recognize how globalization from above enables new forms of slavery that make our T-shirts so very inexpensive. It took one hundred years then to abolish slavery, to put an end to child labor, and to introduce minimum wages.

That struggle waits for us now. We can learn from the history of nonviolence what is needed today. Mahatma Gandhi called this form of freedom the greatest power placed in the hands of humankind, more powerful than the most powerful weapons of destruction. We should try to believe in that power.

One of the many new movements in the United States is called "Justice Not Vengeance." People like Rosa Parks, Alice Walker, and Gloria Steinem belong to it. Cities like San Francisco and Seattle declare themselves "hate-free zones." Justice is the answer to terror that we need. Justice is deliberate, reflective, patient, and for the long term; vengeance is often hasty, its results are for the right now. Vindictiveness has no vision behind it and no future ahead of it.

Those are messages we hear from America, and we ought to make them ours here. In other words, if we do not change, we are no better. Jesus believed that whoever reaches for the sword will also die by it. The necessary conditions of life have so worsened for eighty percent of our world's people that we really ought not put up with it any longer. "Stand up for peace!" today means "Stand up for justice!" which is the basic necessity for peace. Globalization from above is a barbaric system of impoverishing the vast majority of humankind and of destroying the earth. We are in need of a different economic globalization. From below! In the interest of the earth, in the interest of the most wretched of the earth.

Notes

1. Translated by Barbara and Martin Rumscheidt.
2. *taz*, 20 September 2001, n.p. *taz* is a daily newspaper published in Germany.
3. Tom F. Driver, "Our National Tragedy: A Call to the Churches and the Nation," *Union Seminary Quarterly Review* 55, nos. 1–2 (2001): 16–17.
4. *taz*, 28 August 2001, n.p.

2. The Guarantor of Poor Peoples's Rights[1]

An address delivered during the Brecht Festival of 2002

I

I want to begin by expressing gratitude to Bertold Brecht. He is one of my great teachers, which is perhaps the most important thing one can say about a human being. I owe him a great, great deal in two respects: the literary and—"you will laugh," to use his own words[2]—the theological!

Let me tell you something about my search for literary forms of speech. Like many young girls from the educated bourgeoisie, I began to write poems at age thirteen or fourteen. Eichendorff, Hermann Hesse, and the early Rilke were my models. But when I arrived at the later Rilke, that road came to an end. I then entered university and enrolled in German studies and soon knew enough to recognize that I was linguistically disabled. Brecht rescued me from that prison; he made the everyday acceptable as well as ordinary words, free rhythms, and above all else, contradiction. In his "Bad Time for Poetry," I read

Inside me contend
Delight at the apple tree in blossom
And horror at the house-painter's speeches.[3]

I knew those contending voices only too well—in the Adenauer era and its silencing [of the immediate German past] and remilitarization of my country.

My first small volume of poetry, entitled *Meditationen und Gebrauchstexte* *[Meditations and Everyday Texts]* appeared in 1969; the material is arranged under the headings of "Wenn er wiederkommt" and "Als er kam" ["When he returns" and "When he came"]. Here is an example of that volume.

He needs you
that's all there is to it
without you he's left hanging
goes up in dachau's smoke
is sugar and spice in the baker's hands
gets revalued in the next stock market crash
he's consumed and blown away
used up
without you

Help him
that's what faith is
he can't bring it about
his kingdom
couldn't then couldn't later can't now
not at any rate without you
and that is his irresistible appeal.[4]

One more example. It is called "frei nach Brecht" [Brecht with liberties]. It is reproduced on the cover of my book *Sympathie,* published in 1978, seeking to help explain that title. Perhaps "frei durch Brecht" would have been better, free because of Brecht!

my young daughter asks me
why learn Greek
sym-pathein I say
a human capacity
that animals and machines lack
learn to conjugate
so far Greek is not yet forbidden

II

This liberation for sustained contradiction has also shaped my theological reflection. I come from a post-Christian home, and even though Bach and the Bible are my inheritance, I could not bring myself after Auschwitz to believe in "the Lord who so wondrously reigneth." I had no antenna for "omnipotence." Brecht helped me to go about faith differently. God was not exactly all-powerful in the days of the Nazis; he had too few friends.

Brecht helped me with his mute Kattrin in *Mother Courage* to come to a better understanding of what prayer really is.[5] In the final scene of that play—it is the year 1636—the imperial troops set out to attack the Protestant town of Halle. They force a young farmer to show them the way in the deep of night. Frightened by soldiers' terror, his young wife begins to pray with the handicapped Kattrin. "Pray, you poor creature, pray! We can do nothing against bloodshed. Even if you can't speak, you can still pray. He hears you if no one else does. I'll help you. (All kneel down.) Our Father, hear us, for only you can help. We may perish. But why? We are weak and have no spear or nothing, we dare do nothing and are in your hand." Unnoticed, Kattrin gets up during the prayer, climbs on the rooftop of the barn, and awakens the townsfolk with her drumming. Kattrin is shot to pieces, but the town is warned.

In that powerful depiction it became clear to me how prayer has been misused for centuries: One declares oneself to be without power—and prays for others. Instead of acting for those around us, words are addressed to a higher being. I was angry when I composed an essay in 1968 about prayer and spoke about Kattrin. My anger is reflected in the following: "If you ask Christians what they did for Jews when they were persecuted, the supremely mendacious reply is: we prayed." From Brecht I learned a radical this-worldliness that does not let itself in for empty promises. But when I think on this today, living in a post-Christian world, I ask myself something else. Would Kattrin have beaten her drum if others had not prayed? If she had not learned to pray? If she had not grown up in a world of prayer? Do drumming and praying perhaps not belong together as praying and doing justice do in Dietrich Bonhoeffer? Is this contradiction really an either/or?

III

I engage Brecht with an important question; it concerns his curious faith in science. Do we not need languages other than the language of science? "To pray is to wish, only more ardently," says the poet Jean Paul. Do we not all need to learn to wish instead of wallowing in "wish-less misery?" Can we let go of the language of religion? The languages we are so well in command of, the languages of money and science, are they sufficient? Is this transfiguration of science not idolatry that permits no other wishes but those that science fulfills? What is "the piety of science" supposed to mean? Does Brecht use that expression? I have some reservations about the goddess that is worshiped here. Something Martin Luther once said has been in my mind for the last ten years; I find it more true than ever before. "Reason is a whore"; it sleeps with anyone and everyone if the pay is good. Think only of gene technology!

With Brecht, I embrace the famous assertion of Karl Marx that whatever humiliates human beings, renders them servile, abandoned, and contemptible, has to be overthrown. But this is an assertion that cannot be accounted for empirically; after all, does not neo-liberalism teach us with its radicalization of capitalistic barbarism that there are winners and that there are losers, at a ratio of 20 to 80? And, so it goes on, the winners have the right to live long and happy lives, to buy new human organs when the old ones wear out. And the losers? Well, the most important thing is to arm ourselves against them, or else they will all become terrorists.

The real terrorist is the new totalitarian economic system under which we live. But that is still not widely known. That system is, indeed, much smarter than the two older totalitarian systems that used to shout orders. With soft advertising and by patenting all of life, it deregulates human rights and the earth's right to survival.

Karl Marx's wonderful assertion is rooted in Jewish thought even though he denied it, despite the fact that his grandfather was a rabbi, just like Brecht denied his pious grandmother. Yet Marx could not get rid of those religious roots. Passion for thinking so differently does not derive from scientific analysis but can and, indeed, should make use of it. But the unshakable truth of the affirmation that creation's goodness is for all requires something more. In religion we speak of it as "faith." It has nothing to do with credulousness in regard to certain peculiar salvific events. Instead, it has everything to do with an anticipation of life for all. The hope that the conditions that violate human beings will be overthrown, as Marx put it, is an assertion that reaches forward to the land of accomplishment where everyone's rights are established and their tears dried. It cannot be demonstrated scientifically that something like that is to be. No science can give birth to such affirmations and no rationality can prove them. What is needed is the witness to whom the language of religion gives the name *God*. Simple, postreligious people sometimes say, "This isn't what it's meant to be; surely, this can't be all there is." Those are helpless but splendidly religious stammerings.

I cannot agree with Marx that the highest being for us humans is the human being. The insight that the way to God in Jewish thought leads via the neighbor, that is to say, via the woman next door who gets on my nerves and always listens to the wrong music, is one of Judaism's greatest gifts to humanity. I believe in that but also with the desire that my neighbor who reads nothing but the tabloids will someday also enter the way to God.

Radical humanism has its own language difficulties. It cannot pray and cannot wish for more than what seems possible. But we all need the "more" we call transcendence. We need a guarantor of the rights of the poor, the superfluous and disabled, a guarantor that is greater than our reckoning. In that sense, we are all incurably "religious." It is an illness we cannot get rid of in the life of industriousness.

IV

I had a wonderful argument recently with my husband about reason and faith. There had been a series of sermons in the university chapel about that subject. He had entitled his first sermon "Reason Cleanses Faith." Somewhat puzzled by that title, I asked whether faith had spilled something on itself. That it had done so, indeed, and still does so without letup is really no point of dispute between him and me. So he invented a different title for me: "Faith Heals Reason." It does seem to me, really, that reason and science are rather sick today.

Here is an everyday example. A disabled child who can walk only with a limp and is not able to speak comes to the playground with his mother. Soon, another mother says to this child's mother: "Was that really necessary? Wasn't it predicted? Couldn't you avoid the risk and have an abortion?" The young woman who told me this was deeply hurt. Science promises planned children, "designer" children; soon, they will all be cloned, beautiful like Marilyn Monroe and intelligent like Albert Einstein. Accidents, mistakes, imperfections have to disappear from our world. We have no time for that; it is too costly and, given our ability for early detection, quite avoidable.

Such scientific reason is sick and needs healing. A powerful example of illness comes from the science of economics that explains to us that the freedom of the human being and the absolute freedom of the market are inseparable concepts. As if the laws of the latter that were brought into being by the utterly egotistical and merciless social orders and that have degraded human beings to a mere commodity were in concord with the freedom of human beings. The millions of children in the world who are forced to slave away for their livelihood, prostitute themselves, "donate" their organs, and sell drugs—they are the outcome of total liberalization.[6]

Reason, scientific thinking, is sick today, perhaps incurably; the chances of the world with its limited resources surviving are slim. It is the task of faith to heal the patient "reason."

But what is its sickness? One of the most important symptoms is faith in reason's own omnipotence. Years ago, during the build-up of medium-range missiles, I came across a remark by an army general that we are capable technologically of doing everything. We are omnipotent. At any moment, we can clone children, poison our drinking water, install tourist attractions on the moon, turn outer space into a weapons arsenal, abolish creation's power of renewal through planting and reaping, and replace the grain that falls into the earth with genetically manipulated substitutes that have to be purchased anew each year from those who own the world. The God who once upon a time "gave pasture to our cattle and bread to our children," as an old hymn puts it, is superfluous. We can produce a better, less susceptible world. The ancient dream that we shall be like God is made possible through science.

Nothing proves this point in our everyday experiences as palpably as the abolition of the rhythms of creation. Day and night, summer and winter, ebb and flow, youth and old age, live a span of time and then die; those are conditions of living on this earth. Time itself is a rhythmic element that is not switched off and on with a push of a button but binds our life to a given, established rhythm.

I saw a man recently on TV who announced that after his demise he would be put into a deep freeze, have antifreeze injected into his blood, and be preserved in a refrigerator. Then, perhaps in five hundred years, when death has been quite done away with, he would be thawed out and live forever. It costs only $38,000, he said. What was most uncanny for me was that he seemed in no way ill or nutty but quite normal.

Could it be that behind this craving to do away with every rhythm of life there lurks a diseased, diabolical search for God? Could this search for never-ending domination—marking not only individuals but living in scientific reason itself, like a compulsive constraint hanging over the dominant, rich world with its "faster, oftener, more"—be the consummate expression of the religion-free world? If I can be God, I need no longer look for one; if I am boss of time, the Sabbath, the pause and silence are unnecessary. There are agencies in Germany that spend billions of Euros so that travelers from Hamburg can arrive twenty minutes earlier in Berlin. If time is equal to money—a fundamental dogma of capitalism is that "time is money"—then the old saying that God's time is the best time is null and void. If I can play God with the world, its resources and possibilities, then dependency on the goodness of life that I cannot produce is superfluous. That this goodness meets me, even waits for me, that the beauty of a falling leaf waits for me, that—to put it in the old-fashioned way—God waits for the soul "to praise to him" and in so doing forgets itself: All that is less and less known in the world of the "makers" and what they "make." Yearning and longing decay and die, replaced by "productivity."

Hans Christian Andersen tells a beautiful tale of the devil and the mirror he made. The mirror distorts everything beautiful and good into nothingness. The most beautiful landscapes look like cooked spinach; the best people look repulsive or stand ridiculously on their heads. Every good and pious thought shows up as an ugly leer. It is a mirror that revokes creation itself. (The Bible calls creation "good" and "beautiful," two words that are exchangeable in Hebrew!)

Armed with that mirror, the devil and his sorcerer apprentices fly up to heaven in order finally to show God how revolting, stupid, and mean his world is. The mirror falls from the devil's hands and smashes into smithereens that enter into the eyes of human beings. When a piece enters the human heart, it will turn to ice.

I had not thought of that story for a long time; then I read and retold it to our grandchild and wondered whether Andersen had not had scientific reason in mind. Some of the pieces, so the story continues, got into people's eyeglasses. It was awful when they put on their glasses in order to see things correctly and to be just. All they could see was profit, success, and the survival of the fittest. Justice, one of the names of God in the Bible, withdrew. Today, in the language of empire, that name is no longer rendered as justice but only as fairness.

V

There are some changes taking place in us that are associated with the scientific notion of domination. One is our relations to time and the rhythm of life that have to be abolished. Everything can be bought at any time: strawberries in December, ice skating in mid-summer, sex objects in one's old age. We are, as René Descartes asserted, *"maîtres et possesseurs de la nature,"* masters and owners of nature. We are not creatures but lords, slave owners, those in charge, and reason readies us for possessing, dominating, and making. In the ideology that rules over us, time is not a fundamental category of life that in tradition stood before eternity; at best, time is money that one can use in order to get more out of life. That time can also be bread of life, that it can help us make a new beginning and rise up again, is a gift beyond value to be shared among us: all that has been forgotten. An African saying makes the point very clearly: "You have watches, Africans tell us. But we have time."

Another change that science's technocratic dominance brings about is in our relation to ourselves. In the life of "efficiency" we forget that we need God and those events that tradition calls "revelations" and that are beyond planning. We forget that we belong to that great whole which bears and fulfills us. Faith could free us from always having to play the omnipotent lords of this world. It could remind us of those other, old-fashioned and superfluous ways of behaving: to listen, wait, be silent, interrupt ourselves. Abilities such as these that let us remain passive rather than in control grow ever more difficult for us to activate. We forget how to "let go" of ourselves, as the mystics advise. Only when we know that we are not God but creatures—limited, sinful, mortal—can we find God and partake in her. Then we shall forget the language of defining, of records of successes, and come to learn again the language of calling and pleading, the language of silence and prayer.

What disturbs me perhaps the most in the world determined and dominated by science is its language that condemns all emotion, fear, and hope into silence. To the freedom into which we are called belongs also the ability to express what we desire, what our dreams of a different life are, what we aim for. It is too cold for me in the world of scientific language; we have to learn another way still of communicating. For only then shall we cease at playing the masters and owners of the world when our true inner longings find language and take form. What religion can accomplish also in the world pervaded with science—perhaps precisely in that world—is to make visible, audible, palpable the "more than everything." *Es muss doch mehr als alles geben* (There must be more than everything), as one of my poems is entitled.

We have in our old churches a language for life's most important things. We can share those things one with another. As Meister Eckhart puts it: God is "above all the most communicable." God waits to be shared and communicated. God is not, as neo-liberalism wants us to believe, a private matter of individuals to whom freedom of religion is conceded or not. No, God is common to all, not a "private property" as we are being told over and again in "God's own country." In scholastic language one could say that God is *bonum commune*, the common good. The Bible feels no need to condemn either knowledge or reason; it wants to deprive them of their rule and keep awake our wishes for life for everyone.

God liberates us from the compulsion to make everything and to play God. As every mystic knew, we can be one with God. Whenever we concur with her will for the life of all her creatures, whenever we know that our power of discernment, deconstruction, and reconstruction are oriented toward a different life, science walks out of the prison that it currently lives in and becomes an employee of love.

Notes

1. Translated by Barbara and Martin Rumscheidt.

2. In 1928, soon after completing *The Threepenny Opera*, Bertold Brecht was asked which book had exerted the greatest influence on him. He replied, "You will laugh—the Bible!" Klaus Völker, *Brecht: A Biography* (trans. John Nowell; New York: Seabury, 1978), 6.

3. Bertold Brecht, *Poems 1913–1956* (ed. John Willet and Ralph Manheim; trans. Edith Anderson et al.; London: Minerva, 1994), 331.

4. Dorothee Soelle, *Revolutionary Patience* (trans. Rita and Robert Kimber; Maryknoll, N.Y.: Orbis, 1977), 7.

5. Berthold Brecht, *Mutter Courage und ihre Kinder* (Frankfurt: Suhrkamp, 1999).

6. Observations made by Fidel Castro in an address on 1 January 1999.

3. Breaking the Ice of the Soul

Theology and Literature in Search of a New Language[1]

An essay published in Mutanfälle: Texte zum Umdenken

When I think about the relation between theology and literature, a critical question always arises concerning the traditional separation of these two subjects. Why is there theo-logy at all, and no theo-poetry? Many years ago, during a visit to Martin Buber in Jerusalem, one of the first things he asked me was: "Theo-logy—how do you do that? There is no logos of God." In the Occident, why was an attempt to do theology of the logos of God undertaken, but no theo-poetry? Among professional Christians, just as among professional poets, the term *theo-poetry* disconcerts; it evokes apprehension, while theo-logy has been part of their diet for centuries! What would the writer of a biblical psalm have to say to this attitude toward texts so prevalent among us? And who distinguishes between theo-logical and theo-poetical texts? Who knows precisely what is poetry and what is prayer?

I prefer the more limited concepts "poetry" and "prayer" to the more comprehensive ones of literature and theology, because they take me closer to the heart of the matter. I have a metaphysical-aesthetical dream of perfect poetry that is at the same time pure prayer. When I look for examples that approach that goal, I think of John Donne, Klopstock, and above all, Hölderlin, whom one cannot understand at all without the category I call prayer. Among those poets of the twentieth century who come to mind are Paul Celan, Ingeborg Bachmann, and Nelly Sachs; but there are also texts by Gottfried Benn, for example, that attain to the quality of mystical entreaty and come closer to being prayer.

31

Simone Weil described prayer as the highest state of attentiveness; to illustrate this immersion and concentration, she refers to solving a problem in mathematics that demands our undivided attention. A poem should demand and create no less attentiveness. There is a kind of speaking that places us into relation with the ground of the depth of being, and without this attentiveness we are capable neither of beauty nor of truth. Poetry that is also prayer does away with the prejudicial notion that prayer is something private, not to be made public. Real attentiveness, which Hölderlin calls *"Innigkeit"* (depth of intimacy), has no time for that sort of opinion. Everything inward seeks outwardness. When people pray together they give themselves permission again to desire, hope, or dream; they find again the lost language of sharing with one another what they feel. Poetry and prayer are attempts, so to speak, where the separation of public and private, outward and inward become unnecessary and cease to matter.

Could the sentence "perfect poetry is prayer" be reversed? Would "pure" prayer, freed from the intrusion of lies, reach the character of poetry?

I suppose so, and I know enough examples from the Latin American liberation movement in which prayer becomes more and more pure poetry—Julia Esquivel, Helder Camara, and of course, Ernesto Cardenal. I name them here next to the many unknown praying and fighting people who are not poets, but become such ever again in the arduous assertions of their human dignity. Like all great religions, Christianity presupposes that all human beings are poets and that they can pray. But in today's prayers of the oppressed, there is also a mystical tendency that strives for silence and creates a silence after the spoken word. But that, too, is an element of poetry: What would a poem be without its silence?

There is a point, I think, where the traditional distinctions between theology and literature become unimportant; in fact, they only trivialize. The intent of this essay is to get close to the point where they converge. But the concept of literature becomes unsuitable when its sociological breadth extends from the advertising text to the esoteric composition; it cannot encompass the poetic— the newly created, the quality of poetic language. Too much is governed by the category of literature that has nothing to do with *poiein*, to create, produce, make anew, do. Franz Kafka said that a book has to be like an axe in order to break the ice of the soul. In this image is the criterion of poetry that helps us differentiate between Dante and the tabloid. The language we use most of the time is unsuitable for breaking the ice within us: We are not reached, the words do not affect us in our depth, the soul freezes. We search for a language that breaks the ever-thickening ice.

But in our context, "theology" is an all too broad and shallow concept; every ecclesiastical pronouncement declares itself to be theology. That word has undergone a huge inflation that has much to do with the professionalization of theology and its scientific airs. At the beginning of the twentieth century, many concepts were still qualified with the adjective "Christian," which one would be embarrassed to use today. It does indeed sound so much more thoughtful to be looking at things from a "theological" and not merely from a "Christian" perspective. The existential dimension of genuine theology often atrophies in the scientific-scholarly enterprise. And on the basis of that danger in which the servant, scholarship, turns itself into the master and the real substance of theology, I want in what follows to relate poetry above all to "prayer" and "narration," the forms of theological expression that permit the existential to be truly present.

Religion expresses itself on three linguistic levels: mythic-narrative, religious-confessional, and argumentative-reflective.

For example, the phenomenon of human suffering, of guilt and inadequacy, of the finitude of life, can be treated in religion in diverse ways. We can tell the myth of the garden of Paradise and the expulsion of Adam and Eve, the first human beings. This is a narrative and those are images that evoke thoughts and feelings even without interpretation. But we can do something else; we can subjectively appropriate to ourselves the burdensome fate of guilt and enmity between humans and give it religious articulation in the concept of "sin." In *The Symbolism of Evil,* in which he reflects on finitude and guilt, Paul Ricoeur elaborates the transition from mythic fate to religious, consciously acknowledged sin and confession.[2] Finally, the third mode of speaking is theological-philosophical reflection that seeks to comprehend guilt in terms of the dogma of original sin.

Telling a story, making a confession, or formulating a concept are quite different ways of interpreting the world religiously; we name those ways with the words: myth, religion, and theology. To the secularized consciousness, these inner-religious differentiations are rather irrelevant; often these three concepts are used interchangeably and in dismissive ways. The atheism of the masses is correct in regarding them as merely dealing with the same thing with different word games.

The Enlightenment and its tradition of the critique of religion looks upon these forms of speaking from the position of progress in history: One can discern in the course of time an irreversible development from the myth to the concept, the logos. The latter represents the stage of the progressive consciousness, and it renders the myth superfluous by "conceptualizing" it. But is this picture of the diachronic process correct in which myth, passing through religion, dies into the logos? By orienting theo-logy towards theo-poetry, I endeavor to present a different "postmodern" understanding of myth.

Today, there are good reasons for rejecting the idea of progressive secularization. In spite of enlightened thinking, religion has not rendered itself superfluous and has not become irrelevant for the decisions people make about life.

Take two quite different examples: American theologian Harvey Cox, having described the city without God in a work of 1965 called *The Secular City,* followed it with a book on religion in that very city, *Religion in the Secular City* (1984). In the latter, he revises the first thesis in the light of the growing right-wing fundamentalist movement in the United States and the religious base communities in Latin America.[3] Then there is the Italian Communist and filmmaker Pier Paolo Pasolini, who, in his critique of consumerism, demonstrates the resistance of religion and the mythical against the new, soft fascism of consumption.[4] It seems to me that we come closer to the truth of religious consciousness when we look at it synchronically as participating simultaneously in the three different forms of religious expression. I formulate my thesis as follows: Today's post-Enlightenment theology must implement all three levels of religious language.

Without the narrative element—the retelling of the myth and the telling of one's own experience—theology dries up, masculinizing itself in life-threatening absolute sexism. By this I mean not only that women have nothing to say in this theology and, for that reason, must be discriminated against institutionally and journalistically, but also that the theological method of the male appropriation of the world renders the dimension of narrative superfluous. In a manner of speaking, this dimension is raped, forced into conception from the very start. The sexism that rules in the theology of the church and university consists not only in a subconscious assumption that the human being is a man but also in the violation of the mythic-narrative that has gone far beyond Bultmann's program of demythologization. At a time when better explanations were at hand, he fought against the myth that explained the world but had long frozen into a fetish. He did so for the sake of the existentially comprehended truth that disappears in rational-argumentative discourse and becomes inexpressible. Bultmann had learned from Kierkegaard that faith includes a "leap" from the plane of the reflecting consciousness. In that "leap," myth and prayer regain a voice in religious discourse. One could call it a "myth after demythologization."

Human thinking does not follow an irreversible direction where, of necessity, myth becomes something of the past. The forms of language in religion—narrating and composing, confessing and praying, thinking and reflecting—belong together. In my view, Kierkegaard is a wonderful theologian because he speaks all three of religion's languages in the passion of the absolute: He narrates, he prays, and he argues. He does not let himself be pushed aside on one level of language, such as that of ironic reflection. And so Bultmann, too, tried in his writings to give "testimony"; he did not only construct chains of theological arguments. And even though he tried to inculcate in his hearers and readers the difference between theology and proclamation, his best theology expressed precisely the disowned genus: proclamation, promise, testimony, and prayer.

Great theology has always practiced narrative and prayer and involved itself in all three levels of religious speaking.

As an counterexample, one need only read Protestant church pronouncements in our country on the question of peace in order to see the self-destruction this theology is engaged in. It does not know how to give expression to myth, nor how to appropriate it religiously. It allows itself instead to be lead astray into a mode of reflection in which the ability to look for truth has long been relieved by the ability to achieve consensus. It is a language that increasingly excludes narrative and confessional speaking; it has purified itself of all traces of having been encountered and uses theological terminology in a purely instrumental sense. These pronouncements do not express life's holiness; rather, they function like contraceptives. Not a single word goes beyond the technocratic language game.

On the other hand, a theology that succeeds invites myth back. It looks for the form of speaking made use of by myth, for narrative and prayer, rather than banning them as something impure. This is one of the criteria of liberation theology—black, feminist, or from the context of poverty. Here are found narrating and lamenting; both are forms of praying. At the great ecumenical conferences, representatives of liberation theologies are present, giving testimony and addresses. When Domitila, the Bolivian miner's wife, tells of the Bolivian women's hunger strike, what she is doing is narrating and entreating, pleading and accusing, analyzing and reflecting. What she says cannot be summarized in a synopsis; prayer and narrative refuse to be housed in that form of communication—they die from its coldness.

Today, wherever theology has a liberating character, a new synthesis of myth, religion, and reflection comes into being. Myth is not artificially protected there against the reach of the logos as religious orthodoxy had tried to do. Rather, myth is criticized wherever it legitimates humans ruling over other humans in the manner of sexism or racism. Myth is not destroyed when its operative functions in certain situations are exposed.

Myth is not rendered superfluous in the logos; rather, it is validated there, celebrated and recovered. The strongest testimonies of liberation theology are prayers, liturgies, proposals for how we worship God, in all of which the Christian myth, especially the exodus and resurrection, is dramatized. Something like that can happen only among those who depend on the world being changed and do not withdraw from such undertakings in academic resignation. They need God because the generally espoused view of "this world" that impacts them is a death sentence on the poor: The poor must become even poorer so that the rich may become even richer. It is an illusion to assume that we live in a scientifically transparent and controllable world that can do without belief in the God of justice. It is, after all, only the rich who can comfortably do without God.

The return of the myth happens among those who need the hope it offers.

And yet, in the first world's enterprises of literature and theology, a distinct separation is made between the various attempts to break the ice of the soul. There is a theology that is void of poetry, using diverse mechanisms to seal itself off from literature. Theo-poetical statements are dismissed by it as "merely literary" and distinguished from so-called theological ones. Doctrinal or dogmatic thinking serves as such a technique of prevention. By such thinking, I mean traditional systems of dogmatics, on the one hand, and on the other the noncodified dogmatism that is no longer able to formulate doctrines but still constantly issues impediments to free thought and other taboos. Placing theology and its institutions under the governance of legislation is another attempt to protect faith from poetry. In nearly every conflict between Christians and church-administrations, the language used by those "above" against what were at first theo-poetical statements is firmly established and carefully regulated: God language must not be renewed. But the most important wall that poetry-less theology has erected against innovation and change is the transformation of theology into a scientific discipline and its perversion by scientific methods. The attempts to break the ice of the soul are here subject themselves to the process of freezing.

Of course, critical reason has its place in theology and serves a necessary function against superstition and biblicism. But those who are only fluent in the language of science are voiceless in relation to essential aspects of life. Today, the language of Enlightenment no longer suffices for the enlightened consciousness, because that language cannot give expression to certain experiences such as those of meaninglessness or meaning being found, of being disconnected or being bound to all that lives. The greatest weakness of that language is that it isolates us from myth, religion, and poetry and that, in addition, it suffocates the mythic-religious-poetic being that is found in us as human beings. As if it were unnecessary to break the ice of the soul!

When we inquire what separates theology from literature, it is not only a theology void of poetry that needs to be criticized but also a poetry void of religion, having emancipated itself from myth and religion and reposing in postmythical, postreligious resignation. Indeed, it renounces the effort to break the ice of the soul. In terms of the language of German literature, reference must be made in this context to the significance of the Bible. Its images and figures, its narratives and sayings, its feelings and longings have become so much a part of that language that the abandonment of the Bible is a huge impoverishment. I have in mind such elementary feelings as fear, remorse, and jubilation but also deep desires like the wish to be made new. Religious language can educate us to name our feelings, to know ourselves and to make ourselves known.

There is a religion-free one-dimensionality that is aimed against poetry also; however, language steeped in memory opposes it. For in language we encounter not only ourselves; we express not only our actuality. We always live in a house of language, built by previous generations. That is why the memory of a different life and the hope for less destructive ways of living can hardly be rooted out. Poetic, transformative, ice-melting speech is structured into language itself. Wilhelm von Humboldt puts it like this: "Language gives more being to what is" *(Die Sprache macht das Seiende seiender)*. It names, orders, clarifies, and deepens our manner of living. Of course, we can eat without words and rituals, drink, work, make love, buy, and die, but in reality we all know that language really gives "more being to what is" and assures us that we are alive.

What do we need a language of poetry and prayer for? Could we not do just as well without them both? In his poem *"In lieblicher Bläue blühet . . ."* ("In lovely blueness blooms . . ."), Hölderlin says: "Voll Verdienst, doch dichterisch wohnet der Mensch auf dieser Erde" (Albeit with great merit, it is poetically that humans live on this earth). Is it not utter presumption to claim that humans "live poetically?" Do they not live well enough under the administration of technocracy, without poetry and prayer, without wishes for what lies beyond them, and in fears that create deep insecurity? Is it not enough for us to use language as a tool for making ourselves understood and to instrumentalize it?

The connection between poetic and religious language becomes apparent to me precisely in the counterimage of today's loss of speech: the family that no longer shares meals together as its members simply help themselves, when and to what they want; the young people in front of television up to six hours a day. There is no more conversation. Why is the language of prose, of information, of understanding one another without the use of pictures, not sufficient? Why is it that everyday language is not enough? What drives us beyond it?

Our own language is destroyed, corrupted. When a word such as *love* is used in reference to a car, or the word *purity* to laundry, they are void of meaning; they are destroyed. All words that express feelings are damaged among us, and that also goes for the language of religion. "Jesus Christ is our savior"—this is ritualized, destroyed language; it is dead. There are many people who can no longer say what they want to say and what they expect from life. I believe that a certain amount of despair in the old language, a certain amount of disgust with it, is needed for writing. That is a completely natural feeling. Shame, according to Karl Marx, is a revolutionary sensation; one needs to be ashamed of and suffer from the way we blather, how language is being destroyed, how human beings are destroyed or are utterly unable to see themselves in what is being said. In this shame I gravitate toward something so that I may find the language we need.

I need the language of poetry and of prayer and of the Bible. As an author I work with theological material just as creative artists work with stone, wire, wood, or other materials. The materials I use in order to throw a little light on a dark and confusing context are the Bible, the history of the saints, church history, and systematic-theological reflection which, the institution's intensive efforts notwithstanding, has not destroyed the gospel.

Why is this so? Why does an ancient narrative of the Jesus tradition help me today in my writing? What does mythical-narrative language yield? It yields something that is hidden in my empirical reality but does not become visible most of the time. I use the gospel, and other religious traditions as well, to say something that is essential for me to live at all. I use myth and mythical speech; I work with it because I need it. Whatever is not needed is dead. What is it then that drives me to such need and use?

One of the first suppositions of writing and speaking today is that we defend ourselves against the clutches of the media and escape from its laws. Those laws rule over our thinking and destroy our ability to hope or, to put it in biblical terms, to see the world with the eyes of Jesus.

The Bible's mythic-narrative language repels the constraints of the media and critiques one of their fundamental presuppositions: the utter and absolute faith in power and success. One of the messages delivered by the media and received by us is that only what succeeds matters. Let me illustrate this in terms of what I have experienced in recent years in connection with the peace movement. I was interviewed by all kinds of media people, and it took me a long time to understand the mechanisms that are operative in such interviews.

I unconsciously assumed that in interviews those who ask and those who answer are united by an interest in finding out the truth. This assumption turns out to be naïve. As a rule, what interests a reporter is not the search for the truth, for example, whether a weapon is designed for first use or for defense, whether arms are manufactured in anticipation of or in response to threats; or whether the matter at issue is the murder of Nicaraguans or the protection of indigenous peoples' human rights. The essential interest of media people is whether the movement for more peace is successful, whether its representatives, like me, radiate power. Their basic cynicism consists in the arrogance of power in which they themselves participate. How many times they let us know that we are "very nice" but quite impotent! When I try in such conversations to represent the movement for peace, I first must attempt to break the ban of "success thinking" under which my interviewer exists and to dissolve this "being possessed by power" so that the question for truth can be raised at all. In the conversation I must try to achieve a reversal of priorities of success and truth before the subject under discussion can be heard at all.

The coercion to think in terms of success and power captures not only those who work for the media but all of us. Our ability to perceive is deranged and our sense is of being trivialized. Life is trivial by necessity in a culture that expects us to become informed daily and hourly about cat food and hair spray.

What such daily brainwashing produces and what in certain times and circumstances is being consumed (the daily news, sports broadcasts, beer) is in a new sense the very everyday ritual that has replaced the ancient myths. Just as the way a city neighborhood is laid out can communicate to a child that cars are important and children are not wanted here, so all our means of communication teach us a persistent and self-evident disdain for life, for what is weak and worthy of protection. What cannot be marketed just has no being. What is not successful, no matter how true it is, does not make the news in today's world. The sanctity of life that I advocate here is rigorously and mercilessly destroyed in the rituals of consumerism.

The old myth is the story about life being sacred. And this sanctity has to be dramatized again and again so that we do not forget it or consider it superfluous. In the language of myth, we express thanks for the sun, bless bread, wish one another a safe journey home, and in that way remind ourselves that life is a gift and not a possession.

What do prayers and poetry have in common? They connect us with our wishes and lift us out of the misery that comes from nothing being left to wish for. They put us in touch with what we now are not and remind us of who and what we were meant to be.

In his *Aesthetica in Nuce* (1762), Johann Georg Hamann wrote: "The senses and passion do not speak nor understand anything other than in pictures. The whole treasure of human knowledge and happiness resides in pictures." At the core is not the concept but the picture; human beings were not created as a rational animal but in the image of God. We "actually are a pointer to the human being hidden within us, namely an example of God in miniature: *exemplumque Dei quisque est imagine parva.*" That is why for Hamann, speaking "is translating from an angelic language into a human one." Here the distinction between theology and literature is deliberately not made. Both work at translating from another language, that of the angels. "Poetry is the maternal language of humankind, older in the way tending the garden is older than agriculture, painting than writing, singing than declaiming, telling parables than drawing conclusions, exchanging than engaging in commercial transaction." Hamann is a thinker who, engaging the European Enlightenment critically, reclaims poetry against the world of prose, scientific writing, logical deduction and commerce.

The dangers of all these symbols of the rationalistic-technological world are more clearly apparent today at the end of this epoch. Is it possible to turn back to where poetry, expelled as something merely feminine, may come home again, where we get around today's "maternal language of humankind," namely the paternal jargon of technology, and become healed? Is language only an instrument of world domination, finally no more than an expression of "the will to power," as one can discern so easily in President Ronald Reagan's speeches? Theology and poetry, the language of wishes and of hope, of lament and of prayer, are equally under threat today. The instrumental-technocratic reason that steamrolls over us does not linger over how Jeremiah and Hölderlin differ one from the other; in that reason, both deserve to be bulldozed or plowed into a historicizing cultural program as something insignificant.

Today, theology and poetry have more in common than ever. Both have been driven from their home, both are regarded as irrelevant. In schools and other places of education, one can do without learning those languages: A passive acquisition is still tolerated; everything that goes beyond mere reception of cultural heritage is leveled down. Who would even want to teach prayer and write poetry?! Who would presume to translate from an angelic language?! And what teacher would be interested in rendering visible through language the "pointer to the human being hidden within us"?! Who would attempt to do what poetry and prayer have always set out to do, namely, to communicate God, to share God, to pass on the good that makes itself known?!

In the world of language that is governed by consumerism (in the way Pasolini describes it), we can express ourselves only in the categories of ownership. Our relation to the world is defined by the chief idols that our culture worships: money and power. What that means in terms of language is that many people are overcome by a particular helplessness in face of everything that cannot be acquired, bought, conquered, taken ownership of, controlled, and marketed. The language of having that now holds sway has overwhelmed the divided language of being. The best that those rendered mute can muster is the helpless stammering that we know, for example, from situations of grief and mourning.

"Poetically lives the human being," Hölderlin said, nourished by poetry and prayer. Wherever we ourselves escape from the language of dominance and try another language, that is, try to hear, understand, and learn to speak it, there the creation and renewal of language is a source of strength, an encouragement that goes far beyond analytical-critical knowledge. I remember how I first heard the sentence "The soft water breaks up the stone." It is filled with the memory of what the soft water has already accomplished, of Brecht's poem about the origin of the book of Tao-Tê-Ching; it is a visionary sentence that speaks from what the Bible calls "the strength of the weak." In short, it is a theo-poetical sentence. It makes no predictions and leaves unanswered the most obvious question at hand: "When will it finally be?" Being between memory and vision, that sentence reminds me that I will probably die before the stone has been broken up and the war being waged now has come to an end: war against the most destitute of this world, against creation, and against ourselves. To sing of peace in the midst of war is, I believe, the secret of the people in the

New Testament, who, trembling under an empire marked by a similar hostility toward human beings, still sang their different songs. That is how they "lived poetically" and shared another language one with another.

Notes

1. This essay is published in Dorothee Soelle, *Mutanfälle: Texte zum Umdenken* (Munich: Deutcher Taschenbuch Verlag, 1996), 187–201. Translated by Barbara and Martin Rumscheidt.

2. Paul Ricoeur, *The Symbolism of Evil*, vol. 2 of *Finitude and Guilt* (trans. Emerson Buchanan; New York: Harper and Row, 1967).

3. Harvey Cox, *The Secular City* (New York: Macmillan, 1965); and *Religion in the Secular City* (New York: Simon and Schuster, 1984).

4. Pier Paolo Pasolini, *Freibeuterschriften* (Berlin: Wagenbach, 1975).

PART 2

NEW FORMS OF
THEOLOGICAL LANGUAGE

4. "Come, Read with My Eyes"

Dorothee Soelle's Biblical Hermeneutics of Liberation[1]

Luise Schottroff

The Beginnings and the Contexts

The "political evensongs" of Cologne came into being and were conducted with Dorothee Soelle's active participation.[2] In these evensongs, her interpretation of the Bible played a decisive part. I consider these political evensongs to be an important, historical moment that in the German and European context made visible the shape of a fundamentally changed Christian theology and praxis. At the time, this new theological movement was not yet called "liberation theology." In those days, Dorothee Soelle herself frequently spoke of "political theology." But in today's perspective, it is quite appropriate to regard the political evensongs of Cologne as the hour when a liberation theology was born in the German—and quite likely also in the European—context.

The political evensongs or "night prayers" of Cologne existed from 1968 to 1972. The group responsible for them was composed of about forty people, from Roman Catholic and Protestant traditions, who began to work together in 1966; they understood their cooperation as an ecumenism from below.

Together they composed services of worship on current political issues in a hitherto unknown format. This group regarded itself as a "new church community" that was different from the local parish community.[3] These worship services were structured in three steps: analysis, meditation, and guidance toward praxis (information, meditation, action). Prayer and exposition of biblical texts arose from the analysis of political injustice. I cite two examples. In a worship service on October 1, 1968, both the Soviet-directed invasion of Czechoslovakia of August 20 of that year and the war of the United States of America against Vietnam were analyzed as genocide. At the same time, strong support for the West's politics of detente was expressed. Concluding the service's first step, namely analysis, was a reading of Matthew 5:21ff. entitled "The Meaning of These Words Today." The meaning of that text was interpreted: "Whoever even thinks that the Communists have now taken off their masks and that, accordingly, the politics of detente is a mistake, is guilty of an offence." At that time, this was tantamount to a frontal attack on the anti-Communism of Germany and on Cold War politics that was fueled afresh by the Soviet entry into Prague. Jesus' word was transposed directly into the political debate so that, in the presence of the congregation reading the Scriptures and interpreting the biblical text this way, perpetrators and victims are given a name and an address, so to speak.[4]

The second example comes from Dorothee Soelle's "Credo" that was recited during that same worship service. This Credo caused the Roman Catholic vicar general of the region, and the president of the Evangelische Kirche in the Rhineland, to declare the evensongs in general and Dorothee Soelle in particular to be heretical. "I believe in Jesus Christ who was right when 'as an individual who can't do anything,' just like us, he worked to alter every condition and came to grief in so doing. . . . I believe in Jesus Christ who is resurrected into our life so that we shall be free from prejudice and presumptuousness, from fear and hate and push his revolution onward."[5] The Christology of this Credo does not perceive the Christ relationship as one from above to below; rather, it sees Christ next to and in women and men praying. No separation here between the historical Jesus and the Christ of faith, even though at that time such a distinction shaped both popular and academic theological discussion. The relationship to the Jesus of history itself is also understood as something of faith. The historical experiences of Jesus' life are seen as analogous to the social experiences of our own time. Presupposed implicitly and taken for granted is that the violence, injustice, and toil for justice of one's own situation is comparable to the epoch of Jesus (and other epochs of history). To this day, the political evensongs of Cologne exert wide-ranging influence, both in their order of worship where political analysis, meditation, and liberating praxis are joined together as well as in the ongoing use especially of their prayers.

I sum up this historical retrospective in three theses.

1. In a sharp and clear focus, Dorothee Soelle's Credo of October 1, 1968, unites the theological conceptualization of the political evensongs and the new departures in Christianity at that time. Dorothee Soelle's theology, in the years since then and to this very day, has to be understood in connection with the

Christian movement for liberation. It is no desktop theology; it is movement theology.

2. The theological themes of the evensongs and their hermeneutical presuppositions have come through the decades in good shape and are now part of the bases of feminist and liberation theologies. (In 1968 in Germany there was no talk yet of feminist theology; that movement came into being five to ten years later.)

3. However true it is that liberation theologies can be understood only as contextual theologies, often independent of one another, they nevertheless share worldwide a common structure.

Years ago, Dorothee Soelle told me the following anecdote that is related to my first thesis above. Her Credo, recited then and recited again and again in German-speaking countries by many people, was once ascribed in a printed service order to "an unknown author."

The hermeneutical bases of liberation-theological interpretation of Scripture within the European context are to be described therefore as a structure that is relatively homogenous despite the different contexts and presuppositions of those who "do" liberation theology. "When they pray, human beings give expression of themselves in the face of God. They do so out of their pain over the still absent reign of God, they express their hope in that reign. . . . Christ has taken sides, for he takes the side of truth, of justice and we, as his followers, are recognized as such precisely in also taking that side." This was said in the very first political evensong of October 1, 1968.[6] In this interpretation of Scripture, hope and "taking sides" are seen as hermeneutical orientations, grounded in the Bible, especially in the gospels of the Second Testament. At the same time, the praxis orientation of faith is defended against the charge of legalism, leveled by Lutherans. "When Jesus says: 'go and do likewise,' is this to be reckoned as law or are not human beings themselves addressed in terms of the example . . . in a challenge that presupposes our capability freed for another way of being?"[7]

That orientation gives rise to a new Christian anthropology that is critical of Christian and, in particular, Lutheran dogmatics, charging it with causing Protestantism to confuse sin with powerlessness. "We indeed do not understand sin as a matter of individualistic issues, chiefly related to the area of sexuality, nor do we see it as that global Protestant feeling of powerlessness which says, in the words of Luther's famous hymn, that 'our human strength must fail us.' . . . We are collaborators of sin simply by belonging to the rich Northern world."[8] In addition, the negation of the dualism of "this world" and "the world beyond this one," apparent in the resurrection hope, is already present here. (See Soelle's "Credo" of October 1, 1968, above.) No one can fail to notice that here is a hermeneutic in conscious contradiction to the dominant theology of the churches and universities. Repeatedly, Dorothee Soelle has worked out the hermeneutical structures of a European liberation theology in contrast to those of dominant Christian theology and, in view of this, has spoken of "two theologies."[9]

The two different theologies never entered into dialogue. The representatives of dominant theology almost totally barred this newly developing liberation theology from their own context; since the first developments of this theology were not based institutionally, they did not feel it necessary to be drawn into dialogue. The disequilibrium in power relations becomes apparent in such silencing of this other, different theology as well as in the few written assessments of it by persons who represent the traditional theology. Here one encounters consistently what amounts to discrimination: that liberation theology is not serious science and that it is ideologically Marxist.

Dorothee Soelle's participation in the liberation movements in the contexts of Germany and North America shaped her reading and interpretation of the Bible. I want to name one place in particular where that reading and interpretation, as well as her biblical hermeneutic, were presented to a broad audience in a very concentrated form. I am speaking of the German Protestant *Kirchentag*.

Even though it was known that she was to be invited, the governing board of the *Kirchentag* refused to invite her to participate in the 1985 *Kirchentag* at Düsseldorf. Consequently, we arranged with the organizers that Dorothee Soelle share in the Bible-study sessions that I had been invited to present. Her participation in this form did not require a decision by the governing board. And so at the *Kirchentag* in 1985, we presented Bible studies together. (The musical ensemble *Gruppe Habakuk* was also a part of our presentations.) Our Bible studies were published under the title of *Die Erde gehört Gott*.[10] Even though these presentations were successful, Dorothee Soelle was once again not invited by the governing board to take part in the Bible studies of the next *Kirchentag* in Frankfurt, 1987. But I was, and with the concurrence of the organizers, we repeated the 1985 arrangement. After Frankfurt, we were officially invited by the governing board to present joint Bible-study sessions, if that is what we wished. This experience demonstrates just how anxious established institutions were again and again to prevent Dorothee Soelle's public engagements. The angry response to her address to the Assembly of the World Council of Churches in Vancouver in 1983 shows this perhaps most blatantly. She had applied the story of the rich young ruler of Mark 10:17ff. to the prosperous affluence of Christianity in her country and, in doing so, elicited the ire of the Reverend Bishop Professor Dr. E. Lohse, the head of the German delegation. Back in Germany, he saw to it that the funding of ecclesiastical institutions could be in jeopardy if they were to invite Dorothee Soelle.

Her Bible studies were not independent pieces of work but grew out of Dorothee Soelle's work at the grass roots. And, in return, they became the tools of base groups that were engaged in the peace movement of the 1980s or the many tasks of justice work.

The Four Steps of Liberation Theology: A Program for Today

In the title of his book *Vom Leben zur Bibel—von der Bibel zum Leben (From Life to the Bible—from the Bible to Life),* Carlos Mesters summarizes how liberation theology studies the Scriptures. From that perspective, the three-step process of the Cologne "political evensong"—information, meditation, and action—can be related as much to the basic concept of liberation theology as to later feminist theological approaches based on women's experience. This hermeneutic of life consciously sets itself apart from traditional interpretation of the Bible that makes the biblical word the beginning point of Christian faith. The latter hermeneutical approach was reflected over decades in the widely used publication *Göttinger Predigtmeditationen.*[11] The pattern there is exegesis, meditation, and sermon. This process meant to set forth a path from scholarship to daily praxis, on the one hand, and to uphold the authority of Scripture as the sole source of revelation, on the other. This alignment of faith in scholarship and what, in the end, is a fundamentalistic understanding of the Bible, determined the education for future theologians in Germany for many generations. I said "in the end," because the biblical scholarship and interpretation practiced here is not fundamentalistic, according to its self-understanding, as it does not adhere to a doctrine of inspiration nor regard every biblical text as authoritative, but rather practices critical examination of all texts. Nonetheless, this formally "liberal" approach is theologically fundamentalistic since it regards the Bible as the sole source of revelation and the preaching of the Word of God as the source of faith. Furthermore, by asserting that there is one and only one correct interpretation of the Bible, such an approach is fundamentalistic as well.

In contrast, liberationist theological interpretation of Scripture understands itself consciously as a hermeneutics of life. "It is the claim of liberation theologies that they bring a new hermeneutical orientation to the question of how theology can be done in a meaningful, that is, life-changing way. Whereas traditional theology starts with the text (the Word of God, the Gospel), liberation theology starts with the context of our lives, our experiences, our hopes and fears, our 'praxis.' This is not to deny the power of the text and its spiritual quality, but to make room for it."[12] This is how Dorothee Soelle describes the beginning of the process of liberation and of Christian faith. She wrote this at the end of the 1970s as academic instruction material at Union Theological Seminary in New York. Not until 1993 was it was published in various places both in German and English. She provided a schematic summary for it in an article in the German journal *Junge Kirche*.[13] I consider that text unsurpassable in its timeliness and practicability. The process of liberation is shown here as the process of faith and not only as a method for reading Scripture, as Elisabeth Schüssler Fiorenza proposes, or as a pedagogy for groups in base communities, as seen in the majority of Latin American liberation theological procedural models.

Dorothee Soelle's proposal begins the process with a first step that recognizes existing social praxis. Analysis of praxis with the "best possible analysis" follows as the second step. In working on her own Bible study or systematic theology, Dorothee Soelle draws for her analysis only partially on current proposals of social analysis in the social sciences, for example, those of feminist-Marxist studies. Chiefly, she makes use of analysis provided by critical groups, such as the critique of military issues by the German Committee on Basic Rights and Democracy, or the analysis of global monetary policies, such as the economic initiatives proposed by Kairos Europe. At the *Kirchentag* of 1999, she once again stressed how relevant nongovernmental organizations are today. As a result of such praxis-related analysis, her way of proceeding gains concreteness and persuasiveness.

Now I wish to focus on Dorothee Soelle's reading of Scripture in the light of her liberationist theological model as well as her actual presentation of Bible studies. She once called the approach to the Bible "a hermeneutic of hunger." In her model, she describes "hunger" as follows:

> In order to dialogue with the Word of God, the praxis of the prophets and Jesus, we need the clearest understanding of our own praxis. When we delve deep enough into our own situation, we will reach a point where theological reflection becomes necessary. We then have to "theologize" the given situation. We read the context (step 1 and 2) until it cries out for theology. The only way to reach this point at which we become aware of our need for prayer, for hope, for stories of people who have been liberated, is to go deeply enough into our own sociohistorical context. The theologian will discover the inner necessity of theology in a given situation and its potential for unfolding theological meaning. We have to reach this point of no return where we will know anew that we do need God. This is the basis of doing theology, but the only way to come to this point is worldly analysis of our situation."[14]

Dorothee Soelle describes how she deals with the Bible like this: Read the Bible, learn to lament, see images of resurrection, search the Scriptures and traditions for help in the midst of the distress that comes from hungering for God.

"If we don't find an answer, we cling to those parts of the tradition that speak to us in our despair."[15] For that reason, Dorothee Soelle uses the exegetical groundwork of a social-historical interpretation of Scripture but then switches over to meditation wherein the language of biblical texts is brought together with the analysis of the present time. A prayer she composed in 1995 serves as an example:

> God, your Spirit renews the face of the earth.
> Renew our hearts also
> And give us your spirit of lucidity and courage.
> For the law of the Spirit
> Who makes us alive in Christ
> Has set us free from the law of resignation.
> Teach us
> How to live with the power of the wind and of the sun
> And to let other creatures live.[16]

This prayer takes up Romans 8:2 and brings it into the present. "For the law of the Spirit of life in Christ Jesus has set you free from the law of sin and of death." The law of sin is rendered as "the law of resignation" and is protected against the misunderstanding found in Christian dogmatics that the desire to act is sin and works righteousness. Desiring to act is not sin but to resign is. Dorothee Soelle clearly contradicts Lutheran dogmatics and its reception of Paul on the subject of sin, and often she does so explicitly.

What her prayer shows above all is that Dorothee Soelle is a translator of the Bible's poetry. With her eyes one can find poetry even in Paul and his piling up of concepts. Dorothee Soelle coined a metaphor for her treatment of the poetry of the Bible: "eating Psalms."

> For me the Psalms are one of the most important foods. I eat them, I drink them, I chew on them. Sometimes I spit them out and sometimes I repeat one to myself in the middle of the night. They are bread for me. Without them the spiritual anorexia that is so widespread among us sets in and often leads to a deadly impoverishment of the spirit and the heart.[17]

The Bible gives us language for our despair; we can learn the language of lament from it. And it gives images of resurrection that help us to see liberation and to learn hope.

I wish to cite a verse by Dorothee Soelle that shows in a negative way the importance of the Bible for resurrection.

O don't ask about resurrection
A tale of ages long ago
That will soon skip your mind
I listen to those
Who dry me out and diminish me
I accustom myself
To the creeping accommodation to being dead
In my well heated abode
The big stone at my door.[18]

The Bible is dead when it becomes a tale of ages long ago. It quickly skips the mind in our world of violence and money where we dry out and accustom ourselves to being dead. Her text continues: "O do ask me about resurrection; O don't stop asking me." The hermeneutic of the hunger for God cannot be expressed more concisely than this. That hunger is what opens up the Bible.

Notes

1. This essay was delivered at an event held at the Evangelische Akademie Boldern near Zurich, Switzerland, in September 2000 honoring Dorothee Soelle on the occasion of her seventieth birthday. (Dorothee Soelle was born on September 30, 1929.) It is translated from the German by Barbara and Martin Rumscheidt.
2. See Dorothee Soelle and Fulbert Steffensky, eds., *Politisches Nachtgebet in Köln*, vols. 1 *and* 2 (Stuttgart, Berlin, Mainz: Kreuz Verlag, Matthias-Grünewald Verlag, 1969 and 1971). See also Dorothee Soelle, *Against the Wind: Memoir of a Radical Christian* (trans. Barbara and Martin Rumscheidt; Minneapolis: Fortress, 1999), 37–41.
3. See Fulbert Steffensky, "Politisches Nachtgebet und 'neue Gemeinde,'" in *Wissenschaft und Praxis in Kirche und Gesellschaft* 60 (1971): 527–34.
4. Soelle and Steffensky, *Politisches Nachtgebet*, 1:17.
5. Soelle, *Against the Wind*, 40.
6. Soelle and Steffensky, *Politisches Nachtgebet*, 1:23ff.
7. Soelle and Steffensky, *Politisches Nachtgebet*, 2:236.
8. Ibid.
9. See Soelle, *Political Theology* (trans. John Shelley; Philadelphia: Fortress, 1974); and Soelle, *Thinking about God: An Introduction to Theology* (trans. John Bowden; Philadelphia: Trinity Press International, 1990).
10. Dorothee Soelle and Luise Schottroff, *Die Erde gehört Gott* (Reinbeck bei Hamburg: Rowohlt Taschenbuch Verlag, 1985).
11. The series *Göttinger Predigtmeditationen*, published by Vandenhoeck and Ruprecht in Göttingen, was designed to assist preachers in their sermon preparations.
12. Dorothee Soelle, *On Earth as in Heaven: A Liberation Spirituality of Sharing* (trans. Marc Batko; Louisville: Westminster/John Knox, 1993), x (translation altered).
13. Dorothee Soelle, "Wie können wir befreiungstheologisch arbeiten?" *Junge Kirche* 54:11 (1993): 607–8.

14. Soelle, *On Earth as in Heaven,* xi.

15. Ibid.

16. Dorothee Soelle and Luise Schottroff, *Den Himmel erden. Eine ökofeministische Annährung an die Bibel* (Munich: Deutscher Taschenbuch Verlag, 1996), 61.

17. Soelle and Schottroff, *Den Himmel erden,* 31.

18. Soelle, "Über auferstehung," in *Fliegen Lernen* (Kleinmachnow: Wolfgang Fietkau Verlag, 1979), 21.

5. The Language of Prayer between Truth Telling and Mysticism

Andrea Bieler

This article is concerned with a critical reconstruction of Dorothee Soelle's understanding of prayer. Through her participation in the "political evensongs" in the late 1960s, Soelle began dealing with a view of prayer as an exercise in truth telling. Interestingly, the liturgical structure of the political evensong or "night prayer" *(Politisches Nachtgebet)* did not leave much room for actual prayer in the classical sense. It proceeded in three steps: information, meditation, and action. The first step included information about pressing political issues, combined with an analysis of the unjust structures in which those issues were entrenched. During the meditation, the worshipers struggled with the question of how one might understand political events (e.g., the Vietnam War) in light of the gospel. The reciprocity of text and context, of Scripture reading and political analysis, was considered to open up an illuminative process. This process was supposed to lead into the concluding step of the political evensong, which dealt with the possibilities of resistance and conflict resolution.[1]

From my point of view, this model initiated more of a pedagogical than a liturgical experience. It suppressed the dimensions of prayer such as thanksgiving, doxology, and intercessory activity, which do not have a primarily educational intention. I argue that this imbalance refers to the profound crisis of prayer that Soelle reflects in her theological pondering. In her relocation of prayer, beyond a theistic concept, "crisis" becomes a genuine feature that shapes her anthropological comprehension of human beings as *cooperatores dei,* and the practice of interceding as the attentiveness of love.[2]

In her later work on mysticism, Soelle adds another dimension to the language of prayer.[3] The search for words in negative theology, paradoxical language, and the importance of silence inform her insights in a language beyond dominance. From this reconstruction, the following reflections elaborate the potential and the constraints of mystical language for liturgical practice.

"We Do Not Know What We Should Pray": Crisis as a Feature of Prayer

In her early work on prayer, Soelle lifts up the Enlightenment and its followers of the nineteenth and twentieth centuries and their criticism of prayer. The "enlightened" post-Christian consciousness considers prayer as a pure surrogate: Human beings pray to God when they experience the constraints of their own power or reason. In those particular situations of crisis, people express immature illusions and the desire to escape a reality in which people are not willing or able to act efficiently and to fight against injustice. Soelle quotes Immanuel Kant, who speaks of prayer as the production of a fetish *(Fetischmachen),* as a kind of magic in which one relies on the gaps of the social and philosophical systems however rational and causal they might appear. It is within these gaps that one tries to act upon a divine power and falls back into the realm of magic invocation.[4] Besides Kant, Soelle also refers to Gerard van der Leeuw's *Phenomenology of Religion.* He defines prayer in a similar sense as an exercise of power through particular words and body postures. Those magic exercises take place in spaces that are defined as sacred and at times that are set apart; they are attempts to influence a power that is experienced as more distant and mightier than oneself. This kind of praying tries to overcome the distance in order to gain access to a divine and almighty force.[5]

In order to deconstruct this alleged magic, Soelle refers to Jesus, Paul, Luther, and the drumming protest of Bertold Brecht's mute Kattrin.[6] Hence, it is not only the critique of the Enlightenment but the very nature of the biblical witness that opposes the view on prayer as a surrogate action offered in the house of God as a safe space:

> Religion as the house which protects a man, the roof built by his fathers and which his sons will continue to preserve, no longer exists. The immediate prayer available to the members of this household has become impossible for Paul. He no longer knows what he should pray, as he ought. It is not an accident that the early Christians were described by their heathen neighbors as *atheoi* or godless. They had left the house

in which dwelt many worshipers of the gods. Christianity was not thought of as a religion. The Christian way of worshipping God made people irreligious. Religious people know what they should pray. With Christ, the era of religions which know what they should pray comes to an end. Jesus turns people out of the house into the open.[7]

From an exegetical point of view, one has to oppose this dichotomous construction of the early "Christians" who rejected the cultic prayer in the temple or the synagogues. This reading reflects the dominant exegesis of the late 1960s, which did not recognize the Jesus movement and the first communities of disciples as belonging to the synagogue in which Jewish people prayed. Moreover, Soelle reproduces the classical dichotomy between magical, primitive action, and rational, enlightened consciousness that was invented by theologians and phenomenologists of religion in order to present Christianity as the most mature form of religious expression. Although I cannot agree with these constructions, I want to stress one aspect that is well taken in Soelle's argument. The dichotomy between the sacred spheres in which we pray and the profane in which we live our daily lives is an inappropriate hermeneutical lens for the reading of the biblical Scriptures as well as for our own practice and theology of prayer. It is this disconnect between prayer as an isolated ritualized act and other social practices that Soelle passionately challenges. She stresses over and over again that Jesus turned people out of the house of prayer into the open. As Jesus sees it, the house of the religion is empty, since God wants to be found on the road between Jerusalem and Jericho, despite being overlooked there by the priest and the Levite.[8]

We can read Soelle's reflection on prayer as one voice among a multitude of modern positions that no longer start off with the heavenly Father who is above but rather with the social location of those who pray. The anthropological and political move toward the people who pray reveals the destabilization of the classical theistic framework in which neither the theology nor the praxis of prayer can again be located. This focus on the people highlights the supposed transformative power that prayers have, or should have, rather than the practice of prayer itself. This methodology converges with the critique of the enlightened skeptics of religion who were much more interested in the psychological and social effects of praying than in the phenomenon itself. This classical functional approach to prayer and ritual prevailed in the "practical theological" discourse of the late 1960s as well as in the emerging movement of political theology.

Prayer beyond Theism

Soelle's theology reflects the crisis of prayer caused by the critique of a metaphysical and theistic understanding of God that presumes the existence of a superpower dwelling in some world other than this. She challenges the classical notions that are attributed to God, such as apathy, immortality, and almightiness. These belong to a mythological conceptualization of the human-divine relationship that is no longer accessible to people who take the insights of the Enlightenment seriously.[9] Consequently, Soelle rejects a practice of prayer in which God is worshiped as the great magician whom we might ask to perform miracles and to be responsible for our actions. Making room for the reality of modernity in one's own prayer praxis means to acknowledge the infinite pain of the feeling: God is dead. Since the Enlightenment, believers do not have access anymore to an immature father-child relationship as an expression of their faith.[10] In the same way, it is impossible to express an immediate religious consciousness that illuminates God's being through human experiences of nature or through the metaphysical speculation about divine qualities. Soelle refers to Hegel's notion of the "unhappy consciousness" (unglückliches Bewußtsein) that remembers the knowledge of the Absolute that is beyond this world (das überweltlich Absolute) which became unrecognizable in the boundaries of reason. The unhappy consciousness is based on the impossibility of an immediate knowledge about God. Since God transforms God's self into the finite and concrete history of human life, it is impossible to substantiate God beyond the human story. It is impossible to possess God like an object, or like a person across from oneself. It belongs to the truth of the dead God that there will be no more voices from heaven who call us. "But the pain caused by these absent voices, visions and prophets, is blind against God who does not talk less silently—even though more indirectly—in the newspapers, on movie posters or in statistics, than in the burning bush."[11]

This divine manifestation is the central moment of the hymn in Philippians 2:7. God emptied God's self by entering into the alienation of human life and becoming part of it. Consequently, the Christian faith is grounded in the notion of "kenosis" (self-emptying or Entäußerung). Kenosis reflects the process that happens in God's own self. Neither ontology nor metaphysics can be the starting point of doing theology anymore. It is rather the field of history and of human interaction, which reveals God's own self as being in relationship that needs to be considered. It is less God's being but more God's becoming that is disclosed.

> History is now experienced as God's kenosis. This word has a double sense: it means the extreme distance from God as well as his articulation and his work. . . . God didn't transform himself in such a way into history that nothing is to be expected anymore. We might say, he saves something of himself, he holds something back—otherwise we would be in "heaven." The "also" in Hegel's thinking keeps the future open and refers to the idea that God conceals himself in the expectance and the

"unsatisfied" of history (Ernst Bloch). Substance remains, however not in a naïve theistic way, but as *absconditas.*[12]

The infinite pain, the unhappy consciousness, and the unsatisfied experience *(das Unabgegoltene)* frame the possibility of prayer in modernity. Soelle's attempt to believe in God in an a-theistic way is strongly influenced by Hegel as I have just explicated. It resonates as well with Dietrich Bonhoeffer's and John A. T. Robinson's theology of prayer. Soelle picks up Bonhoeffer's question about how to speak of God and how to pray in a world come of age that is religionless. Bonhoeffer asked in a letter from prison in 1944: "How do we speak of God—without religion, i.e. without the temporally conditioned presuppositions of metaphysics, inwardness, and so on? How do we speak (or perhaps we cannot now even 'speak' as we used to) in a 'secular' way about 'God'?"[13] From his point of view, the questioned theological presuppositions as well as the search for another language were connected with the reflection on the place of worship and prayer in a religionless world.[14] Bonhoeffer saw a connection between the loss of a theistic language, an idealistic doctrine of God, and a rediscovery of the meaning of prayer. He was awaiting the rise of a new language that would overcome the powerless words of current prayer. "It will be a new language, perhaps quite non-religious, but liberating and redeeming—as was Jesus' language. Until then, our being Christians today will be limited to two things: prayer and righteous action among men. All Christian thinking, speaking and organizing must be born anew out of this prayer."[15]

The perceived loss of a metaphysical language and a theistic doctrine of God led Bonhoeffer to a renewed praxis of prayer, in which the action of the "other," the powerless, and the ethical transcendent God is located. According to Bonhoeffer, this practice of prayer has a Christological foundation as it is mediated through Christ's presence. At this point, we can recognize an interesting shift in Bonhoeffer's reflection: It moves from the meditation of the divine reality as the prerequisite of prayer toward the reality of prayer as an opening medium of the divine ethics in the reality of human beings. "This concept is ambivalent. The experience of God's fading omnipotence, which is framed into the idea of God's being beyond this world *(Überweltlichkeit),* is not interpreted as a real experience with God which urges one to pray, but it is merely understood as the disappearance of a metaphysical and theistic God talk. This very disappearance makes authentic experience with the ethical-transcendent, powerless God possible."[16]

Theologians like Dorothee Soelle and John A. T. Robinson adapt Bonhoeffer's model of the ethical transcendence of God in which prayer becomes the practice of a new and healing experience with God. Robinson notices that the idea of a God who lives in a spiritual or metaphysical sense beyond the world dies very slowly. He wants to transform the classical understanding of prayer in the sense of ethical transcendence. The work that Christians do, while they are trusting in God's presence, is the real prayer. Ethics and prayer are two aspects of the same thing.[17] He describes his prayer practice as follows: "My own experience is that I am really praying for people, agonizing with God for them precisely *as* I meet them and really give my soul to them.... Prayer is the responsibility to meet others with all I have, to be ready to encounter the unconditional in the conditional, to expect to meet God in the way."[18]

Soelle agrees with Robinson and with Bonhoeffer on the ethical foundation of Christian prayer. In his book on modern theologies of prayer, Perry LeFevre points out that Soelle tries to respond to Bonhoeffer's question "Who is Christ for us today?" by transcending individualistic existentialist categories as she had learned them from Bultmann's theology. "Her hermeneutical principle, authentic life for *all*, embraces the whole of reality including the political and economic structures."[19] According to Soelle, the desire to pray should be driven by the desperate attempt to pay attention to the world in its fractions, and by the longing to get connected to the suffering that surrounds us. Compassion has to be learned, since middle class people have the privilege not to see and to remain in a state of frozen apathy, which is grounded in the apathetic freedom from suffering. This apathy keeps "first world" capitalism going: "We have inverted the relationships between love and suffering.... Our highest goal is to remain free of it right up to the moment of death.... The apathetic freedom from suffering, this freedom from want and from pain and from commitment to people has been promoted to our highest value.... The goals of being capable of love are subordinated to the goal of getting through life 'well' which is to say getting through unscathed, untouched."[20]

The prayer praxis of interceding has the potential to become a dangerous exercise in melting frozen apathy and in growing into an attentiveness that is local and global at the same time. In that sense, praying is an act of consciousness-raising. By focusing on concrete situations in which people suffer, those who pray get the chance to relate to those who are in pain. Interceding in prayer fosters the desire to be connected and to be accountable.

Soelle claims the anthropological notion of human beings as *cooperatores dei* as central to her understanding of prayer. We are invited to work for the coming of God's reign and to participate in the miracle of transformation and resurrection. Resurrection, as a fragmented experience, can be realized in prayer. It becomes the place of identification with people who suffer, the place for acknowledging one's own responsibility and complicity, and it becomes the place for political decisions. Prayer without any political consequences is hypocrisy.[21] The lines between political discussion and prayer become intentionally blurred. Whether prayer is expressed in the form of an address is more or less irrelevant. The focus of prayer should be on its content. If prayer is directed to God, or if it is only the illusionary projection of one's own desire, the question is decided with regard to the content and not with regard to the form. Because of God's kenosis, it does not make sense to differentiate between divine and human activity.[22]

It seems to me that in Soelle's early theology, the praxis of prayer becomes the proof of God's existence. Prayer becomes the bearer of faith in God, of resurrection, and of the coming of God's reign. She starts off with the crisis phenomena and with the insight of God's kenosis as a loss of positivistic substantialized God talk, as essential features of prayer. Prayer framed in the context of the "infinite pain" that has left behind metaphysical thinking, both in its rational and in its moral version, should enable the articulation of fragmented experience rather than of positivistic and compact utopias in which resurrection is equated with wholeness. But through her ethical assumptions she loses this approach. Prayer is no longer a place in which the infinite pain can be expressed. Instead, it becomes the locus of the yearning for wholeness, which finally silences the articulation of fragmentation. Hereby she leaves the ambiguous trace she had recognized before in Martin Luther's work that reflects on faith as a transitional experience, a "hovering in loneliness between earthly and heavenly life."[23]

Hans Jürgen Luibl offers in his study on prayer a very helpful insight when he notices that Soelle holds this ambiguity in her poems rather than in her theology of prayer. Her poems focus again and again on the topic of suffering; they are almost a reversal in that each prayer *has* to realize a moment of resurrection. In contrast to her theology of prayer, her poetry avoids the logic of perfect transformation of God, history, or humanity. It remains more faithful to the infinite pain and to the unsatisfied experience:

> We could think of nothing against the cold
> but a flimsy shirt . . . But I also became poorer
> and walked around the town depressed
> going to demonstrations, too,
> as if they handed out courage there.
> I long to see
> that other half of the story
> the empty grave on Easter morning
> and the empty graves in El Salvador.[24]

Almost thirty years later, Soelle articulates her interest in prayer anew within her reflections on mysticism.[25] The language of the mystics offers an entrance into an understanding of prayer beyond the logic of perfect transformation and beyond the substantialized ethical God talk. Mystics have always been in trouble with religious language, and they struggle with its limits.[26] This language might open a space for prayer that not only is determined by ethical demands but unfolds the gap for the *deus absconditus* and for experiences with God that are not dominated by a narrow purpose-oriented rationality. Soelle's early bias that the prayer of the mystics is an exercise in becoming desireless changes in her later works.[27]

The Silent Cry: Praying in the Language of Mystics

"We do not know what we should pray": Soelle interprets Paul's lamentation as an expression of the fundamental crisis that is caused by Jesus' prayer practice that decentered time and space and diffused the distinction between sacred and profane.[28] Crisis as a fundamental feature of prayer refers not only to time and space but also to language. We do not know how to express ourselves; we have no language, since we do not know how to be in real dialogue. Soelle's existential understanding of language is deeply influenced by Heidegger and Hölderlin. Heidegger traces his thoughts back to Hölderlin's phrase: "Since we became a conversation we exist for each other and became listeners for each other."[29] Language cannot be possessed like an object; it evolves in conversation, it is an event, an action, an exercise of power that happens between people: "If the sentence 'we have no language' will not do, we can say, 'we are not a conversation.' We do not express ourselves because we are not listeners for each other. We do not answer because our words would not be heard. We do not live in dialogue. It is not the language we lack but we *are* not the dialogue we are meant to be."[30]

Soelle translates "We do not know what we should pray" into "We are not a conversation" and equates this phrase with the sentence "We are not a prayer." She agrees with the Protestant reformers that real praying comes from hearing; it is an answering to the Word one has heard before. Becoming a prayer means to live out the conjunction of hearing and speaking in which we express ourselves to God beyond the constraints of special times and formulas. It is not an occasional occupation but something that determines all we do.

This existentialist understanding of language refers to a philosophical discourse that emphasizes the contextuality and relationality of all that is spoken and that refuses to perceive language in an essentialist sense as a pure object.

I assume that these insights into language and prayer as conversation inspired Soelle's interest in mysticism. In her reflection on mystical prayer, she returns to the gap in which the experience of the *deus absconditus* can be expressed and in which prayer evolves: "The darkness or the silence of God cannot be taken up into an alleged immediacy. . . . Thus what mystics call 'becoming at one' is never a possession that cannot be lost. What really happens in mystical union is not a new vision of God but a different relationship to the world—one has borrowed the eyes of God."[31]

In light of this interpretation of *unio mystica*, Soelle describes prayer as the attempt to see the world with God's eyes by paying attention to what is little and unimportant, what is rendered invisible and irrelevant. To use God's senses in prayer initiates one into the mystical insight of the *sunder warumbe* (without any why or wherefore). As Soelle writes, "If there is a verb for the life of mysticism, it is praying. This superfluous activity, this unproductive waste of time happens *sunder warumbe*. It is as free of ulterior motives as it is indispensable. Prayer is its own end and not a means to obtain a particular goal. The question 'what did it achieve?' must fall silent in face of the reality of prayer."[32]

Using the insight of the *sunder warumbe*, Soelle overcomes the compulsory demand that prayer has to realize a moment of resurrection. She goes beyond a utilitarian framework of prayer and transcends the dichotomy between passivity and activity. She states that mystics rarely have cultivated the practice of supplication, since their desire was to grow into the conversation that they *are*—as Hölderlin puts it—or to learn to see the world with God's eyes, as the mystic Mechthild of Hackeborn says. Soelle's deepest yearning is that God might take her heart, her eyes, and her ears in order to speak and listen through them. "Even though in supplicatory prayer the human being—in the nominative—is still at the center, in performing mystical prayer the transformed human being replaces the former. It is the human being now who no longer only calls out but has always been called already—the human being in the accusative."[33]

People who pray acknowledge that they are not independent beings. Soelle recognizes that the language of dependence that mystics use in their prayers is not a language of dominance but of mutual relationship that grants freedom.

I am fascinated by Soelle's reflection on a mystical language beyond dominance, which might inspire our reflection on language and prayer. Many mystics were driven by a negative or "apophatic" theology which expressed the wisdom that whatever is said about God in positive terms is not appropriate. Language is considered to be too small and narrow to name the divine. Mystics pondered on the *topos* of the unspeakable. Mystical prayer goes beyond a language of dominance that tries to control and to possess. Soelle finds this language of unity and mutuality in New Testament passages such as "For from him and through him and to him are all things" (Rom 11:36) or "that they may all be one. As you, Father, are in me and I am in you, may they also be in us, so that the world may believe that you have sent me. The glory that you have given me I have given them, so that they may be one, as we are one" (John 17:21–22).

All dualistic discourse of lord and servant, speaking and listening, and free and slave is left behind here: instead a language is sought that is non-imperialistic and anarchistic (as the repeated use of "in" and "one" indicates). This basic quandary of language of domination versus language of oneness is precisely what mystics suffered from.[34]

Mystics choose the *via negativa*, the paradox, and the silence as three possibilities for their God talk and their prayer. Negative theology proceeds on the assumption that since the deity cannot be named in positive notions, one has to name it negatively. Or as Meister Eckhart puts it: "Whoever can say the most of God speaks the most in the negative."[35] One of the outstanding representatives of negative theology is Dionysios the Areopagite. In his treatise on the heavenly hierarchy (*De calesti hierarchia* 2,3), Dionysius explains why only negations (*apophaseis*) can truly speak about God and why positive affirmations (*kataphaseis*) are always insufficient. "It has no power, it is not power, nor is it light. It does not live nor is it life. It is not a substance, nor is it eternity or time. It cannot be grasped by the understanding since it is neither knowledge nor truth. It is not kingship. It is not wisdom. It is neither one nor oneness, divinity."[36]

This radical negation of naming the divine in substantially positive terms is located in the effort to find names for God that escape the constraints of anthropomorphic and natural metaphors. Many mystics suffered from these constraints of language. Some, as we have seen, employed a negative theology because it exposed the problem of articulating on the experienced relationship to the transcendent within the immanent framework of language. Other mystics, however, tried to hold the tension between apophatic and kataphatic speech, knowing that the insufficient words are necessary even though they would nevertheless return to the negation.

The dialectic between apophatic and kataphatic language leads us to the second feature of mystical language, which is the paradox or the oxymoron. Moving beyond pure negation means to experiment with a language in prayer that opens up a space for an explosion of imagination. According to Soelle, this might happen through the use of oxymorons like "darklight," "sadjoyous" (Friedrich Hölderlin), "bittersweet," "eloquent silence," "filled emptiness," or "acquired dispossession." These examples demonstrate how an oxymoron or a paradox comes into being through the coincidence of contradictions (*coincidentia oppositorum*) by merging two beforehand incompatible notions into a new expression.

In terms of philosophy of language, the paradox is an attempt to approach from two directions a factor that cannot be perceived or understood. Other than in dialectics, no synthesis results here nor a reconciliation of polarities. The opposition remains unmediated and cannot be resolved in language. Dionysius's phrase about the "darkness that outshines all resplendence" is a prime example of paradoxical language. Other bold word images are "whispering silence," "fertile desert," "soundless tone," and "silent cry." With the unserviceable means of a logical language that operates chronologically, such images seek to name mystical experiences.[37]

The third feature of mystical language is silence. The mystical experience of silence refers to moments of abundance in which words are no longer needed to communicate with the divine or with human beings. Soelle states that silence in the mystical tradition has two layers. One layer describes the more technical preparatory exercise as a fasting from words. To be silent purifies and focuses one's senses and prepares oneself with a fuller capacity to listen. Yet it is more than that. The second layer is the self-expression of the living light that shines beyond words.[38] Silence that derives from that self-expression can be perceived as the space of resonance that echoes the paradox. The arrival at that moment in which deep silence unfolds is beautifully expressed in a poem by the German poet Ingeborg Bachmann, whom Soelle quotes:

Let be, I say, let be.
Into the highest ear
whisper, I say, nothing,
don't collapse into death,
let be, and follow me, not mild
nor bitter,
nor comforting,
without consolation
without significance,
and thus without symbols—

Most of all not this: the image
cobwebbed with dust, the empty rumble
of syllables, dying words.
Not a syllable,
you words!"[39]

Conclusion

The unifying thread in Dorothee Soelle's journey from the "death of God" theology to her interest in mysticism is the negative theology operating in both fields. Her journey reflects two poles of theological inquiry and religious expression. These poles are not contradictory or exclusionary; they are like a field of energetic tension that holds together a variety of possibilities for a language of prayer rooted in people's everyday experiences and freed of the corruptions of dominance. These two poles are expressed in Soelle's early statement that Jesus exclusively practiced the prayer of supplication, combined with her later statement that mystical prayer is an end in itself and goes beyond supplication. Both claims show the range of possible speech acts through which prayer can be expressed. It is Soelle's reflection on negative theology in the language of the mystics that develops further her early claims on prayer beyond a theistic framework.

From a liturgical perspective, I am interested how these reflections on language and mysticism may inform our current discussion on public prayer and language. I am aware that mysticism and public worship refer to different language games. Mystical texts incorporate different genres such as aphorisms, biographical texts, theosophical treatises, exegetical analyses, poems, and prayers. The diversity of genres corresponds with transformative, magical, noetic, and theurgical tasks that language may fulfill in the scope of mysticism. Mystics wander on the border of almost inexpressible experience caused by revelations and the expansion of one's own consciousness in meditation and other spiritual practices. Moving toward the outer limits of the unsayable, they nevertheless feel compelled to express the insights they have received in substantive communication. "It is, indeed, their *success* at just this sort of substantive communication that allows us to speak of, to learn of, and to participate in mystical traditions at all."[40] Soelle stresses that we ought to learn from mystic traditions but that mystic experiences are accessible to everyone. They do not belong only to people with a particular spiritual sensitivity. They exist within all people; we only need to dig them out from under the debris of trivia.

Following Soelle's assumption here, I wonder how we can we learn to speak a mystic language that rings true for us today. I think it is precisely the paradox of speaking the unspeakable that needs to be revisited in its relevance for Christian worship. How do we express the paradox of intimacy and ultimacy, nearness and distance in our prayers? How do we make room in our liturgical language for the *deus absconditus* who is distant and incomprehensible? Both our doxological language and our lamentation should not dissolve the described paradox for the benefit of a language that exclusively stresses either the aspect of intimacy or the aspect of ultimacy and power. From my fieldwork observations, this language of intimacy is prevalent in the public prayer life in many liberal, predominantly white congregations that are part of the Free Church traditions located along the Californian coast. In these settings, worshipers often call upon the spirit of gentleness or the mothering father as the one who gives shelter and comfort. It was intriguing for me to see how in the weeks and months after the attacks of September 11, these worship spaces became real sanctuaries, hiding places, and spaces of shelter for people who had to live through traumatic moments, grief, confusion, and the growing sensitivity of finitude and vulnerability in one's own life. It is troubling that there was almost no space for a language of lamentation that articulates the experience of the *deus absconditus,* the absent God. Besides the language of intimacy, a language of patriotic assurance rose in worshiping communities that supported the war against Afghanistan, as well as in the public discourse. The phrase "God bless America" was accompanied with gestures of supremacy such as "We will not fail, we will not falter." Mystical insights in the paradoxical quality of language for the divine might offer a potential critique of both attitudes. Both the exclusive regressive images for God as a hiding place or a shelter as well as the imperialistic use of God's name to legitimate warfare escape the paradox that the mystics express.

It needs to be stressed that the described language of intimacy differs from the language that mystics use. It is well known that many reports of mystical experience use the language of sexualized intimacy in order to describe the encounter between groom and bride, between Christ and the believer. This playful language of erotic longing is highly intimate, and the fantasy of melting into Christ occurs quite frequently. However, we can find many mystical texts which interrupt the language of undisturbed, one-dimensional intimacy by pointing to the paradox that is alive in God's self. Soelle refers to the poetry of mysticism that names the beloved as well as God the *loin-près,* the far-near one. "It is for him, the far-near one, that the soul waits in anticipation. He is simultaneously far and near, deep and high, bright and dark. . . . The beloved cannot be named in a single word. The words of nearness, happiness, fulfillment, and sweetness are in themselves limited. They cannot express the power of the erotic in such a way that it truly remains the power that cannot be possessed, and for that reason is "other," far away, eluding, and ever giving itself anew."[41]

This power of naming and calling upon the divine without claiming possession respects the impossibility of having God at one's disposal like an object. How would our language of prayer be transformed if we called God the far-near one, who is much more than the addressee of our small wishes? It seems to me that the mystical wisdom about the dynamics of apophatic and kataphatic language may enrich the possibilities of expression in public prayer. Yet these dynamics exist also structurally in liturgical prayer. The language of adoration is grounded in the knowledge of God's transcendence. For instance, the *Sanctus* is an example of the language of adoration challenged to its limits through the attempt to describe God's beauty and self-giving love. The paradox of psalms of lamentation that pray to God against God are disturbing, yet they offer at the same time convincing examples of a prayer language that does not dissolve itself into the language of intimacy. Thus, apophatic and kataphatic language can be discovered in all genres of prayer, in the language of adoration as well as in lamentation. Congregations who lose this quality of language in their public worship might unconsciously fear the risk of arriving at the paradox that invites as its consequence silence.

Notes

1. The origin of the "political evensong" can only be understood in the context of post-war Germany. With its predominantly pedagogical and functional comprehension of worship, it marked a radical change in the form of prophetic religious speech that had its *Sitz im Leben* in worship and was at the same time influential in the public political discourse. During the Nazi regime, the Confessing Church in Germany had articulated itself through confessions of faith. The founders of the political evensong in Cologne, however, used the previously mentioned three-step model in a different form. They invented it as a public model of religious expression and as the form giving structure to their liturgies. This three-step model became influential in the 1970s and 1980s in Christian communities that were committed to liberation theologies in Europe. It found its independent expression in the base communities in Latin America. The political evensong dealt with a variety of controversial political topics, such as the Vietnam War, the Russian invasion of Czechoslovakia, the Cold War, and the authoritarian organization of prisons and schools.

2. See Dorothee Soelle, "We Do Not Know What We Should Pray" in *Truth Is Concrete* (trans. Dinah Livingstone; London: Burns & Oates, 1969), 89–100; Soelle, "Gebet," in *Atheistisch an Gott glauben. Beiträge zur Theologie* (Munich: Deutscher Taschenbuchverlag, 1983, first published in 1968), 109–17; Soelle, "Das entprivatisierte Gebet," in *Aktion Politisches Nachtgebet* (Wuppertal: Jugenddienstverlag 1971), 19–26. Important insights into Soelle's understanding of prayer are offered by Hans Jürgen Luibl and Perry LeFevre. See Hans Jürgen Luibl, *Des Fremden Sprachgestalt. Beobachtungen zum Bedeutungswandel des Gebets in der Geschichte der Neuzeit* (Tubingen: Mohr, 1993).

3. Dorothee Soelle, *The Silent Cry: Mysticism and Resistance* (trans. Barbara and Martin Rumscheidt; Minneapolis: Fortress, 2001).

4. Soelle refers to Immanuel Kant's treatise *Die Religion innerhalb der Grenzen der bloßen Vernunft*, part 4 (1793); see Soelle, "Gebet," 109.

5. Soelle, "Gebet," 110.

6. Ibid.

7. Soelle, "We Do Not Know What We Should Pray," 91–92.

8. Soelle, "Gebet," 112. In order to contextualize her work, it is important to recall that Soelle was part of a strong anti-institutional force that moved progressive Christians who had observed that the churches might have prayed—in only a few cases—for the Jews in Germany during the Hitler regime yet failed to enter into further practical solidarity. It is the experience of Christian complicity in the Shoah, and of hypocritical prayer practice, that let her question Protestant and Roman Catholic worship with an attitude of rejection.

9. Dorothee Soelle, *Death by Bread Alone: Texts and Reflections on Religious Experience* (trans. David L. Scheidt; Philadelphia: Fortress, 1978), 132–33.

10. Soelle draws heavily on Hegel's notion of "infinite pain," viewing the history of God after the Enlightenment as a history of suffering. Dorothee Soelle, "Theologie nach dem Tode Gottes," in *Atheistisch an Gott glauben. Beiträge zur Theologie* (Munich: Deutscher Taschenbuchverlag, 1983), 54–58.

11. Ibid., 56 (English translation by the author).

12. Ibid., 73–74. The German version reads: "Geschichte wird nun erfahren als Entäußerung Gottes-im ganzen Doppelsinn dieses Wortes, als äußerste Entfernung von Gott, aber auch als seine Entäußerung, sein Werk. . . . Gott hat sich nicht derart in die Geschichte vermittelt, daß nichts mehr von ihm ausstünde. Er spart etwas von sich auf, wenn es erlaubt ist, so zu reden; er hält etwas zurück von sich—sonst wären wir im 'Himmel.' Das 'auch' in Hegels Rede läßt Zukunft offen und weist darauf hin, daß Gott auch noch im Erwarteten, im 'Unabgegoltenen' (Bloch) der Geschichte sich verbirgt. Substanz also bleibt, nur eben nicht theistisch, naiv, sondern als absconditas."

13. Dietrich Bonhoeffer, *Letters and Papers from Prison,* enlarged edition (New York: Macmillan, 1972), 369.

14. Ibid., 281.

15. Ibid., 300.

16. Luibl, *Des Fremden Sprachgestalt,* 236 (English translation by the author).

17. John A. T. Robinson, *Honest to God* (Philadelphia: Westminster, 1963). Robinson and Soelle both were representatives of the "God is dead" theology that caused great turmoil in Germany as well as in North America. The notion of God's death remained, however, a metaphor for the change of the modern consciousness that rejected an understanding of transcendence disconnected from human life.

18. Ibid., 99ff.

19. Perry LeFevre, *Modern Theologies of Prayer* (Chicago: Exploration Press, 1995), 204ff.

20. Dorothee Soelle, "Life without Suffering a Utopia?" in *The Strength of the Weak: Toward a Feminist Christian Identity* (trans. Rita and Robert Kimber; Philadelphia: Westminster, 1984), 28.

21. Soelle, "Das entprivatisierte Gebet," 24–25.

22. Ibid., 24.

23. Soelle, "We Do Not Know What We Should Pray," 92.

24. Luibl quotes phrases from her poem collection *"spiel doch von brot und rosen":* "uns ist nichts gegen die kälte eingefallen / außer einem hemdchen . . . Aber ärmer bin ich auch geworden und laufe depressiv durch die stadt / geh auch demonstrieren als ob da mut verteilt würde / und sähe für mein leben gern / noch die andere hälfte der geschichte / das leere grab am ostermorgen / und die leeren gräber in el salvador." Luibl, *Des Fremden Sprachgestalt,* 254–55.

25. Soelle, *Silent Cry.* Her general interest in mysticism evolved, however, earlier in the 1970s. See Soelle, *Death by Bread Alone.*

26. This trouble with the limits of religious language is already expressed in the word itself. Mysticism derives from the Indo-European root *mu,* which means inarticulate sounds; the Latin *mutus* (mute, dumb) and the Greek noun *mysterion* belong to the word field of *mystikos.* See Ewert H. Cousins, "Bonaventure's Mysticism of Language," in *Mysticism and Language* (ed. Steven T. Katz; New York: Oxford University Press, 1992), 236.

27. In her early work she states: "If Tauler thinks the purpose of prayer is to lose oneself in God, Jesus does not; he remains himself in the presence of God. Tauler's goal is silence, for he who rests in God no longer needs to call upon him. The highest form of prayer is wordless. But this is not so with the real man from Nazareth and his brothers [*sic*], of whom Luther says that they are hovering between earth and heaven." Soelle, "We Do Not Know What We Should Pray," 95.

28. Soelle, "Gebet," 113. She refers to 1 Thess 5:17, "Pray without ceasing."

29. Soelle, *Silent Cry,* 295.

30. Soelle, "We Do Not Know What We Should Pray," 98.
31. Soelle, *Silent Cry,* 292–93.
32. Ibid.
33. Ibid., 295.
34. Ibid., 63.
35. Ibid., 66.
36. Ibid., 66–67.
37. Ibid., 69.
38. Ibid., 74.
39. Ibid., 72–73.
40. Steven T. Katz, "Mystical Speech and Mystical Meaning," in *Mysticism and Language,* 33.
41. Soelle, *Silent Cry,* 119.

6. A Calling in a Higher Sense
The Poetics of Dorothee Soelle

Martin Rumscheidt

"What her prayer shows above all is that Dorothee Soelle is a translator of the Bible's poetry," writes Luise Schottroff in her essay elsewhere in this book. Dorothee Soelle speaks of Luise Schottroff as "my best friend."[1] Prayer as poetry and, conversely, poetry as prayer: This is Schottroff's imaginative key to the hermeneutic of Dorothee Soelle's theological work.

This essay seeks to examine why Soelle turned to poetry and the literary genre in order to communicate theology, how she connects the two entities, what functional characteristics distinguish them, and finally, what she desires her theological poetry to make known to her hearers and readers. There is little direct citation here of the poetry that by now fills several volumes; instead, the intent is to show why the poetic medium is so much more appropriate today for "God talk" and all that is related to it than is "theology" as it is commonly understood, if it is understood at all.

When Dorothee Soelle speaks of herself as a "theologian"—which she rarely does—one detects in her voice a note of hesitation, of reluctance. The word itself is of ambiguous coinage. Dorothee Soelle once visited Martin Buber in Israel, and during a conversation he asked her, "Theology—how do you do that?"[2] By the time Soelle studied theology at university, that critical question was beginning to form itself on the lips of many of her generation, particularly in post-World War II Germany. Buber wondered about the nimbleness with which the adept, authorized, and blessed of society dealt with the *logos*, with what humans declare they can know with certainty of the Transcendent. Buber's question was not anchored in the craving for method and almost nothing but method that marked (and marks) the theology of the academy. His question arose in the face of the accommodation of a great majority of Germany's theologians with the regime of Hitler, and the burden of guilt and shame it bequeathed to the people of that country. The horrors visited upon Jews, upon the population of countries occupied by the German armed forces, especially the Slavic people, and the terror exercised by the secret police on nearly every segment of the population radically challenged nearly all certainties. What was becoming clear was that the reign of the National Socialists was part of the "long history of calamity and guilt . . . that is on the record of my people."[3] This is how a German World War II soldier put it. In 1944 he wrote and published eight poems written under the impact of the German army's offensive against the Soviet Union and his participation in it. That soldier, Johannes Bobrowski, became a notable literary figure in what was the German Democratic Republic. His work became known to Dorothee Soelle just as she was beginning to explore how she could "do" theology. What she found in Bobrowski helped her significantly in identifying the profound aspect of poetry for the theological, and the necessary but perhaps impossible task of rebuilding theology.

However, what Dorothee Soelle described provocatively in the opening sentences of her address to a plenary session of the sixth General Assembly of the World Council of Churches in Vancounver in 1983 was not the sole reason for her asking Buber's critical question on her own. "Dear sisters and brothers, I speak to you as a woman from one of the richest countries of the earth, a country with a bloody history that reeks of gas, a history some of us Germans have not been able to forget." To this she added, in her typical fashion of always linking past with present: " I come from a country that today holds the greatest concentration of atomic weapons in the world, ready for use."[4] Alongside a history she cannot forget were three additional factors that pushed her theological inquiry. The first was her increasing alienation from the existing theology of the academy, the second the emergence of a new understanding of "spirituality," and the third her entry into the women's movement.

In her memoir, Dorothee Soelle describes these factors in the chapter on her "best friend" Luise Schottroff. She speaks of an erosion of her respect for university theology. "Not only was that theology removed from praxis, it even prided itself on *not* having a praxis, that is to say, it gave its blessing to a false one." It was in the context of just that praxis question that Soelle then spoke of the need for a "new piety" or what in French is called *"spiritualité."* Contrary to the diffuse English meaning of "spirituality," the meaning in French is more precise: "becoming more radical and more pious." "More pious" is defined by Luise Schottroff as the "'conversion' to the power of tradition, to the necessity of rereading Scripture, to hope even in times when the empirical basis of hope seems ever so thin—in other words, conversion to worship and prayer."[5] The "more radical" grew particularly out of the perhaps slowly growing recognition of sexism as *the* place where false theology and its academy and institutionalized church structures, together with the false, hierarchical ordering of life, are to be resisted and broken open.[6]

In this essay, I work with three epistemological conclusions. The first is that Auschwitz and all that it embraces signals the collapse of the so-called Western world's value systems and epistemic structures. Second, as I see it, the indispensable, symbiotic relation between theology and literature, or more broadly, between the ethical and the aesthetic, has been so centrally affected by the reality of the Holocaust that it may well be irreparable. And finally, theology, in its now widely known form as an undertaking of the academy and the institutionalized church, has since the Western world's Enlightenment distanced itself, to its very detriment, from the aesthetic. In so doing, it has undermined its own power in and for the ethical.

Institutionalized theology in the Christian West relegated literature, poetry, music, and the visual arts to the role of a decorative servant. Under the rigorous control of the two chief structures wherein they became housed and maintained, these expressions were to provide a subsidiary or complimentary interpretation to theology, the "queen" of the human spirit's expressions. As it has done for the other domains of life, both physical and spiritual, the Enlightenment loosened the bonds of theology over the work of the creative human spirit. As a consequence, that work could and did develop into something of quasi-religious, indeed, theological significance. For example, historian and theologian Adolf von Harnack (1851–1930) interpreted the art of Johann Wolfgang von Goethe and how the religious renewal movement of Anthroposophy had elevated that poet's famous *Faust* to the level of sublime liturgy.[7]

This is not the place to discuss the turn to the "cultural" that so marked the Protestant liberal theology of the latter part of the nineteenth and the earlier part of the twentieth centuries. In my view, in its positive approach to the broader domains of the artistic, it failed the deep dimensions of the human spirit's search for and encounter with the transcendent "Thou."[8] However, it is noteworthy that in many ways and for many people, literature and poetry in particular, but also music and the visual arts, reflectively subsumed the content of theology and "secularized" it. The poets Johann Christian Friedrich Hölderlin

(1770–1843) and Rainer Maria Rilke (1875–1926) come to mind here; the former became the focus of the philosophy of "Being" of twentieth-century philosopher Martin Heidegger (1889–1976). Hölderlin had asserted that what abides is fathomed by poets. Such a view is not the mystification of people who have become disenchanted with established religion. Rather, it critically exposes the false orientation, if not even the very failure, of theology. Why else would poetry set out to become the "secular" bearer of what is at the heart of the theological endeavor?

The "religion" that predominated in the Western world for more than sixteen centuries is Christianity in its numerous and varied denominations. The charge that can, or needs to, be laid against nearly all of them is that they have held (or still do hold) the human being in bondage. What I mean is that religion was (is) presented in the language of dominance. Being declared the domain of the initiated, the adept, and the experts, theology has for many Christians turned into a mysterious and esoteric discourse, inaccessible to the great majority of the population. The regular preaching of the churches of the Protestant reformations, the celebration of the eucharistic liturgy in Roman Catholicism, in Anglicanism, and to a certain extent, in Orthodoxy manifest clerical control both of the assembled congregation and of the sacred itself. Even reformative or renewal attempts to halt such nimble domestication often fall short of freeing human beings from the petty orderliness of hierarchy, allowing various forms of domination to maintain themselves, however chastened, and even to strengthen themselves.

What is traditionally referred to as the "Word of God" is something "literary." It is spoken and written communication. When turned into language of domination, the "Word" is blocked from what even in that language it is claimed to be, namely the liberation of human beings. Instead, their being in tutelage is cemented, the freedom to become and remain of age is a matter of what Dorothee Soelle and Luise Schottroff call a "false praxis." (The critique of religion Dietrich Bonhoeffer presents in his exploration of a "religionless Christianity" has precisely the same features Soelle and Schottroff envisage. He names them: inwardness, partiality, and otherworldliness.) Many Christians who embraced the Enlightenment and its cry "Sapere aude!" ("Dare to use your mind!") substituted "the good, beautiful, and true" for "religion," if they did not, like Hölderlin, see literature, poetry, music, painting, etc. as religion itself. However this development is to be evaluated, the Western world's "Enlightenment" bequeathed its children the firm conviction that the aesthetic is, unlike religion in its prevalent mode of existence, a means of liberation, of coming of age—in a word, of humanization.

Dorothee Soelle's circle of friends has always included poets, writers, painters, and representatives of other forms of what Germans speak of as *die schönen Künste* (a well-nigh untranslatable term.) One of them was the Nobel Laureate Heinrich Böll (1917–1985) to whom she dedicated a chapter in her memoir and on whose death she wrote a psalm-like poem.[9] As if in intercession or invocation, Soelle calls on the unnamed "Who" (always with a capital *W*)— "Who protects, shields, reminds, comforts, promises, strengthens, intercedes?"— knowing that the call is not into a void but to the Unnamable One who has many names. Soon after she came to know Heinrich Böll in 1967, he and fellow writer Johannes Poethen had a conversation on religion and literature; it was broadcast on German radio. I cite the following excerpts from that conversation since it may be a source of an answer to why poetry became, willingly or not, a bearer of theological substance. It may also indicate what "purpose" Dorothee Soelle pursues in her theological poetics. Böll points out:

> Literature and art are means of humanization. . . . They respect human beings in their lostness. That is why they can never be optimistic, whereas religion, religion-substitutes like Marxism and doctrinaire political teachings have to be so; they therefore render art and literature inhumane. Human beings are qualified by mourning, by love and transitoriness. Creating itself: painting a picture, composing music, writing a poem, or prose, is an erotic process creating relationship. Initially, the erotic relationship is between the artist and the artifact. . . . The eros that comes into being can, of course, create also a relationship to human beings, possibly to God or the devil. . . . Here looms the danger of a new myth emerging, the myth of the author or the artist. This is a mistake, in my view. I believe . . . that authors and artists, all creative people must enter into a relationship of equality with the non-privileged so that they do not create for an educated elite who turn the art created into a pseudo-religious esotericism.[10]

The cult of the genius, of "great men," (Adolf von Harnack is an example of this "cult") that characterized the West's nineteenth century and its pseudo-religion, needed to be resisted with the imperatives of *equality*.[11] To resist in such manner, Böll continues, is

> most likely the task of twentieth century artists; they need to create the myth of equality. No more elitist notions! [Did Böll also think of the elitism of antisemitism here?] . . . Religion, the churches and denominations, having envisaged nothing but authority, are in a state of being completely remaindered. They existed by authoritarian means only, falsely believing that religion was inheritable, to be passed on by doctrine, transferable. [As a result of the collapse of religion caused by this

false belief,] art is put into a position that it really cannot defend: it becomes religion, the only expression of the Word, while the Word of God, corrupted by its representatives, is barely audible, barely understandable. So many intermediary steps were interposed, so many stages of domestication. It might just be that it is precisely the decidedly non-Christian, that is, anti-Christian, even blasphemous literature . . . that will lead forward to humanization and create the human being who can be addressed with the Word of God who became, as we are taught, a human being.[12]

Later in the conversation, Böll and Poethen expand on the "myth of equality" that a genuinely "democratic" literature needs to create. It needs

to create the myth of the human being, of the everyday life of humans, and create anew the mythical elements of everyday human life, the poetry of that everyday life. We basically still think in terms of the categories of "educated" and "uneducated." I believe that a democratic literature must first demolish this myth of "educated" and "uneducated": it must be jarringly popular and popularizeable. . . . Here, there emerges the myth of the human being who is subject to transitoriness, capable of love and hate, living an everyday life. And that life, too, is a myth.[13]

When Böll surmises that theology, as a scholarly discipline, never became something important, he expresses what Dorothee Soelle also affirms. What has been important for people has always been what was secondary in and for theology, "in other words, the unimportant," as he puts it.[14] But it was the unimportant with which control was exercised over people: rules, regulations, church law, catechetical injunctions, etc. People have left behind the institutionalized church and academic theology in order to discover and live the great insights of theology that rarely found their way to the wider populace; to lift the veil off those insights and to live their praxis is what, in Böll's and Soelle's view, "democratic" poetry can do for the basis of humankind.

Without expressly stating it, the radio conversation of Böll and Poethen names the process that became utterly exposed in the Holocaust: the inability of religion to provide through its institutionalized and scientific media a praxis of resistance, that is, an ethics *for* human beings. Those media were elitist, readily amenable to the elitism of the planners and practitioners of the "final solution." This elitism could and did root itself in religion, church, and academy, all of which, being in false orientation, failed the human being. While Böll and Poethen directly name the elitism of religion established in the church institution and its structures, they also identify it, albeit in its varying forms, in the aesthetic domain. Here they incidentally provide a persuasive answer to the question why it was in the very nation of Bach, Beethoven, Goethe, and Hölderlin that the Shoah came into being. This creation of German will, organization, technology, and coercion brutally manifests the apex of a process one and a half centuries long: the utter impotence of art and religion to concretize themselves in a praxis of resistance, perhaps even to imagine one at all.

Dorothee Soelle's latest book, *The Silent Cry: Mysticism and Resistance,* portrays such a praxis in conjunction with a democratic, noninstitutionally based theology. She maintains that in shunning every attempt to impose definitions, the language of poetry is able to render meaning audible and resonant exactly because of its narrative freedom and the range of linguistic means available to it. In particular, she names those used in mysticism: frequent repetition, comparison, exaggeration, hyperbole, antithesis, and paradox.[15] When the relationship between theology and literature is severed, the result is that both suffer. In that separation, theology seeks refuge in "science," which, Soelle argues, is finally something of no ultimate concern to much of humankind. What theology then produces as a secondary product for the general population: ordinances, pronouncements, how-to manuals, etc., declaring them to be for the good of the people, turns out to be detrimental to the real, the profound insights of theology. They are viewed with suspicion instead; the broadly aesthetic, even in its weakness, comes to be seen as more credible and, for that very reason, more decisive and significant.

When a strong relationship exists between them, there is mutual benefit. But the dogma of modernity is a hurdle to be overcome: the separation of the aesthetic, of politics, church, and religion into distinct domains. The Holocaust radically exposed the weakness of that dogma, for existing side by side in a spiritual apartheid, a religion separate from politics ends up venerating power and its idols; a politics separate from religion decays in despising humanity, and a politics and religion separate from the aesthetic turn into mere utilitarian instruments of the principalities and powers of this world.

In 1970 Dorothee Soelle published "Theses concerning the criteria of theological interest in literature." There she says that the theological interest in literature is directed primarily toward "what ultimately concerns us," and that this concern is hidden in the pure profaneness of the artistic form. It is the task of theology to uncover this hidden dimension. In the language of art, theology finds a "non-religious interpretation of theological concepts" (sought by Bonhoeffer). These concepts are those that address human beings in their totality and relate them to their eternal, that is, their authentic life. In its discovery process, theology cannot restrict itself to myth or to the Bible, however significant both are for the self-formulation of human beings. What is theologically important is not just to revert back to myth or the sources of faith but to reach out for authentic life, to anticipate it in praxis. The understanding of what is of ultimate concern to us is in reference to the conditions of finitude; hence, theology is particularly, albeit not exclusively, interested in what brings transitoriness into our consciousness. Art that so covers up transitoriness as to no longer hold before us the victims of a culture is hardly of interest to theology. For both theology and art, banality is a mortal danger. That which is theologically relevant opens us up, lifts us out of the assurances of what we know, confronts us with our own clichés, unmasks us, and changes our relation to the world and, hence, ourselves.[16]

> This kind of poetry is no luxury item; it is bread. It turns our planet, ever so beloved in spite of everything, more and more into home.... [Poetry] creates a boundary dissolving freedom. . . . I really do not believe in the modern program of *poésie pure:* Wherever it happens successfully that the unmixed purity of the beautiful becomes sound and language, poetry is no longer "pure" and "for itself." . . . When I learned Greek, the concept *kalonkagathon* became very dear to my heart. In my seventeen-year-old unintelligence, I wondered how the Greeks could take two words that for us have nothing to do with each other, and turn them into one word: beauty-good. Where on earth would one find aesthetics and ethics in the same dish? . . . In order really to do theology we need a different language. Poetry and liberation are topics central to my life.[17]

Poetry as prayer, prayer as poetry, poetry and liberation praxis: When coupled with the other, does each not lead to the subversion of both? In his *Frankfurter Vorlesungen,* Heinrich Böll made it clear that whenever literature enters into any context whatsoever, it becomes itself the object of diverse interests which, themselves vulnerable and possibly even wounded, may well in turn wound literature.[18] But perhaps even more crucial is the question whether the aim of being about the praxis of liberation does not in itself turn a poem into something propagandistic, so that it ceases to be poetry and becomes just that: propaganda. Some critics, such as Theodor Adorno and Hans Magnus Enzenberger, believe that the theological or political intent of a poem, let us say, has to be contained solely in the artistic *quality* of the poem. The relation of an artistic creation to the theological, social, or political must not lead from but more deeply into the work of art. That to which a poem seeks to relate itself must, so to speak, enter through the cracks, behind the author's back on its own, without the author, as it were. Others known for their "political" agenda, such as Bertold Brecht or Walter Benjamin, insist that in addition to the linguistic-artistic quality (the form), a poem with theological intent (the content) needs a specific technique: How is the envisaged readership to be addressed so that the desired result is achieved? How is the linguistic-communicative aspect to be shaped that the public to be addressed understands the artistic creation? Dorothee Soelle herself makes it plain, in a lecture delivered on Brecht Tage 2002 (included in this volume), that she identifies with the hermeneutic of poetry espoused by Brecht and Benjamin. To her, Adorno and Enzenberger strive more for a form of poetry which she called *poésie pure* and for which she has little interest. I think she identifies in the "dislike" what made "poetry" something that, according to Adorno, could no longer be properly written after Auschwitz. Her response is precisely that Auschwitz demands a response, one that intentionally sets out to bring about a conscientization and transformation that will prevent another holocaust. And her theology, that is, what it is about and seeks to make known and understandable, has a contribution to make, namely, what has already been referred to as the "liberation" from tutelage to the powers and ideologies of the age and for a solidarity with the neighbor whom we are commanded to "love," even when that neighbor is not to our liking or does not meet with our approval, as she puts it in her essay on Bertold Brecht.[19]

In this context it is helpful to turn to yet someone else from her circle of friends: theologian, preacher, teacher, and poet Kurt Marti (1921–). Together with Wolfgang Fietkau and Armin Juhre, he and Soelle edited and published the instructive and rewarding series *Almanach für Literatur und Theologie,* beginning in 1967. An essay Kurt Marti wrote for the Festschrift for Swiss preacher and theologian Eduard Thurneysen in 1968 is included in the 1969 *Almanach.* The essay is entitled "Wie entsteht eine Predigt? Wie entsteht ein Gedicht? Ein Vergleich mit dem Versuch einer Nutzanwendung." ("How does a sermon come into being? How does a poem come into being? A comparison and attempt of practical application.")[20]

Like Soelle, Marti prays in and through his poetry while also seeking to present the profound depths and heights of theological knowledge, which is what he also does in his preaching. Are his sermons then artistic creations and his poetry a homiletical endeavor? His proposal to compare poem and sermon and then seek for a possible practical application is highly illuminating for an interpretation of Dorothee Soelle and what I call her poetry as a "vocation in a higher sense."

Marti declares that neither a sermon nor a poem comes into being on its own but is "made," and "making" them is work. But work on a poem and on a sermon are comparable; in both cases the medium of language is used. Yet each work has different presuppositions and aims.

Preachers preach commissioned by their churches. Lyricists are not commissioned by any institution to write poems. . . . The task of preachers is to proclaim the Word of God as it is attested to in the biblical witness. Lyricists, on the other hand, set out from their unarticulated experiences, emotions, ideas, fantasies, observations, and the like. The *aim* of their work is the articulated text. An already articulated text, that of the Bible, is the *point of departure* of preachers. With their commission, preachers also receive the general theme of their sermons. They are to make known "the great acts of God." (Acts 2:11) No theme is given to the lyricists; they must find it themselves or let themselves be found by it. Preachers, beginning their work of writing the sermon, know that they *must* deliver the sermon, irrespective of whether they succeeded fully, or only half or not at all, in their work. Setting out to work on a poem, lyricists do not know whether what they have begun will ever become a poem. As soon as a poem is published, lyricists submit it to the free, often merciless, often just and often also bribable competition of the literary market and critique. This compels them from the very outset to be rigorously self-critical. . . . From their first sermon on, preachers have an audience while lyricists have to gather a readership first. . . . The fact is that initially no readership awaits the lyricists and even later, the circle of those awaiting their work remains small. Lyricists [unlike preachers] work alone without being called or commissioned. Driven by pleasure or dismay, ambition or despair or whatever else, they write into an anonymous sphere. Both lyricists and preachers have their own uncertainties: lyricists as to whether their work will find a hearing at all and is meaningful, preachers as to whether their work is adequate to their assigned commission and the demands of the congregation.[21]

Kurt Marti's understanding of "theology" is that of Reformation Protestantism. Theology speaks of "the Word of God," which is to say that God is not an unarticulated existence. God is not timeless or abstract but, as articulated communication, is historical, concrete, here and now, this and not that. The Bible gives testimony to this articulated Word, to the here and now of God. The preachers' task is to present this testimony in the sermon that all present become expectant, quasi impatiently and excitedly asking: And now? What of us? Is there a future for us in the Word? And what kind of future here and now? The work of preparing and delivering the sermon includes exegesis and interpretation, to which theological study at university pays much attention. But, in addition, in order to let the hearers come to ask those highly existential questions above, sermon preparation requires meditation: to reflect prayerfully on the text, to weigh it, to think oneself into it, to carry it around within oneself in the midst of the encounters, experiences and problems of everyday. In this phase, the text quasi besets the preachers, their habits and prejudgments.

Conversely, the preachers beset the text with their questions, experiences, doubts. One may also say that the text courts the preachers and the preachers the text and often this mutual courting resembles a struggle.[22]

Marti continues his comparison, still dealing with theology and poetry as separate entities. For him the poet (lyricist) too is "receptive." Poets do not listen to "him," that is, God, but to "it," the world as they experience it. Not the world *as such* but the world as each poet experiences it; it is, therefore, not an objective entity but one wherein it is impossible to distinguish between subject and object. Poets listen to their world (which is "the" world for them) by meditating on their subjective experience of the world. The object of their meditation, their receptivity is therefore not "he," God, but "it," the world. This distinction is not a simple one of method; it embodies a fundamental position that wants to keep "he" and "it," God and world, revelation of God and experience of the world clearly separate. In poetry, poets do not mediate divine revelation but experience of the world. "If in their poems there is talk of God then it is an element of their subjective experience of the world or an invocation of a power which to call God appears appropriate to the poets. . . . What they call God could be God."[23]

Kurt Marti names a profound danger for every poem that makes being understood one of its primary aims. Striving to be understood invites accommodating oneself to the conventional language of society, thereby becoming overtly or covertly subverted by the interests of those who dominate in society. Both Marti and Soelle draw on the prophetic element of theology here to stay clear of this danger. This is manifested well in Soelle's latest work, *The Silent Cry: Mysticism and Resistance.* She shows repeatedly there how a theology that has no practical agenda is relevant only for those who have nothing to resist except what threatens them in their places of elitism.

Marti's conclusion of his comparison is, in my view, illuminating and provocative. He asks, When is a poem, a sermon, "complete"? It is complete when, in its author's judgment, it has become a linguistic entity, autonomous and no longer to be improved upon, self-contained, that is, rhythmically and metaphorically compact. How different the sermon! It seeks to draw listeners into a dialogue. What to an outside observer may seem to be a dialogue between congregation and preacher is really an attempt to enable the deeply existential dialogue between congregation and God within God's own dialogue with the congregation. A sermon can, for that very reason, never be complete as a poem may be said to be. Only *God's* Word, when it meets and transforms a human being, completes the sermon, which is a human word, and allows an "Amen" to conclude the sermon and in that sense complete it.[24]

Marti's "practical application" shows how theology and poetry, poetry and theology relate without mutually subverting each other or ceasing to be what each is. He manifests his suspicion of what I earlier referred to as "nimbleness" on the part of religious elites. Like Dorothee Soelle and Luise Schottroff and their critique of theology "administered" by the institutions of church and academy, Marti believes that the idea of a Word of God under the "management" of the church encouraged the misunderstanding that this Word is "objective" in the sense that it now needs only to be recited and no longer needs to be witnessed to. To witness means to communicate or articulate God's Word with the subjectivity that is given to everyone. And in the witnesses' articulation they do not primarily but clearly secondarily communicate also themselves.

Preachers are to proclaim the Word of God, not their subjectivity. But that Word is refracted in the human subjectivity of Jesus of Nazareth and those who seek to follow him, attaining to its radiancy only in such refraction. The same is true for the testimony of the biblical witnesses. What poets know, namely, that experience and articulation are "genuine" only when the subjective is knowingly introduced, is important for preachers. They speak as witnesses and not as scientists who make operational use of the terminology of objectivity. As witnesses, preachers need to insert themselves, their subjectivity into their testimony no less decidedly than poets do in their poems. This means that preachers will make use of subjectivity clauses such as "In my view" or "As I understand it." This is how Marti puts it:

> The more preachers express their views and understandings as their *subjective* views, their *subjective* understandings, and in so doing open their statements to discussion, the more credible they become . . . when they must speak prophetically, when they do actually declare a word to be indisputably *God's* Word: thus says the Lord now and not in another way, this and nothing else is what *God* wants from us now. . . . Only a sermon that is vulnerably open . . . can open others for that dialogue in the course of which God's Word . . . both activates and assures the consciousness, the conduct and finally also the subconscious of humans so that hearers of the Word become doers thereof (James 1:22) who as active witnesses to God's shalom (peace, salvation, justice, well-being) help change society.[25]

By setting the poem's language apart from or opposed to the conventional, ideological, and interest-bearing language of society, a poet hopes that society may change its language as a result. Poetry seen this way has linguistic traces of a more humane world. In that sense poetry also opens dialogue. This does not automatically cause it to become "engaged" poetry closer in line with what Brecht and Benjamin proposed.

[Poetry] is more than what is commonly understood by engagement. Its category is that of possibility. Reality too is understood [by poetry] to a large extent as possibility. . . . The category of possibility is what points in a poem beyond the past and the present . . . to the future. By mediating on and playing with possibilities, which takes place more or less in every poem, poetry quietly contradicts what is now and envisages an individual and social situation where humans can develop their possibilities more freely, better, where, instead of being pushed into neuroses, they are freed to themselves and so also become free for all that is not the ego. . . . [Poets] should become more aware that they too are drawn into dialogue with their readers and hearers about the future of this changeable world.[26]

What distinguishes poets and Christians but also brings them into conjunction is that for the former the future is a multiformed and still undetermined possibility, while for the latter the future took form and was decided in the subjectivity of the Word of God made flesh.

Dorothee Soelle eloquently expresses that conjunction. She gives very concrete contours to Marti's "category of possibility" in that she relates "possibility," "future" to what above was called "authentic life" as it took expression in the life of Jesus of Nazareth. But instead of repeating the both definitionally precise but inexhaustive *theological* terms, such as redemption, reconciliation, sanctification, and others, she paints word pictures such as the one that gives title to her presentation on the poetry of Johannes Bobrowski: "For a Time without Fear."[27] Soelle is determined, for reasons already signaled, "to speak of God in worldly language," as Dietrich Bonhoeffer's biographer, Eberhard Bethge, put it. (Bethge and Soelle were good friends; he stood by her in all of her "troubles" with the church, and his insight into the work of Bonhoeffer made a strong impact on her theological articulation.[28])

Bobrowski (1917–1965) grew up in Eastern Germany and, after World War II, lived in what was until recently the German Democratic Republic. He openly declared that he was Christian but not a "Christian writer." Society in the East and West, then and now, looks on "faith" as something of the ecclesiastical establishment; it is seen as having to say more about the maintenance of law and order than the encouragement of conscience. Having served in the German army that had wreaked havoc on the people and territory of the Soviet Union, having seen the destruction of European Jewry and realizing that this was part of the long history of disaster and guilt that rested on his people, he saw in the creation and encouragement of conscience and of a different future, a chance for both poetry and Christian faith. He referred to his war and Holocaust experiences as his "war injury."[29] Not until 1949 was he released from the Soviet prisoner of war camps. Before the outbreak of the Hitler war, Bobrowski was associated with the Confessing Church movement in Germany.

Dorothee Soelle characterizes Bobrowski's poetic language as something that is close to what in the Bible is known as "calling," as "a voice calling in the wilderness"[30] Such "calling" is not communication or information *about* something; rather, it is a matter of invocation and adjuration, even conjuring. Above all else, "calling" in that sense promises a future.

Whenever Bobrowski speaks of, or names, God, he does so in what Kurt Marti called "subjectivity clauses." The poet speaks of God in the indicative case, since God cannot be spoken of in the manner we speak of "objects." Bobrowski shows in his clauses of subjectivity that, as Bonhoeffer put it: *"Einen Gott, den es gibt, gibt es nicht"*—there is not God that is there, a God, that is, who can be spoken of in the mindset of objectivity. The language of such clauses is "nonreligious" or "secular"; it has abandoned the sense that one can speak of God, of the dimension and aspects of the transcendent, in "objective" terms, as does the scholarly theology of academy and institutionalized church rejected by Soelle and others. The objectivity that is alleged to be necessary for genuine scholarly pursuit and, subsequently, for "correct" communication of the Christian "truth," claiming to have no praxis—as that would only subvert the objective pursuit of truth—is actually blessing a false praxis, as Soelle maintains. She asserts that theological reflection has to cross the threshold of conscience where praxis is critically analyzed. Here language itself changes from description, mythic naming, and even injunction; it becomes language of the yet unseen. "Vision of a more humane world, utopia of the life that is promised . . . home. Not the home that nature provides beforehand, not that of blood and soil, but the one yet to be won." Soelle quotes the same text that she uses nearly three decades later in her work on mysticism and resistance. "The root of history is the human being working, creating, reshaping, and surpassing what is now. When humans have laid hold of themselves and rooted what is theirs, without relinquishment and alienation, in real democracy, something comes to be in the world, that shines into the childhood of all and in which no one had yet been: *Heimat,* home."[31]

This is a prominent feature in Bobrowski's poetry and in it Soelle recognizes historical consciousness. Not that of the observer: "The observer sees nothing," she quotes from Bobrowski. It is the consciousness of one who, gripped in the long history of disaster and guilt and its traditions (such as elitism), has crossed the threshold of conscience and now "calls up," "invokes" the yet unseen, the promised world of authentic life. It is a time without fear. In Bobrowski the language of Christian faith and tradition has the function of representing the messianic expectation of the human being, the "more brightly colored years."[32]

Soelle describes the complex meaning of "calling" or "invoking" in Bobrowski; in my view, it fits her poetry precisely.

> Human beings attain to their reality through calling and speaking, asking and responding. . . . One . . . dimension of this word [the word *calling*] is the religious . . . the Jewish-Christian tradition, which is not further secularized because it is . . . already secular enough. In some places "calling" has the limited and clear sense of "praising God" . . . of "calling hosanna." . . . This absolute use of the word—without dative or accusative—is known from the language of the Psalms. This calling is synonymous with praying, the one addressed is not specifically named. The specific term "praying," monopolized by church language, does not occur in Bobrowski's poetry, but "calling" as a broader gesture contains within itself the dimension of praising and pleading. . . . Calling is a form of being alive, it belongs to that kind of life that cannot come to its reality in aloneness. . . . Everyone who calls . . . is not content with the "object"; calling is a kind of transcendence over the time of fear; being able to call is something that is not at our disposition any time, any place.[33]

"Calling" means composing, writing poetry. The word—Soelle calls it a Jewish word—perceives the person in her relationship to another; it perceives God in that same way. If one understands Bobrowski's poetry as "calling," then it serves as an example for a Christian poetry that is possible today, one that does not talk "about" God but calls God, to or upon God, for a time without fear.[34]

> For me, praying and writing poetry, prayer and poem, are not alternatives. The message I wish to pass on is meant to encourage people to learn to speak themselves. For example, the idea that every human being can pray is for me an enormous affirmation of human creativity. Christianity presupposes that all human beings are poets, namely, that they can pray. That is the same as seeing with the eyes of God. When people try to say with the utmost capacity for truthfulness what really concerns them, they offer prayer and are poets at the same time. To discover this anew, to bring it into reality or make it known, is one of the goals I pursue in my poems.[35]

Recently two women in Germany published what may well be called a "Soelle reader." They entitled their 240-page anthology of texts by Dorothee

Soelle *To Feel the Rhythm of Life: Inspiring the Ordinary.* Each of the twelve chapters derives its title from a line of one of Soelle's poems, followed by two words (or phrases) conjoined by the little word *and*, words that name "what really concerns" human beings. I cite these twelve titles because they are a form of "calling," of "adjuring."

1. "We are all called to hallow time." The Now and Eternity.
2. "And it is not plain yet what we shall be." To Be Human and Destiny.
3. "Give me the gift of tears, give me the gift of language." Fear and Consolation.
4. "You are to let love bloom." Yearning and Giving the Self.
5. "God's pain embraces my pain." Suffering and Vulnerability.
6. "What are you doing? the angel asks me." Justice and Responsibility.
7. "Someday the trees shall be the teachers." Creation and Solidarity.
8. "Peace is a millet-seed, teeny-weeny." Gentleness and Non-violence.
9. "The bright morning star rises in my soul." Joy and Happiness.
10. "Not we give life meaning, life gives us meaning." Seeking and Being Found.
11. "I shall sing and wrest a chunk of land from death with every note." Dying and Being Raised Up.
12. "We go to the city of our hope." Wishes and Visions.

In their afterword, Bettina Hertel and Birte Petersen write:

> What we wish for our lives need not be little and timid but can be just as big as the wishes and promises of the one to whom we belong. . . . It is not that greater and greater demands be put on life; what concerns [Dorothee Soelle] is that wishes become reality through one's own action and in responsibility toward fellow humans and fellow creatures. . . . Her texts took us into a spirituality that joins profound personal questioning to an alert attention to the world. It is a spirituality that never gives smooth answers to life's questions. On the contrary, there is great tension in those twelve themes. Happiness cannot be thought without pain, death without life, future without memory. It is precisely in the strongest and deepest experiences of love, mystical union and happiness that Dorothee Soelle also reflects on the dark side. . . . Dorothee Soelle has an artful and, at the same time, willful way of articulating her thoughts. She interrupts herself with objections, contradicts tradition and speaks in paradoxes. In a poem on "resurrection" she writes "O don't ask about resurrection a tale of ages long ago" only to conclude it by calling out "O do ask me about resurrection. O don't stop asking me!" . . . The rhythm of life that

Dorothee Soelle feels is multi-layered. It is a joy to let ourselves be drawn into that rhythm.[36]

In that rhythm, according to Soelle, human beings and God, human beings and human beings, human beings and all of creation experience their mutuality and interdependence. It is through "calling," "invoking," and "adjuring" or even "conjuring" that this mutuality is expressed and, in fact, made real. And then it is possible to see images of resurrection, to learn hope, to love, and to resist.

In English, the distinction is made between "calling" and "vocation" even though both may mean the very same thing. *Vocare* means "to call" and to be called is to be invited into a "vocation." In German there is a parallel differentiation between *Beruf* and *Berufung*. The former is an utterly secular term, referring to one's job, whereas the latter has the clear dimension of having been called, most closely related to the religious aspect of having been addressed by the divine. It is this aspect that is heard in the phrase "a vocation in a higher sense." I imply unambiguously that Dorothee Soelle's vocation—"job" or *Beruf*—as a theologian and poet is a "calling," a *Berufung* to witness to the future that is the substance of our hope, the future that is not entirely at the disposal of us human beings. And the witness that we give, and which is found abundantly in Soelle's poetry, appropriately takes the form of "calling" (German, *rufen*) or "invoking" (German, *anrufen*). The "higher sense" refers to the inescapable and central aspect of being *berufen*: being called by the One whom humans cannot name objectively but only through subjectivity clauses, on the one hand, and decisive acts of solidarity with the neighbor, on the other. "Vocation" in this sense rests in the call into freedom for the neighbor, liberation for a praxis of living already in the promised future that is in the hands of God and is shared by God with us humans to be fulfilled, to live out in anticipation the *Heimat* of which Ernst Bloch speaks and thereby create it in the world already. What Luise Schottroff characterized as the hermeneutic of Soelle's writing, namely, poetry as prayer and prayer as poetry, depicts the vocation in a higher sense in that prayer itself is a "calling," an *anrufen* or invoking of the One whose spirit leads those who pray into a more radical and more pious *spiritualité*, as Schottroff and Soelle see it. Dorothee Soelle calls on, enters into conversation with God; her "calling" invokes the conversation God has with human beings in which they are called into the vocation of the future promised to humanity. And, hence, her conversation with God, addressed as it is also to her readers, becomes a form of God's conversation with and calling to them. This is her vocation.

In Dorothee Soelle's hands the poem becomes, both in substance and form, shelter or refuge, even rescue in the face of hopelessness and utter inconsolation. That is why the accolade applies to her: Hers is a vocation in a higher sense.

Notes

The author of this chapter acknowledges with gratitude the rich participation of Barbara Rumscheidt in the translation of Dorothee Soelle's essays in this book; she also carefully edited this chapter, helping to soften my "Germanisms." Barbara Rumscheidt died in January 2003. She was Dorothee Soelle's friend. May they both rest in peace.

1. Dorothee Soelle, *Against the Wind: Memoir of a Radical Christian* (trans. Barbara and Martin Rumscheidt; Minneapolis: Fortress, 1999), 158.

2. Dorothee Soelle, *Thinking about God: An Introduction to Theology* (trans. John Bowden; Philadelphia: Trinity Press International, 1990), 2.

3. Hans Dieter Schäfer, "Johannes Bobrowskis Anfänge im 'Inneren Reich,'" in *Almanach für Literatur und Theologie,* vol. 4 (Wuppertal: Peter Hammer Verlag, 1970), 67. Cited as *Almanach.*

4. Soelle, *Against the Wind,* 93.

5. Ibid., 159.

6. Ibid., 158–60.

7. See Martin Rumscheidt, *Revelation and Theology. An Analysis of the Barth-Harnack Correspondence of 1923* (Cambridge: Cambridge University Press, 1972) on Harnack's views and use of Goethe's poetry and the place of Goethe's *Faust* at the high temple of Anthroposophy at Dornach, Switzerland.

8. See Martin Rumscheidt, ed., *Adolf von Harnack: Liberal Theology at Its Height,* vol. 6 of *The Making of Modern Theology* (London: Collins, Harper and Row, 1989), 9–41. Cited as *Liberal Theology.*

9. Soelle, *Against the Wind,* 143.

10. *Almanach,* vol. 4 (1970), 97.

11. Rumscheidt, *Liberal Theology,* 232–68.

12. *Almanach,* vol. 4 (1970), 97–98.

13. Ibid., 99.

14. Ibid., 102.

15. Dorothee Soelle, *The Silent Cry: Mysticism and Resistance* (trans. Barbara and Martin Rumscheidt; Minneapolis: Fortress, 2001), 64.

16. *Almanach,* vol. 4 (1970), 206–7.

17. Soelle, *Against the Wind,* 151.

18. Heinrich Böll, *Frankfurter Vorlesungen* (Munich: Deutscher Taschenbuch Verlag, 1977), 7–9.

19. See Dorothee Soelle, "The Guarantor of Poor Peoples's Rights," published in this volume.

20. *Almanach,* vol. 3 (1969), 94–109.

21. Ibid., 94–95.

22. Ibid., 97.

23. Ibid., 100.

24. Ibid., 103–4.

25. Ibid., 106–7.

26. Ibid., 108–9.

27. Dorothee Soelle, "Für eine Zeit ohne Angst—Christliche Elemente in der Lyrik Johannes Bobrowskis," in *Almanach,* vol. 2 (1968), 143–166.

28. Soelle, *Against the Wind,* 92.

29. *Almanach,* vol. 2 (1968), 145.

30. Ibid., 147.

31. Ibid., 158. See also Soelle, *Silent Cry,* 11.

32. *Almanach,* vol. 2 (1968), 161.

33. Ibid., 163–64.

34. Ibid., 165.

35. Soelle, *Against the Wind,* 153.

36. Dorothee Soelle, *Den Rhythmus des Lebens spüren. Inspirierter Alltag* (ed. Bettina Hertel and Birte Petersen; Freiburg: Verlag Herder, 2001), 243–44.

PART 3

SUFFERING
AND REDEMPTION

7. Witnessing Trauma
Dorothee Soelle's Theology of Suffering in a World of Victimization

Flora A. Keshgegian

In the last decades of the twentieth century, Christian theologians turned their attention to the challenges posed by those victimized by violence in history. Events of genocide, particularly the Holocaust, and growing awareness of the injustices wrought by practices of colonialism and imperialism in the so-called "third world," as well as the exploitation of women and all those deemed "other," called for serious theological attention. The truth and authenticity of theological claims seemed to be at stake. The cries of those who suffered demanded response. Johann Baptist Metz posited that the twentieth century was witness to a new subject of history: victims. For Metz, these victims suffered history rather than being agents of it. Theologies arose around the globe that tried in one way or another to attend to the victimized and to bear witness. Dorothee Soelle's work on suffering stands out among those attempts as an articulate and passionate expression of the need for Christianity to pay serious attention to those who suffer. Her work, especially her early volume *Suffering,* offers one of the few and arguably earliest phenomenologies of suffering from a theological perspective.

For many theologians, the problem of suffering leads directly and most naturally to the question of theodicy. How could a good God allow such pain? Soelle, in concert with the political and liberation theologians with whom she identifies, directs her theological attention to questions about the human condition and about justice. What happens to people in situations that are oppressive and that threaten the goodness of existence, if not life itself? Soelle has rightly tried to move away from excessive concern with justifying God's power and goodness and toward the effects and dynamics of suffering on those who are directly affected by it. Her theological interest seems to be less in asking "Why?" than "How?" How are humans to deal with suffering, especially when it threatens human life and meaning and when it is caused by social and political forces? In *Suffering,* she presents a range of responses persons have to travail. She describes the movement from "mute" suffering to articulation to resistance and action for transformation. Soelle also includes, in her works, numerous narratives of those who are afflicted by political suffering such as poverty and torture. These narratives serve as sources for her theological analysis and point to her diligence in dealing with the challenges suffering poses to meaningful human existence and agency. The ability to act and the possibility of transcending self, often in mystical encounter, are central to Soelle's approach to suffering. Yet this emphasis on the mystical belies her continuing interest in justifying God's presence. What is at the heart of her spirituality and theology is affirmation of presence: God's presence in relation to and in support of human subjectivity. Although she argues against traditional theodicies, her theological agenda is still framed by a desire to make suffering meaningful in relation to God.

Trauma studies, as developed by psychologists and theorists, are also concerned with the conditions of victimization. They attempt to understand the impact of traumatic suffering, most often caused by violence that is meant to terrorize the victimized. Trauma theory offers particular insights into victimization and the human struggle with such challenges to selfhood. Rather than asking why violence happens, it focuses on the "how" question and the ways in which people deal with violent injury.[1]

When traumatic suffering is intentionally inflicted by perpetrators, it is often meant to strip away all that allows someone to be present to self in the world. Survivors of such suffering sometimes describe themselves as being in a black hole, which by definition is absence. The experienced losses are of safety and a sense of connection, of dignity and of meaning. States of traumatic and posttraumatic existence are characterized by such losses and a sense of void or absence that they produce.[2]

Even more profoundly challenging to any sense of presence is another dynamic of traumatic events: namely, that such events often are not experienced in their happening.[3] Therefore, there is a struggle to bring those events into awareness and thus to make them present to the self and others. Dori Laub describes this phenomenon:

Massive trauma precludes its registration; the observing and recording mechanisms of the human mind are temporarily knocked out,
malfunction. The victim's narrative—the very process of bearing witness
to massive trauma—does indeed begin with someone who testifies to an
absence, to an event that has not yet come into existence, in spite of the
overwhelming and compelling nature of the reality of its occurrence.[4]

Laub, a psychiatrist who has served as director of the Video Archive for
Holocaust Testimonies at Yale University, points to a central dilemma of witnessing to the trauma of the Holocaust. Witnessing, by its very nature, assumes
presence. Trauma manifests as a kind of absence. How does one witness to such
a void? The dilemma is shared both by the victimized and those who attend to
them, though each experiences it differently. For survivors, the dilemma is how
to witness not only *to,* but also *in* silence and absence. Laub describes trauma as
"an event that has no beginning, no ending, no before, no during and no after"
and that is "outside the range of associatively linked experiences, outside the
range of comprehension, of recounting and of mastery." For those who witness,
the challenge is to be "both unobtrusive, non-directive, and yet imminently
present, active, in the lead."[5] Further, the process of witnessing to trauma, making it present, is often experienced as a betrayal of the trauma and/or a betrayal
of others who suffered. Such witnessing necessitates a type of distance that is felt
as a separation and loss. Attending to trauma thus remains a delicate and complicated dance of facing absence, allowing loss, and being present.

This consideration of Dorothee Soelle's work is informed by the perspectives of trauma theorists, especially their attention to dynamics of absence and
loss and the impact of traumatic suffering on human subjectivity. Such theorists have led me toward a postmodern embrace of the provisionality and
ambiguity of human subjectivity, coupled with the mystery of the human
thirst for life in history, even amid the losses that haunt events of trauma.
Consequently, I will focus my treatment of Soelle on her understanding of the
suffering person and examine several dimensions of her thought: the centrality of binary oppositions; Soelle's own subject position; the nature of agency;
and the need for suffering to be meaningful. The thread running through
these dimensions is Soelle's interest in maintaining a centered human sub-
ject/agent, an I to the Thou, even in ecstatic, mystical encounter with the
divine. My examination of these dimensions of Soelle's thought will be pref-
aced by an examination of a Holocaust story which seems key not only to her
understanding of suffering, especially in relation to the Holocaust, but also to
her approach to the divine. This story and the way in which she interprets it
frame my considerations here.

Elie Wiesel's *Night*

In his Holocaust account *Night,* Wiesel tells the story of the killing of three males by hanging. Among them is a young boy, described as "the sad-eyed angel" and as dear to those in the camp. Because the boy weighs so little, he does not die immediately. Rather, he dangles from the noose to die a slow death. The inmates of the camp are forced to watch this spectacle. One of these witnesses asks, "Where is God now?" As Wiesel recounts the moment, he tells the reader that a voice inside him responds: "Where is He? Here He is—He is hanging here on this gallows. . . ." Then Wiesel adds, "That night the soup tasted of corpses."[6]

This passage is the one most often quoted by Christian theologians from Wiesel's or, arguably, any Holocaust author's writings. Soelle is no exception. She makes reference to it a number of times in her works. In *Suffering,* she interprets the story as an indictment of a cruel and sadistic God who would allow or even cause the suffering of "his" people. Such a God is evidenced in those strains of Christianity that emphasize the dominating power of God above all else. In this God's place, Soelle offers a view of the divine as present in the suffering. God is on the gallows, dying along with all those who suffer and die. She views that divine presence from a Christian perspective: "To interpret this story within the framework of the Christian tradition, it is Christ who suffers and dies here."[7] The God on the gallows is Christ, the embodiment of God's love, as opposed to a God of arbitrary and absolute power.

Soelle does understand the dangers of appropriating this Jewish story for Christian uses and of interpreting it from a Christian perspective. She suggests, "The justification for a Christian interpretation can only be established when it undergirds and clarifies what the story from Auschwitz contains." For Soelle, this meaning is that "God is on the side of the victim, he is hanged."[8] Therefore, the boy in the story and all who are victimized are not alone in their suffering. God is present, rather than absent. Further, God needs human action to preserve the memory of those who died and to effect change in the present. Soelle suggests there is no alternative to this claiming of past suffering for present purposes if the suffering is to have meaning.

Thus, this story of brutal and brutalizing suffering is read as a moral and theological lesson. Theologically, the story reveals the character and behavior of God, who is not the cause of suffering or above suffering, but who is to be found in its midst. This God is, for Soelle, present as a God of love rather than of power, a God who also suffers in contrast to taking sadistic pleasure in exercising dominating and absolute power. In her analysis of such power, Soelle leads the way for later feminist critiques of God as a male tyrant whose use of power is abusive. Such critiques are an important ingredient in feminist theologians' approaches to the abuse of women and other forms of oppression. As is the case with Soelle, these theologians tend to oppose love (good) and power (bad). Or they oppose dominating (bad) power to the (good) power of suffering (Soelle) or eros (e.g., Rita Nakashima Brock and Carter Heyward).[9] In Soelle's theology, this opposition seems to cause a split within God, between God the bad and mean "father" and Christ, the embodiment of God's love. The former God is to be left behind in her posttheistic theology and replaced with the latter. In this way, Soelle draws upon and echoes aspects of Bonhoeffer's Jesus as the "man for others" who is to be encountered in the suffering power of the cross. Soelle, however, carries Bonhoeffer's thought further by coupling the suffering of Jesus with an indictment of the dominating power of God as abusive.

Soelle uses Wiesel's story not only to justify God's presence but to engage her readers in action for justice. By doing so, she switches the narrative perspective from that of a fellow sufferer who is being terrorized and victimized along with the boy hanging from the gallows to that of those who seek to understand and act in relation to the suffering of others. This is a problematic move because it changes the character of the story and elides crucial distinctions. As a result, Soelle reads the story as a morality play and grounds for hope and redemption rather than a tragic pronouncement of loss that remains unjustified and unredeemed.

Soelle's is the characteristic Christian move. In Wiesel's story, the pronouncement of the inner voice that God is on the gallows remains ambiguous. At face value, it is an assertion of God's death. Indeed, the import of the narrative is of death: unrelenting and unremitting. In Wiesel's words, quoted above: "That night the soup tasted of corpses." *Night* is not a story of redemption. Even though the camp is liberated at the end, Wiesel's central image remains that of a corpse. He closes the book with these words: "From the depths of the mirror, a corpse gazed back at me. . . . The look in his eyes, as they stared into mine, has never left me."[10] There is no resurrection or redemption here. *Night* is a narrative of trauma that recounts experiences in a way meager of meaning. It seeks to tell a tale of horror that is stark and honest. As the title suggests, the book is about the absence and loss that haunt those who suffer without choice, reason, or meaning. Yet Christian theologians read these words through their own meaning system. They make it a story of God's active, incarnate presence. Soelle names that presence as God's *Shekinah* that is fully incarnate in Christ. When Christian theologians see God/Christ on the gallows, they appropriate the narrative for their own perspectives and uses. They do not read the story from the point of view of the victimized. Their interest remains in justifying God by making God present in suffering, finding meaning in suffering, and supporting action for change. By pursuing these goals, they do not offer due honor to the corpses.[11]

Binary Oppositions in Soelle

The sharp distinction Soelle draws between God the tyrant and the loving God of the Jewish *Shekinah* embodied in Christ functions as a binary opposition. It is illustrative of numerous oppositional relationships that Soelle draws and that remain central in her theology. Among the others are oppression/liberation, power/love, and dolorous suffering/compassion. These binaries indicate not only difference but value. One side of the binary is bad and the other good. So bad power is contrasted with good love, which is understood as "powerless." The bad tyrant God, who in certain dominant strains of the Christian tradition exercises absolute and arbitrary power, is opposed to the loving God present in Christ. Dolorous suffering is not of value; compassionate suffering is.

These binaries allow Soelle to paint a prophetic picture of the importance of moral agency for justice and love that stands in bold, stark, and unambiguous contrast with forces that are harmful and destructive. Grounded in Marxist perspectives, Soelle's view of the world tends toward oppositional explanatory categories that fuel revolutionary struggle. At the same time, however, these obscure what are the more ambiguous and fluid perspectives of those who live with legacies of suffering and trauma. One of the insights of trauma theorists is that holding on to defined and rigid categories and moral oppositions can get in the way of working through trauma. Only when the victimized are able to let go of overly clear-cut definitions of good and evil and simplistic analyses of complex and often very conflicting social realities, only when they accept the murky moral terrain before them, are they able to face the past in all its horror and then perhaps move toward a different position in relation to it. There are no heroes in the world of trauma survivors. Often those who survive do so at considerable psychic and moral cost. These survivors dissociated and/or succumbed, lied and/or stole. There is a stark pragmatism to such survival that, at the time, cannot count the full cost of its actions. As long as moral evaluations and worldviews are grounded in simplistic judgments of good and evil, these survivors are offered few resources for dealing with their lives.

Soelle's own pragmatic bent enables her to appreciate this complexity to some extent. Yet the resources she draws on for understanding suffering do not offer enough nuance and analysis for the realities she seeks to portray. For example, in *Stations of the Cross,* a book that chronicles suffering in Central and Latin America, Soelle recounts the story of a woman who had been imprisoned for political activity and then sometime after her release from prison was robbed. This woman's reaction to the robbery seems extreme to Soelle. As Soelle writes: "[The woman] cannot cope with ordinary criminal violence in her life. The old unresolved problems descend on her again. . . . So she screams for hours, as if under torture."[12] Soelle recognizes that this woman has been terrorized and so her fears may be understandable, but the judgment Soelle imposes, adopted from the psychiatrist who tells Soelle of the woman, is that she is a victim of "learned despair." The label of "learned despair" makes the woman's behavior into a moral and existential condition shared by many rather than a specific trauma reaction. Such a judgment misses the dilemma of entrapment that attends survivors of terror and trauma. Theirs is not a condition of despair so much as captivity and isolation. It cannot be dealt with cognitively or morally but only in a slow and painful process of reconnection. Even then the wound of trauma will always remain as a vulnerable scar that may be easily reinjured by a triggering incident or another traumatic event.

Soelle's Subject Position

One of Soelle's goals, in writing about the suffering of others, is to invite her readers into active solidarity with the victimized for the sake of justice and transformation in the world. Her own activism is ample witness to the values she seeks to promote and the ways in which she herself acts for justice. As with Dietrich Bonhoeffer, to whose work and example she is so indebted, she seeks to stand with God at the cross, with all those who suffer.

Soelle's own subject location, however, is as a first-world person, a German, a woman, and a Christian. Except for her position as a woman, with which she identifies later in her life and a little reluctantly, she is located with those who oppress rather than with the oppressed.[13] Of these locations, being a German Christian is perhaps the most formative and important. In much of her work, Soelle deals with the Holocaust and the role of Germany and Christianity in the killing of so many of God's people. She is arguably one of a few Christian German theologians who pays serious attention to the Holocaust in her work. Along with Johann Baptist Metz and Jürgen Moltmann, she is considered a founder of political theology, a movement that focuses on Christianity's place in the world and its use of power.

As are most Germans who attend to the Holocaust, Soelle is haunted by guilt—both for what her nation did and for the ways in which her generation was not attentive to it for so long. In that way, her theology is an attempt to atone for the past: to make sure the Holocaust is not forgotten, to be careful that inattention never again leads to the overlooking of suffering.

Soelle's location determines her theology and informs it from a particular perspective—that of a first-world person of privilege. That location also informs her perspective on suffering. The relationship to suffering is different for a person of privilege. There is potentially a choice to suffer that does not apply to the situation of many of the victimized to whom Soelle attends. The danger for a person of privilege is apathy, which literally means the inability to suffer. To risk suffering then is not only a choice but also a means of action and solidarity and even redemption. Soelle does not proffer this view as a choosing of masochism. She is clear to avoid and condemn such suffering. But suffering and agency are connected for her. A key issue for her is claiming agency and deciding how to use it.

The Nature of Agency

Action is the goal of Soelle's theology. Even when writing about mysticism and the lives of the mystics, such as in *The Silent Cry*, it is an active mysticism that Soelle is promoting. An acting agent, who exercises choice, determines the nature of action for Soelle. Starkly put, Soelle's theology requires a centered subject who actively chooses how to be and act. While that statement calls for modification and nuance, I take it as a true assessment of Soelle's perspective. Arguably, her theological interest is all about those who suffer being able to claim their agency and engage in action. Her understanding of redemption is also about action for liberation.

This interest is reflected in the phenomenology of suffering Soelle delineates in *Suffering*. There are three phases in a person's relationship to suffering. The first Soelle labels "mute suffering." In this phase, the ones who suffer are controlled by the situation of victimization. They are silent and powerless. Any action is reaction. The sufferers are passive victims. In phase two, the ones who suffer find voice and express their condition in cries of pain and lament. In this phase, the suffering is articulated. In phase three, the victimized move into action for liberation. Soelle recognizes that moving into phases two and three can itself cause suffering: "This process itself is painful. At first it intensifies the suffering and strips away whatever camouflaged it."[14] But the character of such suffering is different. It does not isolate but brings people into connection and solidarity. The victimized move back and forth between phase two and three. As they do so, they give more articulation to their pain and are able to claim more agency. As Soelle observes, a "new question" is posed: "How do I organize to conquer suffering?" Soelle concludes: "The *conquest* of powerlessness—and this may at first consist only in coming to know that the suffering that society produces can be *battled*—leads to changing even the structures."[15]

There is a progression to Soelle's phases. Even though persons move back and forth between phases two and three, phase three and action for change is the clear and necessary direction and goal of the movement from reactive to active behavior. That is patently a desirable direction. Soelle's description of the phases offers helpful perspectives for those dealing with suffering, although she gives least attention to describing the mute phase. This lack of attention is intentional, for Soelle sees "numb and mute suffering" as evidence of submissiveness to the power of God—a stance often embraced and advocated by Christianity but which she wants to criticize and leave behind. Movement away from such submission begins with language, the ability to give voice to the suffering.

Soelle's condemnation of submission to suffering is an important corrective to Christian approaches that read all suffering as the result of sin and therefore deserved. Such approaches do little to support resistance and transformative action and instead often contribute to the victimization. However, the silence of victims is not only about submission. It may be a strategy of survival and resistance. In that way, there is a form of agency operative within the silence. The term "mute phase" does little to illumine the subterranean dramas that constitute the lives of so many who live with trauma. Nor does it recognize the absence, often described as a black hole, that so textures the experience of traumatic suffering.

Soelle's approach focuses on language that, for her, is indication of agency and subjectivity. Yet often traumatic suffering is carried in the body and not in conscious, verbal awareness. The emergence of the traumatic injury into consciousness may begin as body memories, experienced as physical sensations or as cognitive intrusions and disturbances such as flashbacks or nightmares. As Judith Herman observes, traumatic memories "lack verbal narrative and context" and are characterized by "imagery and bodily sensation."[16]

Further, the process of coming to terms with trauma and knowing and naming it as such is a social process, not just a personal journey. For so long traumatic suffering was not recognized as such. This social dynamic affected processes of dealing with suffering and contributed to the silence of the victimized.[17] Indeed, the history of trauma is one of recognition of traumatic injury, followed by a type of forgetting. Herman, commenting on this dynamic, concludes: "The study of psychological trauma has a curious history—one of episodic amnesia."[18] For example, the early Freud talked about the traumatic experiences of his clients but then changed his mind and suggested that such narratives of trauma were fantasies. World War I brought new awareness of the impact of war trauma on soldiers only to have that knowledge set aside. Since safety is such a core concern for survivors, if there is no context for naming trauma as such, survivors are less likely to talk about their experiences, especially as trauma.

These dynamics are, however, more complicated still. Trauma theorists have also pointed to the limits and even impossibility of representing the trauma experience in language. Traumatic events fracture and shatter. Any representation is already a distancing and an objectification. As previously indicated, theorists also suggest that trauma is that which is unexperienced in its happening, so even recognizing it and experiencing it is a form of separation from it. That is the fundamental paradox and irony of trauma.[19] Trauma needs to be recognized in order to be experienced and mourned. But that process itself constitutes a kind of loss and even a betrayal. Often loyalty to the trauma and all that has been lost keeps survivors from working through it. Any approach to trauma, therefore, needs to honor these complex dynamics around loss and loyalty. It is from the silence and from the abyss of loss that suffering needs to be known and named.

The subjectivity and sense of agency of trauma survivors remain unstable and decentered. Their experience of self is "permanently provisional."[20] This does not preclude agency but gives it a particular character. There is nothing simple about the lives of such survivors who live amid the tensions honoring what will never be and perhaps never was, such as a sense of basic trust, at the same time that they find resources for survival and maintain concrete hope for the present and future. Action for change is but one dimension of their agency that is always shaped by absence and loss and multiplicity. For example, Lawrence Langer, in writing about the oral testimonies of survivors, suggests that they experience time and themselves in the world differently. Survivors simultaneously inhabit the present and the past, living both in the world of the trauma and in their current lives. In fact, "successful" survival may entail such compartmentalization or what Langer refers to as "duality."[21]

In *The Silent Cry,* Soelle comes closer to this more complex perspective on agency by understanding human agency more as mystery, albeit an active mystery. She shifts from transformation to resistance as the goal of such agency. In that book, silence also takes on a different valence. For Soelle, the silent cry is a name for God. Therefore, silence is a sign of presence rather than absence: "The silence speaks of God's presence."[22] Such silence is in contrast to "muteness," precisely as presence is to absence. Soelle does not seem to be able to allow absence, even in silence. This is because suffering has to be meaningful and meaning is mediated by the presence of the divine. So suffering has to be a way to a God of presence for Soelle.

The Meaning of Suffering

Soelle offers four options in how one deals with suffering. One is to understand it in relation to a tyrant God and to submit. A second is to avoid or deny it and fall into apathy. A third is to resist it. A fourth is a "mystical affirmation" of suffering.

As I have indicated, Soelle is critical of the Christian tradition that understands suffering as necessary for salvation. In that perspective, all suffering is a result of sin and the source of the suffering is God. It is through acceptance of and submission to suffering then that persons are included in the economy of salvation. Soelle attributes such views to a sadomasochistic form of Christianity that embraced, valued, and sought suffering. An example of such Christianity is found in the ascetic tradition in which suffering became a means of showing devotion to God. She labels this type of suffering as "dolorousness," in which suffering is chosen out of masochistic asceticism.[23] Such suffering ought to be resisted.

Soelle is also critical of apathy and the avoidance of suffering or the inability to suffer/feel. Into this category, she puts those who are "numbed" by losing themselves either in a consumerist society or in a belief in progress that denies suffering, or by being so overwhelmed by suffering that they are devoid of feeling. Because of her critique of apathy and numbness, suffering has positive value for Soelle. The experience of suffering indicates that someone is alive, engaged, and able to care.

In her preferred option, a "mystical affirmation" of suffering, suffering is understood to be the way of Jesus. Soelle clearly rejects the other approaches described and affirms this one.[24]

> If God, too, is one who suffers, then suffering is not simply something to which we can surrender or stand up in resistance. It becomes instead a reality that has something to do with the far-near God and that fits into God's incomprehensible love. The way of suffering that is not just tolerated but freely accepted, the way of the passion, becomes therefore part of the disciple's way of life.[25]

Soelle's work on suffering might be seen as moving into a deeper appreciation and analysis of such an affirmation of suffering. To aid her, she turns to the mystical tradition itself and especially those mystics, such as John of the Cross and Edith Stein, who "suffered unto God." Thus, she moves from understanding suffering as submission to God to suffering as participation in God. This is the suffering of compassion, as opposed to the dolorousness of masochistic asceticism. "Suffering unto God" in compassion results from the risk of "partiality" for the victimized and from working for justice. Suffering unto God in compassion means suffering with the suffering Jesus.[26] It accepts suffering as necessary for solidarity. Such suffering is purposeful. In a story that appears several times in her work, Soelle recounts the experience of a Roman Catholic priest in a base community church in Brazil who injures his back and suffers great pain due to a lack of painkillers. This priest speaks of "offering up" his suffering to Christ and connecting his pain to God's pain. Soelle suggests that the priest, by accepting his suffering, is making it active and potentially redemptive.[27]

Again, Soelle offers binary choices: dolorousness versus compassion, numbness versus agony. The faithful embrace compassion and agony as the way to God, mysterious as it may be. Such agony is *sunder warumbe,* "the utter absence of any why or wherefore," a concept Soelle adopts from Meister Eckhart.[28] In the end, Soelle affirms mystery. There is no rational way to explain suffering. It is not redemptive in the way the Christian tradition has sought to make sense of it. The conditions that cause it ought to be changed. Those conditions ought to be resisted when change is not immediately possible. But suffering also needs to be affirmed. In a social context that wants to get rid of suffering, Soelle emphasizes its value—for growth, for learning, for leading to God, for motivating change, for making us human. Suffering thus has meaning and even redemptive value. It makes a profound difference and seems to be at the heart of the encounter with the mystery of God. It is an experience of presence. She states boldly, "All who suffer are in God's presence."[29]

Conclusion

I am moved by Soelle's passion and drawn into her portrayal of the faith of those who live unto God, but I am also cognizant that, given the examples she discusses in *The Silent Cry,* her focus is on those who chose suffering or who chose a course of action they knew could well lead to profound suffering. Edith Stein's decision to remain in Germany and to stand with her people, the Jews, was an active one. While John of the Cross did not "choose" the dark night of the soul or to be imprisoned, he did decide to align with Theresa of Avila and the reform of the Carmelite Order. Yet the victims of childhood abuse, of crushing poverty, of genocide, and of torture have not chosen. Their suffering is inflicted upon them, often in ways that can barely be perceived. It represents the intrusion of a power in relation to which they have little or no resources. At best, the resources available to them enable survival at great cost. Their actions for survival can be characterized, to use Lawrence Langer's phrase, as "choiceless choices."[30] Their suffering is world- and self-destroying. It literally overwhelms the self and eats away at life, leaving gaping holes.

In the face of such emptiness, I find it dangerous to make such suffering meaningful or educative, let alone redemptive. Soelle's views of suffering continue to be shaped by the Christian tradition of redemption in suffering and by her perspective as a first-world person. While she is unflagging in her commitment to the victimized, her own concerns are more with those who do have a choice about their suffering, those who have an option for apathy and denial. Despite *sunder warumbe,* she continues to look for meaning and purpose in suffering, even if it is in the realms of the mystical. Even her notion of inconsolability reflects an active, choosing agent. In the face of suffering, it is better to be inconsolable than numb or apathetic. Soelle's notion of inconsolability witnesses to the unrelenting nature of suffering in the world. It does not, however, recognize sufficiently the plight of the inconsolable.

The process of dealing with traumatic suffering requires that the victimized let go of the need to find meaning in relation to it. They also need to accept the absoluteness and irredeemability of the losses.[31] Only then, in the mystery of the human thirst for life, can life be engaged with a measure of hope. In that sense, suffering is necessary to the process of returning to life. It is something that must be gone through to reach another place. The destination, however, does not justify the suffering or render it of value. In fact, the suffering of the traumatized only confirms the horror of their trauma. In other words, such suffering is not meaningful or redemptive, even though it is unavoidable. Trying to find meaning in such suffering may even get in the way of dealing with trauma because it shifts attention to asking "why" rather than staying focused on the "how" of working through trauma.

Suffering has a different status and valence for those who choose it than for those upon whom it is visited. Indeed, there are many different types of suffering—some suffering is deserved or is consequent to other behaviors; some suffering may be of limited value; other suffering is chosen or is the necessary outcome of another choice; but much suffering is not chosen, deserved, or necessary. Given this diversity in the nature and status of suffering, it is important to develop more nuance in the ways in which suffering is understood and the different conditions that give rise to suffering. In so doing, it is crucial that no particular approach to suffering be universalized.

Because the Christian tradition has grown to be rather univocal in its equation of suffering with redemption, there has been no incentive to develop such typologies and explore the complex terrain of suffering, including traumatic suffering. That is, until recently. In the last century, political, liberation, and feminist theologians began to attend to suffering in a different way. Thus far, feminist theologians have been the boldest in challenging traditional understandings, but all these theologians maintain deep and abiding commitments to end the undue and undeserved suffering of the oppressed, the abused, and the poor.[32] Dorothee Soelle has stood at the front of that line of those committed to changing the conditions that cause suffering. Compassionate love and a thirst for the life-giving God, as well as her eagerness to be in solidarity with those who suffer, not only in her native Germany but around the world, have given her lenses of discernment that have illumined the way for many of us. Her theological attention to suffering and her descriptions of its contours have provided vital orientation for those who wish to explore the terrain of suffering. Soelle's field of vision remains, however, set by her first-world location that searches always for the action figure, ready to lead the movement for change. As does Soelle's reading of Wiesel's narrative, it clings too tightly to a God of presence and so leaves certain questions unanswered. What word is there for those in vision's periphery, whose world is textured more by limitation than possibility, who mourn eternally it seems, not out of compassionate and inconsolable agony but unrelenting pain? Their journey takes them into territory many of us dread to traverse: landscapes strewn with corpses, whose stench pervades the air. With them we might witness to the thirst for life of those whose suffering leaves them gasping for breath, but only if we, along with Elie Wiesel, "taste" the corpses. The Christian theological tradition needs to attend more to this experience of absence in the lives of those who suffer from violence before it can speak fully to their situation.

Notes

1. For treatments of trauma theory see Paul Antze and Michael Lambek, eds., *Tense Past: Cultural Essays in Trauma and Memory* (New York: Routledge, 1996); Cathy Caruth, ed., *Trauma: Explorations in Memory* (Baltimore: Johns Hopkins, 1995); Cathy Caruth, *Unclaimed Experience: Trauma, Narrative, and History* (Baltimore: Johns Hopkins, 1996); Shoshana Felman and Dori Laub, eds., *Testimony: Crises of Witnessing Literature, Psychoanalysis, and History* (New York: Routledge, 1992); Judith Herman, *Trauma and Recovery* (New York: Basic Books, 1992); Dominick LaCapra, *Writing History, Writing Trauma* (Baltimore: Johns Hopkins, 2001), and Michael Roth, *The Ironist's Cage: Memory, Trauma, and the Construction of History* (New York: Columbia University Press, 1995).

2. I am using the terms *absence* and *loss* differently than does Dominick La Capra (see *Writing History, Writing Trauma*, ch. 2). LaCapra differentiates sharply between absence, which he understands to be a structural condition, and loss, which is historic. For him, events of trauma produce loss; absence is a condition that affects all human existence. I want to suggest that the types of losses produced by trauma sometimes result in experiences of absence.

3. See Caruth, *Unclaimed Experience*, 4, 62, and her introduction to *Trauma: Explorations in Memory*, 4.

4. Dori Laub, "Bearing Witness or the Vicissitudes of Listening," in Felman and Laub, eds., *Testimony: Crises of Witnessing Literature, Psychoanalysis, and History*, 57.

5. Ibid., 69, 71.

6. Both Wiesel and Soelle use male language in reference to God. While I have chosen not to change or highlight such language in direct quotations, I would note it as limiting and problematic. Elie Wiesel, *Night* (trans. Stella Rodway; New York: Bantam, 1982), 62.

7. Dorothee Soelle, *Suffering* (trans. Everett R. Kalin; Philadelphia: Fortress, 1975),146.

8. Ibid., 146–48.

9. See ibid., ch. 2, especially 22ff., and responses by Joanne Carlson Brown and Carole R. Bohn, eds., *Christianity, Patriarchy and Abuse: A Feminist Critique* (New York: Pilgrim, 1989); Rita Nakashima Brock, *Journeys by Heart: A Christology of Erotic Power* (New York: Crossroad, 1988); and Carter Heyward, *Touching Our Strength* (New York: HarperCollins, 1989).

10. Wiesel, *Night*, 109. See Herman, *Trauma and Recovery*, especially chs. 7–10, for an overview of these dynamics of traumatic memory.

11. For a related criticism of Soelle's interpretation, see James Moore, "A Spectrum of Views: Traditional Christian Responses to the Holocaust," *Journal of Ecumenical Studies* 25:2 (spring 1988): 212–24, especially 214–16. Moore focuses his criticism on Soelle's universalizing of the place of Christ and, therefore, reading the story through christocentric

theological lenses. He sees this approach as ultimately cooptive. I agree with his perspective and argue that Christian theologians, including Soelle, are coopting Wiesel's narrative. I am also suggesting that such christological approaches allow only for a theology of presence and not of absence.

12. Dorothee Soelle, *Stations of the Cross: A Latin American Pilgrimage* (trans. Joyce Irwin; Minneapolis: Fortress, 1993), 83–84.

13. See Soelle's memoir, *Against the Wind: Memoir of a Radical Christian* (trans. Barbara and Martin Rumscheidt; Minneapolis: Fortress, 1995).

14. Soelle, *Suffering,* 72.

15. Ibid., 72–73. Emphasis added to draw attention to the active and even militaristic language used.

16. Herman, *Trauma and Recovery,* 38. See her discussion of the ways in which traumatic memories emerge and are experienced, 37–42.

17. Herman, *Trauma and Recovery,* ch. 1 presents a history of trauma and the social dynamics that have affected how it is or is not remembered. Herman suggests that traumatic memory is contested and threatened because the perpetrators want to control the memory. Currently, this dynamic is being played out between advocates of "recovered memories" of childhood sexual abuse and those who deny such memories, especially the False Memory Foundation. False Memory Foundation advocates insist that traumatic injury from childhood abuse is not real or is not very harmful. On a sociopolitical level, such dynamics can be understood to be about social control of knowledge. See also Ruth Leys, *Trauma: A Genealogy* (Chicago: University of Chicago Press, 2000) for an alternative perspective on that history.

18. Herman, *Trauma and Recovery,* 7.

19. See Caruth, *Unclaimed Experience,* and her introduction to *Trauma: Explorations in Memory.* See also Laub, "Bearing Witness or the Vicissitudes of Listening"; and Roth, *Ironist's Cage,* 207ff.

20. Lawrence Langer, *Holocaust Testimonies: The Ruins of Memory* (New Haven: Yale University Press, 1991), 82.

21. See Langer, *Holocaust Testimonies,* and my presentation and discussion of Langer's work in my *Redeeming Memories: A Theology of Healing and Transformation* (Nashville: Abingdon, 2000), 73–76. In my estimation, Langer draws too sharply the distinctions among dimensions of survivors' lives and how these are named and understood, but he does point to important issues in relation to the multiplicity of survivors' experiences.

22. Dorothee Soelle, *The Silent Cry: Mysticism and Resistance* (trans. Barbara and Martin Rumscheidt; Minneapolis: Fortress, 2001), 76.

23. Ibid., 139.

24. Ibid., 133 and 137ff.

25. Ibid., 138.

26. Ibid., 139–41.

27. Dorothee Soelle, *Theology for Skeptics: Reflection on God* (trans. Joyce L. Irwin; Minneapolis: Fortress, 1995), 80–83. See also Soelle, "God's Pain and Our Pain," in *The Future of Liberation Theology* (ed. Marc H. Ellis and Otto Maduro; trans. Victoria Rhodin; Maryknoll, N.Y.: Orbis, 1989), 332.

28. Soelle, *Silent Cry,* 13 (also 25 and 59ff.).

29. Soelle, "God's Pain and Our Pain," 327.

30. Lawrence Langer, "The Dilemma of Choice in the Deathcamps," in John K. Roth and Michael Berenbaum, eds., *Holocaust Testimonies: Religious and Philosophical Implications* (New York: Paragon House, 1989), 224.

31. See Roth, *Ironist's Cage*, ch. 12; and Keshgegian, *Redeeming Memories*. One of the conclusions I come to in *Redeeming Memories* is the need for multiple memorative practices that keep the suffering in memory and pay due honor to all that has been suffered and lost but that do not make the suffering meaningful in itself. Rather, meaning is to be found in life and in the ability to continue to embrace life.

32. See Browne and Bohn, eds., *Christianity, Patriarchy and Abuse;* Brock, *Journeys by Heart;* Rita Nakashima Brock and Rebecca Ann Parker, *Proverbs of Ashes* (Boston: Beacon, 2001); and my *Redeeming Memories* for feminist critiques of the redemptive value of suffering in the Christian tradition.

8. Christ *in* the World

The Christological Vision of Dorothee Soelle

Dianne L. Oliver

Why are you so one-sided
people often ask me
so blind and so unilateral
I sometimes ask in return
are you a christian
if you don't mind my asking

And depending on the answer I remind them
how one-sidedly and without guarantees
god made himself vulnerable in christ . . .

. . . god didn't come in an armored car
and wasn't born in a bank
and gave up the old miracle weapons
thunder and lightning and heavenly hosts
one-sidedly
palaces and kings and soldiers
were not his way when he
decided unilaterally
to become a human being
which means to live without weapons[1]

Even with all of her many accomplishments and the profound wisdom and passion she exhibits in a variety of theological areas, one must admit that Dorothee Soelle is not well known for her Christology. As other articles in this collection bear out, it is Soelle's work with suffering, or mysticism, or political theology, or ideas of God's transcendence, or her own political activism that has established her reputation theologically. Yet I argue it is Soelle's understanding of Jesus as the Christ that provides the seedbed from which these other key moves in her theology have grown. From her first published theological work, *Christ the Representative,* the key hallmarks of Soelle's theology emerge from her revisioning of Christology.[2]

Representing Soelle's initial foray into Christology, *Stellvertretung—Ein Kapitel Theologie nach dem 'Tode Gottes' (Christ the Representative)* was written in the mid-1960s and attempted to reclaim the image of "representative" *(Stellvertreter)* for understanding Christ's role in relation to God and the world. Soelle intentionally pursues representation *(Stellvertretung)* over against other traditional understandings of Christ's work such as substitution and sacrifice. Soelle insists that in a world so fully secularized that the only way it knows to speak of God is to speak of God's demise, an image of Christ must address the driving questions of the day: Who am I, and how am I to find meaning and identity in such a changed world? Otherwise, Christology is meaningless. The traditional categories of substitution and sacrifice used to explain Christ's work only exacerbate the struggles to find meaning, for they highlight actions by Christ on our behalf that require no action on our part. The desire for uniqueness and identity, important concerns of persons in the Western world with the rise of science and technology and after the horrors of World War II, is undercut in these traditional categories. If instead Christ *represents* us before God, our uniqueness and identity remain intact, for Christ does not replace us as in sacrifice and substitution. In Soelle's understanding, representation is always provisional and temporary, so our identity is maintained.

Through her embracing of representation, Soelle makes clear that the traditional theistic God is no longer viable. God as separate from the world and intervening at will to alter the "natural" course of events cannot address the loss of immediate certainty. According to Soelle, the religious establishment's insistence on maintaining this theistic view contributes to the turn away from everything "religious" and the continuing secularization of society. Soelle's nontheistic Christology opens up a vision of God in which God is dependent on us—on our assent to Christ's representation, and on our actions to represent God in the world. The dependence of God on us undergirds our importance and uniqueness in the world, because God cannot act without us. Christ's work is for naught if we do not assent to being represented. We are each unique contributors to the work of God in the world, and our decision to accept representation is ours alone.

With the image of representation, Soelle also begins what will materialize as a move to a social subject. I am not a unique individual whose importance is guaranteed before God regardless of the relationships and communities of which I am part, but it is exactly *because* of these relationships that I am unique and irreplaceable. If it is only my actions and roles in the world from which I find identity, then all is lost, for in those actions and roles I am replaceable. It is relationship that provides the unique locus of irreplaceability. The recognition of this shift finally leads to Soelle's call for a sharing of dependence and responsibility between God and humanity. We are dependent on Christ representing us to God, but we are also responsible to represent God in the world. The dialectic of responsibility and dependence and the recognition of God's dependence on our ongoing activity in the world foreshadows Soelle's turn to a political interpretation of the gospel, or a political theology, which demands my action in the world. In essence, then, most of the key moves that will characterize Soelle's theology began with her initial work on Christology: a post-theistic understanding of God, a social and political understanding of the human subject, and a clear call for shared responsibility and dependence between God and the world.

As Soelle's theology emerged over time, the image of "representation" ceased to provide the main metaphor for her understanding of Jesus as the Christ. The image does, however, provide the foundation for key moves she will make in her theology, although its implications for Christology are nuanced or even altered significantly in her later work. As Soelle moved from an eschatologically oriented theology to one focused more explicitly on the suffering of the world, especially the poor and the marginalized, her Christology began to focus more explicitly on the suffering of Jesus as a historical figure and the ongoing suffering of Christ in the world. In the first section of this essay, I pursue Soelle's construction of the image of Christ as representative and the concomitant theological developments. The second section provides explanations of the changes in Soelle's Christology over time and how these shifts are consistent with her radicalized understanding of incarnation and her turn to mysticism.

Responding to the "Death of God": Christ the Representative

Soelle's turn to the title of "representative" to describe the person and work of Christ occurs in a situation characterized by the "death of God," or more helpfully stated from Soelle's perspective, in recognition of the secularization of the modern world. The claim of American "death of God" theologians, such as Thomas J. J. Altizer and William Hamilton, that we live in a world completely devoid of any understanding or possibility for a transcendent God emerges from similar contextual concerns. According to Altizer, the world is viewed as completely profane, not only without God, but even without need of God. It is the context of "secularization" and the question of the possibility of God that provide some link between Soelle's initial work in Christology and the "death of God" movement. The idea of "secularization" identifies several shifts within Western history and culture over the past two centuries: (1) an epistemological relativism whereby truth is no longer seen as something completely objective or as discoverable by a subjective "leap of faith"; instead, there is a complete lack of any immediate certainty, any sense of the absolute that is beyond question, any necessity of God as a "working hypothesis" for our worldview; (2) a shift in focus to the individual who faces insecurity and loneliness in a technological world where everything, including people, is assumed to be replaceable; and (3) a religious recognition after Auschwitz and with the rise of science that "the self-evident existence of God has been destroyed. . . . Naïve theism, a direct childlike relationship to the father above the starry sky," who intervenes vertically from above, "has become impossible."[3]

In a situation characterized by these shifts, the conditions under which God, or the absolute, appears are defined by a loss of God's "immediacy." There is no longer a grounding of our knowledge of God in ourselves or in the created world, so God is, for all practical purposes, "dead." God no longer acts and speaks directly. For Soelle, however, this is not the complete end of God, but essentially "the dissolving of a particular conception of God in the consciousness."[4] What is gone is the undergirding of individual identity and historical certainty that the idea and vision of God traditionally provided. There is no longer any certainty of universal values or absolutes. Without using the term, Soelle is identifying the postmodern condition. Traditional theism's anthropology claimed no matter what happened to a person on earth, her or his soul was seen as safe and secure with God. But the loss of the immediate certainty of God, a God who acts and speaks, makes this approach superfluous. Thus, the question of the unique identity of a person, a question driving theology in the mid-twentieth century, could no longer be answered by placing one's security with God, since God was no longer seen as part of our immediate experience. Carter Heyward explains this shift well when she states, "Soelle contends that we westerners, Christians in particular, are lost, without either a *deus ex machina*—a mechanical, externalized authority—or a clear internal sense of what difference any of us can make in a world that has produced the Holocaust. . . ."[5] The connection of identity with authority is helpful in understanding what Soelle is really saying: We have lost our identity because we no longer have any authority (traditionally God) that declares we are important, unique people with a contribution to make to the world. In a technological world where everything is seen as interchangeable, those faced with uncertainty about their own uniqueness and role in the world continue to long for a sense of meaning and purpose in life.

In the vacuum left by this loss, Soelle, like German theologians Dietrich Bonhoeffer and even Karl Barth before her, turns to a radically christocentric theology. Soelle insists that the situation of God's death, of God's absence, is an opportunity to speak about God in a different way. We are forced to find new ways to talk about the person of Jesus as the Christ and what his work in the world is. For Soelle, while experience of God is no longer directly available and ceases to provide any immediate certainty, God can be represented. Against the technological world in which everything is replaceable, Soelle insists that we are unique and cannot be replaced by one who is our substitute. Thus, the classic interpretation of Christ's work as substitute for us, taking on God's wrath for our sin, only exacerbates the sense of replaceability and lack of individual identity and uniqueness. Thus, we cannot simply have one who acts as our substitute; we can, however, be represented by one who does not desire to replace us. Christ as "representative" is the image Soelle explores in her initial Christological constructions, and provides the first step in her turn to a post-theistic theology.

The traditional view of atonement as substitution insists that Christ assumes our place permanently, enduring the punishment from God for the sins that we commit and taking our place forever before God because we are unable to do so. Such a view denies our uniqueness and our irreplaceability because Christ is able to replace us and to substitute for us before God. Soelle maintains the problem with Christ as our substitute or as a sacrifice is that substitution and sacrifice are both permanent moves, whereby Christ forever replaces us completely and unconditionally. Such replacement is "indicative of the depersonalized world in which things and persons can be arbitrarily interchanged."[6] If Christ replaces us, then we are simply done away with, another part of the machine that is completely interchangeable with its replacement. There is no need for any relationship between the substitute and the one for whom substitution is offered. In that way, our reconciliation with God, Christ's act of substituting for us, is not an event that changes us but one of which we simply must take note. This does nothing to ameliorate the situation of loss of identity after the "death of God."

Unlike substitution, representation is "a temporary, conditional, and incomplete act" in which the one being represented is not replaced but is represented by another who *acts on behalf of* the one being represented. "Representation keeps alive the memory of this living person," rather than replacing the person so that she or he is forgotten, as substitution does.[7] This is not to deny that those who are represented run the risk of being replaced by their representative. Representation thus always involves some level of insecurity and dependence on the one who functions as the representative.

Christ represents us before God, a temporary action in which Christ holds open our place until we are able to assume that place ourselves, at the time when all is fulfilled and God is "all in all." Thus, human beings maintain their unique identity and are able to be represented without giving up that identity. Soelle insists that God is not content with Christ, our representative, but wants *us*. In the interim, our representative

> speaks for us, but we ourselves have to learn to speak. He believes *for* us, but we ourselves have to learn to believe. He hopes when we are without hope, but that is not the end of the story. . . . By his representation he holds their place open for them lest they should lose it.[8]

It is not just the human soul that is guaranteed to be irreplaceable before God and thus maintain identity, as in traditional theology. Rather, every person can only be represented and not replaced, not just before God but for those with whom one is bound together in relationship. "Irreplaceability presupposes a standing-in-relationship. [A person] cannot be thought of as a self-sufficient being. Identity is not achieved independently: it is not something available to, or attainable by, the individual as such. No one can make [oneself] irreplaceable."[9] For Soelle, the move is made from independence and individualism, in which our identity is found strictly before God as a unique soul, to interdependence, in which I have identity and am unique and irreplaceable only for those who love me. This indicates my embeddedness in relationship with other people and my dependence on them. The move to the subject's identity as bound up in relationship rather than an identity found alone before God is a key shift at this point in Soelle's work. The relational character of our identity and of God's identity is seen in other aspects of Soelle's theology as well.

In reviewing other uses of "representation" to describe Christ's work, Soelle critiques Karl Barth's objectivistic use of the image, insisting that representation for Barth is only seen in Christ representing us before God and our complete dependence on Christ in this action. This version of "Christian perfectionism" excludes our participation—Christ acts and redeems without us, thus overemphasizing our dependence "at the expense of [our] irreplaceability and responsibility."[10] On the other hand, Soelle describes Dietrich Bonhoeffer's work as highlighting representation as responsibility without taking into account dependence as part of the nature of representation itself. Thus, those who assume responsibility without reference to the temporality of such action fail to recognize that representation is always provisional or it collapses into substitution. Soelle sees dependence and responsibility as a dialectic with regard to representation, which informs the further development of this image in her work.

But representation has a double meaning in Soelle's image—not only does Christ represent us before God, but Christ also represents God to us. Previously Christianity has assumed a direct relationship to God, but this is "in jeopardy the moment God ceases to be needed as a working hypothesis in morality, politics and science."[11] We thus live in a post-theistic age in which God is absent but is able to be represented by Christ. "The absence of God can be interpreted as one mode of his being-for-us. In this case, [humanity] depends on there being someone to represent the irreplaceable God."[12] Christ represents the absent God and holds open God's place in our midst. This is a new way of God's existence in the world, with Christ as God's forerunner who keeps God's future open. Christ is present implicitly whenever someone acts in God's stead. We therefore assume responsibility for holding God's place open by representing God to one another in a manner similar to what Christ does. Christ becomes a metaphor for the "consciousness of those who represent God and claim him for each other. . . . Christ's friends and brothers also . . . represent God by allowing God—and this means necessarily those as well who need [God]—time."[13]

For Soelle, Christ is identified with God in such a way that they are indistinguishable in the provisional representation of God by Christ as the "transcendental possibility of love."[14] But Christ does not replace God. Christ is not God's complete self-emptying in human form, or else we would now be experiencing all that is possible of God. Instead, God appears as "mediated immediacy," with Christ as the mediator or representative, playing God's role in the world. Soelle insists that we are now called on to do what Christ did, that is, "play the role of God in conditions of helplessness. We can claim God for each other. . . . We, too, can now play God for one another."[15] Jesus, then, is a paradigm for mediating God—what we, too, are now called to do.

Thus Christ represents the absent God, making Christ the one who acts, not in his own name, but in the name of God. Christ is dependent on God whom he represents since God can accept or reject him. Christ takes on the role of God in the world; "Christ acts *as if* he were God. . . . [Christ] depends upon God by depending on us and living by our decisions."[16] When we do what Christ did, that is, represent God to one another, we, too, become dependent on God. We are dependent because we must live by the decisions of those with whom we are bound together in relationship.

Christ's and our dependence on God is related to the dependence that representation means for God. Christ's dependence on our decisions and our actions "is to say that God depends on us, that he is at risk because he has linked his destiny with ours."[17] In making Godself representable, God has also become dependent by becoming human. The omnipotent God is certainly "dead," indicted by God's helplessness in the world. But this "death" is not the end of God, only a new way of being for God. God has allowed Godself to be represented, and only in Christ does the suffering, powerless, helpless God, the only God that is possible, appear. "Only in Christ does it become clear that we can put God to death because he has put himself in our hands. Only since Christ has God become dependent on us."[18]

The results of Soelle's turn to Christ as representative are several and provide the foundation for her post-theistic theology. First, Soelle can respond constructively to the situation of a secularized society in which God is largely seen as superfluous. While the longing for meaning and identity among persons is no longer satisfied by the uniqueness of the soul before an absent God, neither is there satisfaction in the various God-replacements that abound in a technological world that has taken over many of the activities previously associated with God. God as the one who explains the world is not irreplaceable—science has certainly proven that. God as the absolute that provides certainty is not irreplaceable—the certainty of security is destroyed after Auschwitz and Vietnam, the events that Soelle claims politicized her activism and her theology. So God, whose greatest attribute is power and who controls the world, is dead, but this "death" provides a new way of God being-for-us. God is irreplaceable, in the end, for those who love her. Thus, God's transcendence cannot be understood in terms of God's actions and interventions in the world. Instead, God becomes dependent on us and suffers with us.

Second, dealing with the question of identity in the modern world results in a turn to a social, relational subject for Soelle. It is no longer the individual whose soul remains irreplaceable and unique before God in heaven but the person who is unique and irreplaceable only for those who love her or him (similar to the shift highlighted above with regard to God). "Irreplaceability presupposes a standing-in-relationship."[19] Persons by themselves cannot achieve unique identity, for such identity comes only in relationship to others for whom I am irreplaceable. I am irreplaceable only for those who love me and have set their hope in me, through whom I have a remembered past and a possible future.

Third, Soelle's turn to the image of Christ as representative rather than substitute or sacrifice is a critique of Christian perfectionism that claims that Christ's action two thousand years ago has completed the act of redemption once and for all. Soelle insists that this view of redemption fails to recognize the provisionality of Christ as our representative who is only temporarily standing in for us in order to hold open our place. If Christ's action is that of a substitute who takes our place permanently, there is no assent required on our part, no involvement in even accepting such action on our behalf. Instead, Soelle views redemption as a process in which we are involved as we represent Christ to others, making present the "absent" God.

Finally, emerging from the embrace of representation is the dialectic of dependence and responsibility, which exists both for God and for us. God has made Godself dependent on Christ by being represented *by* Christ. Consequently, God is dependent on us because this representation only works with our assent and our action in the world. Thus, God's future, kept open by Christ as representative, is linked with ours and our representation of God to one another. Responsibility is thus placed on Christ, as representative of God, to play the role and hold open God's future until God will once again take responsibility for the world. But responsibility is also placed on us, because we now represent the helpless God to one another until the time when God is no longer absent and helpless. This eschatological note reverberates through Soelle's work here, not simply as an attempt to "postpone" fulfillment and hold out the proverbial carrot, but to recognize our role and responsibility in transforming the world.

Incarnatio Continua

I have highlighted the four main shifts begun in Soelle's Christology in *Christ the Representative.* Because her work unfolds in some different directions over time, I will now look at how Soelle's Christology evolves in her later work and its relation to her theology as a whole.

While no other monograph-length work of Soelle's focuses exclusively on Christology, several essays or chapters within larger works deal with the person and work of Jesus as the Christ. In these later writings, "representation" ceases to provide the key metaphor for Soelle's christological work and seems to have enabled a shift in her thinking about atonement without itself continuing as the driving argument.[20] In later work, Soelle acknowledges that her turn to representation was a "feminist democratizing effort" in which she recognized the shared character of redemption.[21] What her shift away from representation reflects is a changing orientation in Soelle's theology as a whole. Like many involved in the German political theology movement, the first phase of Soelle's work was eschatologically oriented.[22] As she insisted in *Christ the Representative,* representation, over against substitution, demands an eschatological orientation because it requires provisionality and temporality. Christ provisionally represents the absent God to the world until God can once again be present. Christ provisionally represents the world to God until the world is able to stand on its own. If temporality is not maintained, then representation becomes substitution and our involvement is not required. The meaning of history is pushed somewhat to the future, because right now God is helpless in the world. When God is no longer absent, representation is no longer needed, and the kingdom of God will be here. In the meantime, representation ensures that the place remains open for the ones being represented. While in her early christological ideas, Soelle insists that we are called to participate in the world and be responsible for the world in the meantime (certainly a "present" focus), and that the absent God is present now wherever that God is represented, the culmination of identity, both God's and ours, is still in the future.

What eventually completes the move begun in *Christ the Representative* is Soelle's recognition that God's action and power in the world are really empowerment of the world, both now and in the future. There is not a postponed fulfillment of God's work in the world, but that work itself is now understood differently. God's work in the world is vulnerable not because God is temporarily absent but because God's power only functions to empower. When Soelle shifts more explicitly to the question of suffering and ways to seek its transformation and meaning, she also shifts the orientation of her theology. There is no longer a strong eschatological component in her work, and the provisionality of the present is not emphasized in the same way. Meaning and transformation of suffering are not postponed but are sought *in* the world and *in* history. The seeds of this shift were in the dialectic of responsibility and dependence in *Christ the Representative,* but the lingering understanding of God as absent kept the focus off suffering as the driving question. The turn to focus explicitly on suffering calls for a Christology whose locus is here and now, embedded in the historical world in which we live. The suffering of Christ on the cross provides a key connection to the suffering subject for Soelle as her theology develops, and the cross as central is seen explicitly as early as her work in *Suffering* in the 1970s. This image becomes vital to Soelle's Christology in her subsequent work, and it is to this image I now turn.

Cross and Resurrection

Central to Soelle's christological formulations are her understandings of the cross and the role of suffering. For many, and Soelle identifies the category "orthodoxy" specifically, the role played by the cross is one of sacrifice—Jesus is put to death in order to pay the price for our sins. In this view, the cross is a necessary element, for the supreme, almighty God, whose dignity and honor have been offended by the sins of the people, requires a sacrifice to have that dignity and honor restored. Jesus offers a "yes" to the will of God, which is that he be the innocent victim who takes on the punishment we rightfully deserve. His vicarious acceptance of the suffering, pain, and punishment results in our acquittal before God so that God's honor is restored. Soelle sums up orthodoxy's perspective using Anselm's theory of satisfaction: "Christ as the innocent victim submits to the will of the Father and thus reconciles the Father with us."[23] While this is something of an oversimplification of the variations within orthodoxy, it is this view that functions as the focus of Soelle's response.

Soelle, in line with much liberation theology, focuses on the cross as a "realistic event and not as a symbol," which is embedded in history and "can be given a precise location."[24] The cross was an actual political tool, used in the power politics of the Roman Empire in the service of those who oppressed anyone subversive to the values and structures of the Empire. Soelle insists,

> It is possible to see who this Jesus really was: the illegitimate son of a poor girl, a teenager; a worker who belonged to the landless; a poor man in every sense of the word, living among poor, insignificant people, a nobody from a provincial town; a crackpot who was "'out of his mind,'" as his family decided; a subversive who was sought by the authorities; a political prisoner who was tortured and finally condemned to death.[25]

And this real-life, flesh-and-blood person was killed in a political action. Jesus' death on the cross was the result of his life and actions opposed to the oppression and domination characteristic of the Roman Empire. The cross should thus not be individualized and spiritualized as a timeless symbol transcending history but as a specific event with an explicit historical location.

> The cross is neither a symbol expressing the relationship between God the Father and his Son nor a symbol of masochism which needs suffering in order to convince itself of love. It is above all a symbol of reality. Love does not "require" the cross, but *de facto* it ends up on the cross.[26]

In this way, the cross is the world's response, "given a thousand times over, to attempts at liberation."[27]

The cross is not a "necrophilic, death-seeking symbol," but something we can choose to avoid, just as Jesus could have made such a choice. Soelle offers an interpretation of the "for us" of Paul's writing (Greek, *hyper hymon*), insisting that it does not have to mean "acting for us," as traditional sacrificial interpretations have understood it. Instead, she sees this phrase as implying not Jesus acting in our place but Jesus acting in such a way that we all benefit, for the best of everyone. Likewise, the "must" used to explain the necessity of Christ's suffering (Luke 24:26) is not because God requires or demands Christ's suffering for the purposes of atonement. Rather, the "must" emerges from Jesus' own inner authority and his decision to remain true to the nonviolent, domination-free vision of God—thus, to retain his integrity, he "must" go to the cross. Jesus does this "for us" not in our place but for the benefit of all persons.[28]

Today, it is in similar situations of suffering and oppression in which we continue to identify the cross. Like Latin American liberation theologians,

Soelle acknowledges that the realities of the cross cannot be spiritualized or separated from the lives of oppression of those who are condemned through unjust structures in Jesus' time or in ours. The cross symbolizes not a one-time event in which the sufferings of the world are forever taken up in the life of Jesus, but concrete, historical situations of oppression that we continue to experience today—Christ continues to suffer in our world. The question we must ask is: Where are our crosses? Soelle insists, "To choose life means to embrace the cross. It means to put up with the cross, the difficulties, the lack of success, the fear of standing alone. . . . To embrace the cross today means to grow into resistance."[29] The cross is thus a call to join in the struggle against the suffering and injustice in our world. We are not forced to take up this struggle—we are perfectly free to avoid the cross, as Jesus was, and as his friends urged him to do. "[The cross] expresses love for the endangered, threatened life of God in our world," and while we are called to take up that cross, to take sides, to break with neutrality, we are also free to say no.[30] Jesus said "yes," remaining faithful until the end. He was faithful not because he was "obedient" to the will of God demanding his death, as some traditional theologies claim, but because he maintained his commitment against the injustice of the Roman Empire.

Suffering is not embraced here in a masochistic way for the sake of suffering itself. Instead, "the radical passion for justice, the partisanship for the disinherited, leads to the passion of the way of suffering. Passion and suffering are not separate. . . . It is not because I loved the cross, but because it was and is a historical actuality."[31] God did not erect the cross, but the powers of this world did. Taking up the cross means taking sides with one or the other. "In the face of suffering you are either with the victim or the executioner—there is no other option."[32] To take sides is a political act—such a move does not occur in a spiritual sphere separate from the messiness of our historical world. To take sides is to face the historical actuality of the powers of our world and to choose the side on which we will stand—and Christ calls us to stand with the victims.

Soelle's focus concerning the cross and resurrection results in a shift concerning the nature of power. Traditionally, Jesus plays the role of "hero" or "superstar." He is the unique God-man, exclusively and "magically" reconciling us to God. For Soelle, however, Jesus' power is no heroic, hierarchical, male power to control and manipulate but is instead the power of powerless love.[33] There is no Jesus who goes to his death knowing that God will be victorious and "win" a decisive victory for all time by raising him from the dead. Instead, there is a Jesus who does not have the power to "win," in the traditional sense of conquering or having final victory, but who does have the power to love. Thus, Jesus' powerlessness is what constitutes his inner authority. "We are not his because he sired us, created us, made us. We are his because love is his weaponless power, and that power is stronger than death."[34] Thus the beginnings of a revisioning of power are found here in Soelle's Christology but are really completed in her post-theistic vision of God.

Soelle's understanding of resurrection is directly related to her vision of the role of the cross: "The Resurrection cannot be discussed in isolation, as if it had nothing to do with the cross."[35] Instead, there is a "dimension of the resurrection which becomes visible in the cross itself"—the resurrection, just as much as the cross, is embedded in social history and political context. The glory of resurrection is not that God magically resuscitates a lifeless body, showing that God has ultimate control and clearly has power over natural events. The glory of the resurrection is that "they could not do away with him."[36] The Roman Empire could not destroy Jesus because the message of justice, the becoming one with love, lived on after Jesus' body was gone. "Jesus believed above all— and for all—in a life *before* death. The Resurrection, this spark of life, was already in him. And only because of this God-in-him were they unable to kill him. It simply did not function."[37] Thus, resurrection is for all, not just for Jesus. There is no "divine rescue" only for the God-man Jesus. Instead, Jesus' resurrection provides a powerful image for the existential change that the hope of resurrection offers. Such hope is born out of a life that has gone to the cross on behalf of love and justice, in the face of social contempt, oppression, and derision, with only the "power of powerless love." Such a life, such a love, "is greater than anything that this world can do to us."[38] That is the power of resurrection that is true not only for the individual Jesus but that lives on in us today.

Thus, for Soelle, to ask the question of whether there really was a resuscitation, a literal return to life of a lifeless body, is to ask a question that essentially has no significance. Would we be changed depending on how we answered such a question? Would we live differently? She claims we would not. Just as her vision of the cross insists on the ways in which the cross drastically changes our lives, so, too, does resurrection absolutely change us—or it does not matter.[39] But the focus is not simply on individual change. In much traditional theology, the focus of both cross and resurrection has been too individualistic: "The cross becomes my unique suffering and the resurrection my individual immortality."[40] Soelle insists,

We must free the idea of resurrection from the stranglehold of individualism. This also means that resurrection was not an event, an individual, isolated event which took place once, two thousand years ago. It must rather be understood as a process and it happens afresh, again and again, that people who were dead before rise again from the dead. Some people have already risen from the dead; if we remember them, we nourish our own hope of resurrection. This hope itself is unproven and unprovable. It is a genuine act of faith. The only possible proof of

Christ's resurrection and our own would be a changed world, a world a little closer to the kingdom of God.[41]

Jesus' resurrection is thus evidence that "nothing came to an end when he was tortured to death. Everything really only began, properly speaking."[42] We must share in this resurrection, or we make an idol of Christ because he does not really meet us in our everyday lives, in our ongoing suffering. If he is the only one for whom resurrection is possible, then there is no hope for us. People today still stand up for justice and are tortured; they continue to die from indifference. Yet we continue to see "uprisings of life against the many forms of death."[43] This means Christ is still alive, and resurrection is still possible.

Christopraxis before Christology

Soelle realizes the tendency toward a fundamentalism in much Christology, which focuses on the "universal, unique and unsurpassable" character of Jesus as the Christ.[44] Soelle's key critique is of Christian perfectionism, which insists that the work of redemption was completed in the work of Jesus as the Christ two thousand years ago. I have shown how Soelle's Christology argues that Christ is not unique and that redemption is not relegated to an invisible spiritual world. As she explains it, "God's becoming human can no longer be understood as a once-for-all and completed event; instead, it is a continuing process of divine self-realization in history."[45] Focusing on two key pieces of this explanation provides further understanding: (1) Jesus is not a once-for-all revealer of God or a unique mechanism of God's redemption in whom all the work of salvation is completed, and (2) the process not only is continuing, but it occurs *in history,* in the political, historical world. As she highlights from Jewish theology, "It is not the Messiah who bears salvation, rather salvation bears the Messiah."[46] The messianic empire is made more visible in Jesus, who occasionally heals and has made persons free from fear, but is not engulfed completely in him. We still wait for a different justice, a different peace, with which we help Jesus when we say "yes" to his vision, to the "christic power."[47] This waiting does not assume a teleological culmination of the world but a continuing hope for new possibilities and ongoing transformation.

Thus, the real center of Christology is "from below"—from the lives and experiences of persons in history who continue to participate in the struggle, who continue to be the means by which God is revealed by being God's hands in our world.[48] Incarnation is not entirely encapsulated in the story of Jesus of Nazareth; thus salvation does not come from worshiping him. In line with Kierkegaard, Soelle insists there is a difference between admiring and following. A Christology "from above," one that places a halo on Jesus' head and deifies him, makes him only purer and higher, the "one for all." Such halo-placing results in us worshiping Jesus but not necessarily in following him. Soelle thus concludes that salvation requires participation: "We do not marvel; we go with him."[49] To be "in Christ" means that we are with him on the way. The "we" is significant for Soelle, because it is not "I" alone but "we" who practice resistance, who work together for God's reign. We make ourselves available to God, put ourselves at God's disposal, and this changes our lives and our commitments— and involves us in redemption.[50] Soelle uses the metaphor of the "ape grip" and the "cat grip" to highlight her vision of salvation:

> If a mother ape is in danger, she holds her young tight, and saves them by leaping away. The mother indeed acts, as God acts in our salvation, but the baby ape collaborates by clinging to its mother. Cats are quite different: if danger threatens, they take their young in their mouths; the little ones are passive and do nothing to rescue themselves—all co-operation is excluded.[51]

The cooperation imaged in the "ape grip" is imperative for Soelle, for God wants us, in fact, needs us, to be involved in God's activity, including the activity of redemption. Power, healing, change, miracles—these are not reserved simply for Jesus as the Christ wielding the power of a God who intervenes vertically from above. Instead, "the female and male disciples of Jesus are involved in healing, driving out, purifying."[52] Their participation was imperative for the redeeming activity of God to take place, and our participation is just as imperative.

Our participation in redemption is not relegated to the spiritual sphere. In fact, there is an inherent political character to Soelle's understanding of Christology. When we say "yes" to christic power, we place our hope in a different understanding of salvation—it is not salvation for an immortal future of heaven but liberation from injustice, violence, and suffering. This liberation is not just for me personally but for all. The latter effects are not "magically" produced by God but require our historically concrete participation, our praxis, our action in the political sphere. "To participate in the struggle is a necessary presupposition of the concept of liberation."[53] This political participation and resistance to suffering and injustice are foundational for Soelle's theology.

Soelle's vision is thus of incarnation as a continuing phenomenon— *incarnatio continua*. Soelle calls for an understanding of incarnation that goes beyond the unique vision of incarnation restricted to Jesus of Nazareth. "Christ stands for Jesus of Nazareth *plus all those who belong to him*."[54] To believe in Christ, to follow him, is to continue the incarnation and to carry God's power. "If Jesus of Nazareth was the poor man from Galilee who was tortured to death, then Christ is that which cannot be destroyed, which came into the world with him and lives through us in him." The incarnation of God continues and the christic power is still alive—through us, and in our solidarity with one another in suffering and in struggle.[55] Soelle's recognition of this radical character of incarnation and the call for solidarity underlies her embrace of mysticism. As Soelle remarks,

> Solidarity asks that we change the image of God from that of a power-dispensing father to one of a liberating and unifying force, that we cease to be objects and become subjects involved in this process of change, that we learn cooperation rather than wait for things to come to us from on high. These are all elements of mystical piety.[56]

And these are all elements of Soelle's Christology: focusing on a new vision of power that begins from "power of powerless love," recognizing our role in redemption as an ongoing process, and turning to a relational understanding of human beings.

Some Conclusions

In the end, the key to Soelle's Christology is what it says about the relationship between God and humanity. "Christ in the world" is not a way to talk about thirty-three years in the life of a Jewish man from Nazareth for Dorothee Soelle, though the life, death, and resurrection of that man are of utmost importance. Instead, "Christ in the world" describes the ongoing vulnerability of a God who has become incarnate in the world in a continuing way. Christ is the way God is embodied *in* the world. While this embodiment occurs in a key way in Jesus of Nazareth so that a new paradigm of the God-world model is envisioned, God is in the world beyond this historical figure. God is in the world not just in Jesus but in Christ as the ongoing existence of the community of those who belong to God. The incarnation of God in the world continues so that God is actually bound into the world itself.

Soelle's focus is on the fact that Christ tells us about God and provides a way to God who ceases to be experienced as immediately present. A powerful, mighty God who speaks and acts from the heavens is no longer possible. Christ enables us to see God in a new way if we are willing to look carefully. Incarnation is not a moment in the life of God or in the life of the world but is "the process of God's ongoing self-realization in history."[57] Initially, this was impossible for Soelle to see because of the "father" God baggage of her tradition, with its focus on God's might and power and the certainty of God's ultimate victory. After Auschwitz, that "father" God was gone. While initially in her turn to representation Soelle only claims the "father" God is temporarily absent, she ultimately recognizes that particular conception of God is gone forever, dying in gas chambers and carried away in the cries of the innocent sufferers. Jesus is what helps her to see this: "The son was closer to me than the father, he revealed what the father could not communicate to me: love without privileges; love which empties itself, and takes on the shape of a slave."[58] It is in Christ where we encounter a new vision of God that we are able to see who God really is—not the supreme being up in the starry sky but the God who is forever vulnerable and dependent by hanging on a cross and tying God's very life with that of the world.

While it is clear that Soelle's Christology provides the basis for important features of her theology, it is less clear why Christology does not remain key in some of her important theological work. The idea of radical incarnation is obviously connected to Soelle's embrace of a mystical sensibility, but the Christology that is concomitant with such a vision of incarnation is itself not a key aspect of much of her work with mysticism. For example, in her self-identified magnum opus, *The Silent Cry: Mysticism and Resistance,* Soelle includes minimal reference to any key Christological claims.[59] Soelle touches on mystical aspects and key figures from a variety of religious traditions but seems reticent to explore the key figure in her own tradition even though her own Christological work would support important assertions she makes regarding the inherent relationship between the mystical and the political. Reclaiming some form of the image of Christ as representative that functioned as Soelle's early Christological vision could actually provide a more robust image for her later Christology. Since she claims that it is Jesus as the Christ who enables her to see God in a different way, Jesus really *does* re-present God and fundamentally changes our understanding of the God-world relationship. This is exactly the power of Soelle's theology when it comes to her political, mystical vision. Through Jesus as the Christ, God's transcendence is seen as radicalized immanence (the mystical), and our role and responsibility in the historical praxis of redemption is thus embraced (the political). Soelle focuses more on the political aspects of her Christology than on the mystical qualities evidenced in her ideas of radical incarnation. And at times Soelle almost sounds like those who seek to minimize Jesus *as the Christ* in order to overcome the troubles with claims about Jesus' unique, heroic actions. Yet as I have shown, Soelle's Christology deals constructively with these issues without diminishing Jesus as the Christ. By integrating her liberation vision of the historical, political nature of Jesus' life, death, and resurrection with her feminist subversion of Jesus as heroic figure who claims unique status and power to magically bring salvation, Soelle's Christology is a compelling vision of how God is *in* the world. This

Christology is not just backdrop to her revisioning of God's transcendence, her embrace of a mystical-political theology, or her profound contributions to dealing with suffering after Auschwitz. Ultimately, Soelle's Christology is fundamental to understanding her work.

Notes

1. Dorothee Soelle, "Unilateralism or god's vulnerability," in *Of War and Love* (trans. Rita and Robert Kimber; Maryknoll, N.Y.: Orbis, 1983), 58.

2. Dorothee Soelle, *Christ the Representative: An Essay in Theology after the 'Death of God'* (trans. David Lewis; London: SCM, 1967), trans. of *Stellvertretung—Ein Kapitel Theologie nach dem 'Tode Gottes'* (Stuttgart: Kreuz Verlag, 1965).

3. Ibid., 11–12, 131.

4. Ibid., 133.

5. Carter Heyward, *Touching Our Strength: The Erotic as Power and the Love of God* (San Francisco: HarperSanFrancisco, 1989), 78.

6. Soelle, *Christ the Representative*, 21–22.

7. Ibid., 21.

8. Ibid., 104.

9. Ibid., 34.

10. Ibid., 92.

11. Ibid., 130.

12. Ibid., 132.

13. Ibid., 132–136. The quote is from 136.

14. Ibid., 138.

15. Ibid., 142.

16. Ibid., 144.

17. Ibid.

18. Ibid., 151.

19. Ibid., 33.

20. Soelle admits that her early work largely enabled her to let go of some of the traditional visions of atonement and of God's relation to the world and to deny an overemphasized anthropological pessimism more than to construct a lasting vision of Christ. Interview by author with Dorothee Soelle, tape recording and transcript, Hamburg, Germany, 21 July 1997.

21. Dorothee Soelle, "Christologie auf der Anklagebank," *Junge Kirche* (March 1996): 136.

22. See Rebecca S. Chopp's helpful characterization of the two phases in political theology, eschatology and suffering, in *The Praxis of Suffering: An Interpretation of Liberation and Political Theologies* (Maryknoll, N.Y.: Orbis, 1986), especially ch. 2.

23. Dorothee Soelle, *Thinking about God: An Introduction to Theology* (trans. John Bowden; Philadelphia: Trinity Press International, 1990), 122.

24. Ibid., 125.

25. Dorothee Soelle, *Theology for Skeptics: Reflections on God* (trans. Joyce L. Irwin; Minneapolis: Fortress, 1995), 95.

26. Dorothee Soelle, *Suffering* (trans. Everett Kalin; Philadelphia: Fortress, 1975), 163.

27. Ibid., 164.

28. Dorothee Soelle, "Christologie auf der Anklagebank," 132.

29. Dorothee Soelle, *Choosing Life* (trans. Margaret Kohl; Philadelphia: Fortress, 1981), 104. See also Dorothee Soelle and Luise Schottroff, *Jesus of Nazareth* (trans. John Bowden; Louisville: Westminster/John Knox, 2002), 122–23.

30. Soelle, *Choosing Life,* 53.

31. "Christologie auf der Anklagebank," 137. "Die radikale Passion für die Gerechtigkeit, die Parteinahme für die Enterbten, führt in die Passion des Leidensweges. Leidenschaft und Leiden sind nicht zu trennen. . . . Nicht, weil ich das Kreuz liebte, aber weil es eine historische Realität war und ist."

32. Soelle, *Suffering,* 32.

33. Dorothee Soelle with Shirley A. Cloyes, *To Work and to Love: A Theology of Creation* (Philadelphia: Fortress, 1984), 5.

34. Dorothee Soelle, *The Strength of the Weak: Toward a Christian Feminist Identity* (trans. Robert and Rita Kimber; Philadelphia: Westminster, 1984), 98.

35. Soelle, *Theology for Skeptics,* 107. See also Soelle and Schottroff, *Jesus of Nazareth,* 123.

36. Soelle, *Thinking about God,* 131–32.

37. Soelle, *Theology for Skeptics,* 107.

38. Soelle, *Thinking about God,* 135.

39. Soelle, *Theology for Skeptics,* 107.

40. Soelle, *Choosing Life,* 82.

41. Ibid., 88.

42. Ibid., 79.

43. Soelle, *Strength of the Weak,* 76.

44. Soelle, "Christologie auf der Anklagebank," 133.

45. Dorothee Soelle, *The Window of Vulnerability: A Political Spirituality* (trans. Linda M. Maloney; Minneapolis: Fortress, 1990), 27.

46. Quoting Doris Strohm and Regula Strobel, *Vom Verlangen nach Heilwerden. Christologie in feministisch-theologischer Sicht* (Fribourg: Edition Exodus, 1991), 209. In "Christologie auf der Anklagebank," 134, "Nicht der Messias trägt die Erlösung, sondern die Erlösung trägt den Messias."

47. Soelle, "Christologie auf der Anklagebank," 136.

48. Soelle, *Suffering,* 149.

49. Soelle, *Theology for Skeptics,* 93.

50. Soelle, *Thinking about God,* 94.

51. Ibid., 85.

52. Ibid.

53. Dorothee Soelle, "Resistance: Toward a First World Theology," *Christianity and Crisis* 39, no. 12 (23 July 1979): 179.

54. Soelle, *Choosing Life,* 73 (emphasis mine).

55. Ibid.

56. Soelle, *Strength of the Weak,* 103.

57. Dorothee Soelle, *Beyond Mere Dialogue: On Being Christian and Socialist* (Detroit: CFS, 1982), 18.

58. Ibid., 38.

59. Interview by author with Dorothee Soelle, 21 July 1997.

9. A Postmodern Response to Suffering after Auschwitz

Sarah K. Pinnock

There is heated debate over theodicy among post-Holocaust, feminist, and liberation theologians, whose concerns center on the social causes of suffering and its alleviation. These contextual thinkers encourage strategies of survival and resistance to suffering. Theologically speaking, they validate protest and questioning of God, as opposed to theistic explanation.[1] While theodicy justifies suffering as good or purposeful, thus defending God's goodness to creatures, contextual thinkers' attention to social and political factors exposes massive and pervasive suffering in history that reveals weaknesses in theodicy justifications. Whether the focus is on Holocaust victims, women, or the poor, contextual theologians find it immoral to declare that suffering is punishment for sin or spiritually enriching. There is a consensus that severe, socially caused suffering is neither just nor redemptive.

Since the 1970s, Protestant theologian Dorothee Soelle has been widely recognized for her innovative contributions to the development of post-Holocaust, feminist, and liberation theologies. Her contextual approach is particularly indebted to two late modern intellectual movements: existentialist dialogical philosophy and Marxist critical theory. The twentieth-century figure with the largest impact on her writings is Jewish thinker Martin Buber. Drawing on Buber's *I and Thou*, Soelle argues that theology is primarily language addressed to God in relation, rooted in biblical narrative, not I-It discourse. Moreover, in *The Silent Cry*, she relies on Buber's *Ecstatic Confessions* to support her investigation of common inter-religious, phenomenological characteristics of mysticism. She also finds resources for a relational approach to theological language in the work of Protestant theologian Rudolf Bultmann, whose existential hermeneutics views the gospels as calling readers into direct dialogue. However, she vehemently opposes his individualistic definition of sin and salvation.[2] Dissatisfied with the bourgeois setting of liberal theology, Soelle turns to humanist Marxist philosophers, such as Jewish thinker Ernst Bloch, in order to examine Christian complicity in institutionalized social evils. Twentieth-century Marxist interpretations of Christian faith as utopian political hope serve as a corrective for the political passivity of German Christians exemplified during the Nazi era. Such apathy is condoned by Luther's doctrine of two kingdoms that exempts the state from moral interference by the church. While the Holocaust is the starting point for her theology of suffering, Soelle is equally concerned with other cases of violence and injustice and Christian complicity with massive social suffering, especially in the third world. Her liberation approach to theology goes well beyond both existentialist and Marxist approaches.

In philosophical terms, Soelle's methodology has postmodern traits, notwithstanding the "modern" theological and philosophical influences detailed above. Her work is not self-consciously postmodern, however, nor does she apply this label to her thought. In fact, her emphasis on naming injustice and taking political action is contrary to the relativism popularly associated with postmodernism that has decidedly negative connotations from her perspective.[3] She is certainly not a "radical" postmodern theologian, inspired by Nietzsche, Heidegger, or French deconstructionists. Despite her sympathy with the "death of God" movement and negative mystical theology, she does not imitate the linguistic denials found in the work of Jacques Derrida nor ultimately discount the possibility of naming God. On the other hand, Soelle's work shares family resemblances with the "moderate" postmodernism of postliberal, feminist, and liberation theologies. Such theologians reject modern epistemological assumptions about the autonomous self and the priority of pure reason, as well as the possibility of epistemic foundations or proofs for theological claims. Instead, moderate postmodern theologians locate the truth of theology in its self-reflexive relationship to Scripture and tradition, and its liberatory potential. Recognizing that theology is constituted by language imbedded in culturally conditioned meanings, the role of theology is to articulate the worldviews and practices of faith communities in a specific social context.[4]

Soelle's theology resembles moderate postmodern theology in accentuating religious experience and practice over theory and doctrine. Soelle rejects the modern philosophical demand to systematize religious knowledge and to defend Christian beliefs from skeptical attack. She criticizes theologians who busy themselves primarily with conceptual statements about Christian doctrine without reflection on the cultural setting and practical implications of such endeavors. Soelle is no systematic theologian as compared, for instance, to her contemporary and cofounder of German post-Holocaust theology, Jürgen Moltmann. Positively, her inspiration arises from her own life context and historical situation and from her exploration of mystical experience and its political ramifications. She articulates how Christian faith provides a hopeful vision of the world that empowers resistance to injustice and endurance of suffering, as well as affirmation of hope, joy, and fulfillment.[5]

Soelle is distinctly postmodern in her preoccupation with theology as a contingent, historically situated discourse. She takes a narrative approach to theology, anchored in real-life experiences. Theology, by her definition, is language addressed to God and the recounting of relation with God in history.[6] This narrative approach is exemplified in *The Silent Cry: Mysticism and Resistance,* in which she weaves together mystical testimonies to exhibit select thematic structures of faith. Over her career, her theology has broadened from dealing mainly with Christian perspectives, informed by Jewish thought, to include reflection on mystical narratives based in Islam, Hinduism, Buddhism, Native American religion, and other traditions.

To illuminate her postmodern approach, this essay analyzes Soelle's theology of suffering from *Suffering* (1973) to *The Silent Cry* (1997), in which she makes explicit the mystical aspects of resistance articulated in her early work. It is largely reflection on suffering that prompts her rejection of theism and her rethinking of God's relation to humanity. The postmodern characteristics of her position on suffering emerge clearly in her dismissal of theodicy in favor of a mystical liberation response. Not only is her approach unique, but her work has had significant influence and it sets a precedent for later feminist and liberation thinkers who explore the practical religious meanings found in suffering and the insufficiency of theodicy answers.

Economies of Suffering

In *Suffering,* Soelle deftly interweaves theological reflection on the Holocaust, "third world" oppression, and workers' exploitation. In situating suffering as a topic of theological study, Soelle focuses on the victims' experience rather than on the perpetration of suffering. The majority of her attention is devoted to severe cases of suffering that threaten to incapacitate the individual. Soelle adopts Simone Weil's phenomenological definition of affliction, the most severe type of suffering, which has three dimensions: physical, psychological, and social. Physical pain is accompanied by self-hatred, depression, isolation, humiliation, and degradation in the company of others. A person who suffers affliction is repulsive to onlookers, and a victim of ridicule and scorn. For illness to devolve into affliction, the condition must be prolonged so as to isolate the victim or create a social stigma. Social conditions, such as oppressive manual labor, also can produce affliction, as Simone Weil demonstrated voluntarily in her stint as a factory worker.[7]

In reflecting on how to remedy affliction, Soelle identifies three developmental phases of suffering: isolation, expression, and solidarity. While mired in affliction, the individual is mute, hopeless, and powerless. Physical pain, social alienation, and psychological distress reinforce one another to make affliction seem inevitable. These symptoms are not class specific. They may occur, for example, in an abusive divorce experienced by a middle-class woman, or in the ill health of a male factory worker whose body is exposed to the degradation of repetitive labor. Although affliction can isolate a person and destroy self-worth, it can be overcome where personal stamina and social resources exist. In the second more hopeful stage of affliction, the capacity for complaint enables the subject to articulate suffering and overcome the suppression of agency imposed by affliction, while in the third and final phase, affliction is overcome and transformed into suffering that has meaning. When the sufferer recognizes that the causes of suffering extend beyond the individual and that suffering is shared, solidarity and resistance result. In her simplified three-step schema, recovery from affliction ends in political activism and the acceptance of suffering.

By insisting on the social dimension of affliction, Soelle considers the role of class, nationality, race, religion, or gender in causing and exacerbating the suffering of persons who may be afflicted as a group. Her response is Marxian in its emphasis on social factors that transform suffering into affliction, although she opposes Marx's atheist assumption that religion functions to reinforce the oppression of the working class in society. Soelle argues that liberatory, or genuine, Christian faith actually motivates people to prevent and resist suffering at all costs. Positively, she adopts the Marxian assumption that all affliction can be alleviated and ended by human efforts. Since its causes are societal, all suffering is to be worked on. Soelle acknowledges that a favorable social context is necessary for a person to reach the third phase of recovery from affliction. But she passes over the fact that some affliction never becomes meaningful. Her use of Holocaust narratives capitalizes on hope rather than despair, even though it is precisely these narratives that provide ample evidence of the destructiveness of affliction. In general, a considerable amount of affliction cannot be alleviated or healed, given the severe and large-scale violence and harm perpetually caused to fragile human bodies by societal and natural causes. Thus, Soelle's claim that affliction leads to solidarity and resistance applies only selectively.[8]

In examining the situatedness of suffering, Soelle finds that white middle and upper class "first world" citizens tend toward apathy to others' suffering and avoidance of personal suffering. Such bourgeois apathy includes avoidance on multiple levels. The attempt is made to suppress consciousness of suffering and to avoid emotional extremes, to project the illusion of well-being while insulating the self against extreme suffering or joy. Ironically, although apathy serves a protective function, it also causes suffering symptomatic of isolation and meaninglessness. The greatest moral harm resulting from apathy is that it destroys the will to resist conditions that cause affliction, and resists acknowledgement or participation in the suffering of others.[9]

Not limited to the bourgeois and especially dangerous to the lower classes is Christian masochism, which Soelle finds in devotional literature. The passive submission to God's will in suffering is a subservient attitude that angers Soelle because of its abusive consequences for the individual and the moral impotence of such a response. If suffering is perceived as a result of sin, it appears unavoidable. The universality of sin effaces the fact that some persons suffer innocently because of the sins of others. Empirically, it seems obvious that suffering is not evenly or fairly distributed in proportion to sin. Hence, victims should not accept suffering as God's will, according to Soelle. To explain suffering as a mode of divine teaching or testing puts humanity in a servile position with respect to God. It is meant to "break our pride, demonstrate our powerlessness and exploit our dependency. Affliction has the intention of bringing us back to a God who only becomes great when he makes us small."[10] Soelle sidesteps the fact that some Christian mystics whom she admires (such as Henry Suso, John of the Cross, or Simone Weil) embrace voluntary suffering in a seemingly masochistic fashion. Rather, she insists that an authentic mystical response accepts chosen and unchosen suffering equally. Solidarity enables an active appropriation of suffering for the sake of others that is not passive or masochistic. Characteristic of her postmodern approach, faith responses to suffering are contextual; thus, different kinds of resistance are suitable to different situations. But in all cases, she asserts that protest and acceptance coexist.

Post-Theism after Auschwitz

Soelle holds that certain models of God are inappropriate in response to suffering: the portrayal of God as divine king with the power to intervene in human affairs, and the image of God as the omniscient spectator who watches human history unfold. Such a God is apathetic in the face of suffering. In Hellenistic philosophy, *apatheia* is intrinsic to divine perfection because it indicates a perfect state of being, free from both internal needs and external influence or harm.[11] Soelle challenges the divine apathy of scholastic theism. She rejects the idea of God as an omnipotent father figure who guides the world from above, as well as the metaphysical concept of a perfect unchanging divine being. By now, this critique has become commonplace. Many feminist thinkers as well as process theologians, Trinitarian theologians, and others have launched analogous attacks. For Soelle, the Holocaust spurs rejection of this theism of impassibility and omnipotence. Was God a spectator watching the horrors of the concentration camps? Certainly not. Such a God is no better than a cruel torturer from the perspective of victims. To presume that God does not intervene, but could intervene, is scandalous. Using human suffering as a criterion for God language, Soelle concludes that the concept of an omnipotent God is unacceptable.[12]

Soelle's alternative concept of God, which she calls "post-theistic," hinges on God's dependence on human cooperation to bring redemption to the world. In declaring the end of theism, Soelle keeps postmodern company with those who reject ontological, objectified discourse about God but utilize praxis-based, narrative, and mystical forms of theological language.[13] Like Buber, she defines theology as I-Thou language where faith experience is articulated, but she does not follow Buber's explanation for God's apparent silence during and after the Holocaust as a periodic eclipse of God. Instead, she proposes divine suffering as necessary for post-Holocaust faith, in agreement with thinkers such as Jürgen Moltmann, Hans Jonas, and Elie Wiesel. Divine suffering reconciles God's love with the sheer horrors of human suffering experienced in the Jewish ghettos and concentration camps. But this reconciliation is not a justification of God. It makes God sympathetic to human suffering but does not claim that God has good reasons for letting people suffer. Suffering and evil are part of the structure of creation, in tension with goodness, beauty, and human flourishing. God, too, lives in this tragic tension. God is spoken of as a happening or event, a creative energy, rather than an entity or transcendent being. Since God language properly expresses relation and dialogue, as Buber argues, God's suffering is not conceived ontologically but actively. To articulate faith in God theologically, the proper question is not "Do you believe in God?" as if God is an object to be known, but "Do you live out God?"[14]

The rejection of divine omnipotence and affirmation of divine suffering has a christological emphasis in Soelle's earlier writings, although the cross plays only a minor role in *The Silent Cry*. The cross represents the possibility for resistance and the centrality of nonviolence in response to prejudice, violence, and social oppression. The life of Jesus demonstrates that love for reality entails suffering. Relational power is shared mutually among human and divine with no reified division. In the face of suffering, God is found hanging on the gallows in Auschwitz, as depicted in the hanging of the sad-eyed angel in Elie Wiesel's *Night*. That does not mean that all victims found God to be present or that God was secretly present with each of them. Soelle affirms a mystical response to suffering that applies only to those persons who intentionally seek God and find God within suffering.[15]

Turning from victims to perpetrators, it is striking that Soelle does not explore the role of Christians who had faith in God and yet assisted the Nazi genocide implementation. The reason, presumably, is that since the faith of perpetrators is a negative example, it is not helpful to her constructive project of modeling exemplary post-Holocaust faith. But on the contrary, examining the shadow side of faith displayed by Nazi Christians could enrich her theological understanding of acceptance and resistance. Another related subject seldom explored in Soelle's writings, but central to post-Holocaust thought, is the need for repentance and reconciliation between Christians and Jews. On this issue, Soelle's biography reveals more about her position than her theological writings. For many years, she participated in Jewish-Christian events in Germany and had regular contact with the Hamburg Jewish community. Moreover, in her public lectures she repeatedly emphasizes the importance of remembering Germany's Nazi past, which must be grappled with by German citizens, clergy, and politicians. But judging from her publications, her response to the Holocaust mainly deals with victims' suffering while neglecting to analyze how persons of faith can promote and condone prejudice and violence.[16]

Post-Theodicy

In rejecting God's omnipotence, Soelle decisively opposes theodicy justification of suffering as permitted by God. She insists that it is masochistic for Christians to accept suffering as something that is instrumental for God's will. Theodicy explanations for suffering blame human sinfulness and view suffering as having chastising, testing, or character-building functions. Theodicy advocates acceptance, whereas protest is the appropriate response to the idea of an omnipotent God who allows suffering. Soelle reads the biblical book of Job as a story of rebellion, where the sufferer is not servile but strong enough to oppose God as well as his friends who promote theodicy explanations. Soelle's interpretation prioritizes Job's speeches and dismisses the God of the prologue and epilogue as a capricious monarch. More controversially, Soelle dismisses the image of the whirlwind God as an amoral God of nature, unworthy of worship, although in *The Silent Cry* she is less critical of Job's acquiescence to this God. However, she unconditionally approves of a third concept of God hinted at in Job's speeches. This God is neither an absolute ruler nor an omnipotent nature God. The God who Job calls upon is the witness of his suffering (Job 16:19–20) and his champion or advocate (Job 19:25–29). Job calls for God to defend his claim of innocence. Like the God of the Exodus, the witness-God takes sides with those who are unjustly wronged. This God cannot be blamed for the captivity of Israel, for the slaves' suffering is explained in terms of its social causes. Job's advocate is the hope of the oppressed.[17]

Soelle's interpretation of Job echoes the position of Marxist philosopher Ernst Bloch, who concludes that Job ultimately refuses to submit to the almighty God of the whirlwind who intimidates him. Although Job retreats to silence in the face of the whirlwind speeches, Job does not abandon protest inwardly. Job's retreat is not acquiescence. Job never accepts the explanation of his friends, that God sends suffering for a good reason. No theodicy justification is effective. Up until the end, Job is left waiting for his divine witness to advocate his innocence.[18] Yet unlike Bloch, Soelle also finds a mystical quality of acceptance in Job's rebellion. Job loves God without expectation of reward and without egotistical demands. His faith stems from hope rather than knowledge.

In response to suffering, Soelle concludes that the theodicy "why" question is the wrong one to ask. She is determined to "snatch God out of patriarchy's clinch and overcome the theodicy question as a false question."[19] Theodicy is mistaken for a number of reasons. It assumes that God selectively permits certain suffering for good purposes, which signifies a grave misunderstanding of the God-world relationship. Moreover, theodicy does not recognize that what makes suffering positive or redemptive depends on the response of the sufferer. The issue is not whether God is justified in permitting suffering for good reasons and purposes but whether suffering is meaningful and productive or meaningless and destructive. Human agency is responsible for the differentiation between meaningful and meaningless suffering, not divine decree.

The central theological question in response to suffering should be "Whom does suffering serve?"[20] Suffering serves God, if it is faced in love and recognition of others' suffering. Another way of phrasing the query is "How do our pains become God's pain, and how does God's pain appear in our pains?"[21] God can become immanent in human suffering. However, not all pain reflects God's pain. Persons of faith share in divine suffering through sorrow over injustice and the destruction of life and through a response of love and resistance to suffering. Participation in God's suffering is productive. Soelle compares it to the labor pains that precede the birth of redemption, peace, and justice. In the midst of suffering, joy can be found. The mystic sufferer has relinquished faith in an omnipotent interventionist God but has not relinquished hope for an end to suffering.

Counter to my reading of Soelle, Kenneth Surin argues that she formulates an alternate theodicy in her book *Suffering* —a "practical" theodicy, in contrast with the theoretical theodicies of analytical philosophers. Supposedly, she "solves" the problem of evil with her theology of the cross. Surin finds her approach closely comparable to that of Jürgen Moltmann, even though she does not employ a Trinitarian approach or offer a systematic theology. Surin understands Soelle to claim that God justifies human suffering by divine participation in suffering on the cross.[22] However, I disagree. In discussing the suffering of Jesus, Soelle does not explain why God permits suffering, nor does she assert that all suffering is somehow imitative of the cross. Rather, she argues that the cross provides a model for how suffering can be taken on voluntarily for the sake of God and in solidarity with other persons. In rejecting theism, Soelle refuses to give theodicy justification in universal terms.[23] It is precisely her point that not all suffering is redemptive, and all suffering must be resisted. It is accepted only strategically and becomes meaningful only voluntarily.

Surin further criticizes Soelle's response to suffering by questioning the doctrinal orthodoxy of her theodicy alternative. Surin remarks that, as it appears to him, Soelle reduces God to a mere symbol of the process of emancipation from social suffering. He faults her for overplaying divine immanence and neglecting traditional doctrines of sin and grace. In Christian theology, this type of critique has been directed toward a number of feminist theologians (as well as Whiteheadian process and liberation thinkers) who prioritize immanence, relation and historical development over transcendence, immutability, and divine power. Indeed, there is legitimate debate over consistency with church doctrines. But I argue that from a postmodern perspective, Soelle's post-theism is not a proposal for a theistic ontology but a counterdiscourse. It is mistaken to conclude that she reduces God to secular terms, based on her existential-mystical approach. Instead of focusing on the transcendent referent of theological language, as modern theologies do, she examines the function or operation of God language used by persons of faith who face suffering. This postmodern move shifts the subject matter from knowledge of God to examination of faith practices and vocabularies.

The type of theological language that she employs is situated and relational. Soelle cites testimonies of suffering persons in order to examine how faith survives. Her theology uses narrative to address problems of coping, not explaining. Thus, her statement that "God suffers" articulates the mystical reality experienced in the throes of suffering. It is not a justification, or a theistic ontology, but a description of how faith empowers persons to discover God in suffering. Nevertheless, Soelle does affirm divine suffering that has conceptual and doctrinal ramifications, whether or not she pursues them. As a scholar, I would like to see more thorough treatment of epistemological, ontological, and doctrinal issues to underpin her claims about God's attributes and her post-theistic proposal. This shortage of methodological reflection makes it challenging to bring her work into conversation with contemporary branches of American and continental philosophy of religion. Soelle provides compelling narrative descriptions of mystical faith, but the theoretical positioning of her work remains ambiguous.

Liberation and Protest

Soelle's postmodern response to suffering is accurately categorized as a liberation approach, a label that applies to her earlier political and post-Holocaust theology as well as her feminist, ecological, and mystical reflection. Soelle's understanding of faith and hope is Marxian in its focus on social transformation, but she broadens solidarity beyond the oppressed proletariat to include those of any class who are conscious of the causes of suffering and unite in resistance. Like other liberation theologians, her work deals with faith praxis: the human activities of reflection, critical analysis, and action in history. Praxis is a holistic activity that produces cultural structures, symbols, and meanings, including religious ones. Soelle agrees with Gustavo Gutierrez who defines theology itself as a praxis that involves reflection on God, moral agency, and social context. Within the scope of faith praxis, there are many specific practices such as solidarity, suffering, hope, and protest.[24] As explained by mujerista theologian Ada Maria Isasi-Diaz, liberatory praxis is embodied in the everyday life of Christians, and praxis itself is "theology" on a grassroots level. Like Soelle, Isasi-Diaz and Gutierrez use faith narratives generously in order to gain theological insight into how Christian faith is shaped by class, gender, economic, and political structures.[25]

Soelle's theological focus on praxis is a departure from the stereotypical modern Cartesian understanding of the object of knowledge where reflection involves the operation of reason understood as abstracted from the body. She proposes an alternate conception of the subject as inexorably linked with other beings, not ontologically independent. If the human self is essentially separate, argues Soelle, relation to other beings is optional and external, and the theological result is an understanding of God's being as independent of creation, and human and natural beings as independent of each other. The God who rules over creation is the God of theism. In contrast, the God conceived of as *always* in relationship is the postmodern, post-theistic deity of feminist and liberation theology.[26]

In response to suffering, the radical immanence of God goes hand in hand with experiential certainty of God. Reflective theological language cannot establish this certainty, but firsthand testimony makes it visible. In the 1980s, Soelle recalls hearing a black woman from South Africa speak about resistance to apartheid. The woman was involved in community organization, group Bible study, and nonviolent acts of protest. The assurance and confidence of the woman made visible her patient certainty that liberation would eventually come. Soelle remarks that such hope is indestructible, as a bond with God and solidarity with others. She writes that later "it became clear to me that this young woman in sweatshirt and trainers is what the religious tradition teaches me to call an angel . . . a messenger who makes God visible."[27] The confirmation of meaning in the face of suffering is not external or requiring objective proof. It is already present, like light that is received by those who are open to relation and not hindered by rationalistic blinders. Certainty of meaning depends not on divine intervention or supernatural proof but on the truth of justice and advocacy for the welfare of all beings.

Suffering is a praxis of liberation, when it is accepted in solidarity with others who suffer. Acceptance can apply to involuntary suffering as well as suffering that is intentionally risked to help others. As an example, Soelle tells the story of a priest in Guatemala who served in a base community. Lifting heavy canisters of water, Padre Alfredo severely injured his back and was bedridden without painkillers or medical care because his rural district had no doctors. He told his friends that he offered his suffering "in sacrifice" to Christ. Soelle remarks that in her book *Suffering* she would have criticized his response as submissive or even masochistic. But moving beyond a bourgeois individualistic response, she now sees his actions as acknowledging deliberate acceptance of suffering for the sake of solidarity. Padre Alfredo chose to live with the poor who have no medicines and who endure hardship. Although subject to an accident, his suffering shows God's preference for the poor. Suffering is not private imitation of Christ but Christlike suffering shared for the sake of the community. This liberative meaning resonates with a quotation from Meister Eckhart: "If my suffering is in God, and if God suffers with me, how then can my suffering be misfortune?" Soelle links solidarity between human beings who suffer with participation in divine suffering. She reads into Eckhart's words the political implication that to suffer in God implies connectedness and resistance along with all of creation. When personal pain becomes a part of God's pain, suffering becomes both mystically meaningful and liberatory.[28] Suffering in God is shared suffering, reflecting divine love.

Mystical and Postmodern Responses to Suffering

Soelle's narrative approach to suffering is mystical, even in her earlier work where mysticism is not necessarily named. In the conclusion to *Suffering*, "love of reality" is clearly a mystical attitude that enables a person to accept suffering without servile submission to God or cynical fatalism. Narratives taken from Christian Scripture or from the life of persons who withstand suffering with profound love serve as models. In this vein, Soelle employs the memoir written by Holocaust survivor Jacques Lusseyran, who was blinded in an accident as a boy and deported to Buchenwald concentration camp at age nineteen as punishment for leading a French resistance group. Recalling his accident, Lusseyran consciously refuses to pursue blame, anger, or self-pity, although he is acquainted with other blind children who are angry and resentful of their disability. While imprisoned in Buchenwald, he recalls how people in the camp confided in him and summoned him, nicknamed the "blind Frenchman," to visit the bedsides of those who were sick and dying. Soelle concludes that Lusseyran wastes not "a single thought on avoiding suffering or evading it. The theodicy question is superseded here by an unlimited love for reality."[29] He manages to transform involuntary suffering into accepted suffering, and to risk other suffering for political reasons. To understand how to respond to suffering is to remember the stories of persons, such as Lusseyran, as examples of how to love reality and live with mystical faith and hope.

Although written nearly three decades after *Suffering*, the methodology of *The Silent Cry* is also narrative in approach. In both books, the plurality of narratives avoids reducing mystical responses to suffering to a formal systematized pattern. The voices that speak through narrative are employed as heuristic indicators of exemplary faith responses. As is typical of moderate postmodern theology, communal faith practice takes priority over theory. However, the breadth of mystical examples cited makes *The Silent Cry* intriguing and even puzzling. Upon first reading *The Silent Cry*, I was surprised to see the eclectic collection of non-Christian mystics discussed, such as Jalal Al-Din Rumi, Rabi'a, Black Elk, Mahatma Gandhi, the Ba'al Shem Tov, and Thich Nhat Hanh. Even looking solely at the Christian mystics cited, parallels are drawn between diverse historical figures and eras, eliding their differences and stressing similarities. Soelle's purpose is to demonstrate that resistance is consistently central to Christian mystics. Moreover, her assumption that mysticism inspires resistance is the hermeneutic key to the selection of citations from non-Christian mystical narratives. One might well assume that Soelle operates as a modern "inclusivist" theologian who makes the universal claim that there is one deity whom all mystics seek, explicitly or implicitly. For instance, she states, "Speaking in terms of an image, I picture the religions of the world in a circle with the center as the mystery of the world, the deity."[30] Does she assume that there is one "transcendent" that has many names, or is she making the functional, rather than ontological, claim that various religions exhibit similar mystical responses? I conclude that a functional approach would be most consistent with her practical narrative method. Yet the epistemological arguments needed to clarify and defend her position are absent.

In response to these puzzles, the most persuasive and internally consistent interpretation of her theological position requires a postmodern lens. A postmodern reading accounts for the lack of epistemological and ontological discussion of foundational assumptions in her work. It also best makes sense of the juxtaposition of narratives employed. Mystical narratives are context dependent and fluid with rich potential for comparison and inspiration. She does not prove ontologically that all mystics refer to one concept of God in their written expressions of prayer and wisdom. The mystical love of reality that Soelle speaks of in *Suffering* is a practical posture involving commitment and hope. God is not an ontological other to be categorized. In *The Silent Cry*, mysticism is not defined by God as its goal but by three mystical attitudes—selflessness, possessionlessness, and powerlessness—and five places *(Orte)*—nature, eroticism, suffering, community, and joy. The word *Orte* is awkward in English translation because it loses its familial connotation of birthplace, home, and tradition. These "places" are not spatial or separated by distance but embodied, symbolic, and culturally rooted. Mysticism happens in specific contexts with complex interplay between individual, situational, and religious factors. Suffering is one "place" or event coexisting simultaneously with others. It is important to note that suffering is not the chief or sole place of mysticism but a central place that is potentially inhabited in a mystical way.

Soelle draws together mystical testimonies to explore the phenomena of mystical political resistance found in Christianity and other religions. My postmodern reading interprets her mosaic of mystics as conversing in a dissonant yet productive accord. However, the arrangement of the book and the short space devoted to each figure manages to subsume the mystics' voices into Soelle's phenomenological schema of mysticism. Brief excerpts cannot do justice to each mystic's historical particularity, and brevity and comprehensiveness are necessary for her project. Even within the scope of her aims, more attention should be paid to areas of divergence and incongruity among mystical figures. Moreover, *The Silent Cry* would benefit from arguments justifying its broad and eclectic approach. How do so many different religions correspond to one model of mysticism? What are the criteria for discerning patterns of "genuine" mystical faith in Christianity and other religions? On the other hand, the book is effective at meeting what I see as its two major goals. First, it provides a rich mystical vision of liberation that is the fruit of Soelle's lifetime of searching and reflection. Second, it provides some nourishing bread for the unsatisfied spiritual hunger of Europeans and North Americans, infected by cynicism, materialism, and disillusionment with the church. Ultimately, the ability to inspire and rejuvenate faith in a post-Holocaust and potentially post-Christian cultural setting is Soelle's priority.

Conclusion

As evidence of its enduring impact, Soelle's theology of suffering resonates powerfully with the writings of later generations of feminist and liberation theologians, who argue against theodicy and develop practical strategies for faith's survival. Three examples from feminist American theologians writing during the 1990s will suffice to display the prescience of Soelle's ideas. Like Soelle, Wendy Farley sharply rejects the notion of divine omnipotence and the rational justification of evil based on divine love. Her book *Tragic Vision and Divine Compassion* proposes a tragic view of God and creation that emphasizes the world's beautiful fragility and pervasive suffering, redeemed through the incarnation of God's love in human communities. She presents a phenomenology of faith overcoming suffering with compassion that mirrors elements of Soelle's mystical love of reality. Liberation theologian Sharon Welch, in *A Feminist Ethic of Risk,* analyzes African-American women's fiction as instructive for "first world" responses to evil in society, centering around strategies of resistance. She identifies common themes among faith responses to suffering, such as creativity, connectedness, love, joy, resistance, and recognition of God's immanence in struggle. Her understanding of divine immanence is very similar to Soelle's post-theism. Kathleen Sands, in *Escape from Paradise,* criticizes both traditional theodicy and feminist theologies of Rosemary Ruether and Carol Christ that minimize the scars left by suffering by redeeming it. Using narratives as the basis for theology, like Farley and Welch, Sands uses women's fiction to explore suffering caused by gender, class, and race. Sensitive to the dangers of theological generalization, she offers glimpses of a mystical, ethical, and aesthetic response to suffering. These feminist writers may not draw on Soelle explicitly, and Welch and Sands do not work toward specifically Christian theological responses. Yet Soelle shares with this new generation of writers the conviction that alternatives to theodicy should provide a holistic, contextual, complex, and provisional understanding of how faith copes with suffering.[31]

Soelle's theology is important for its historical placement at the early stages of post-Holocaust, feminist, and liberation theologies. Philosophically, it is intriguing as a postmodern narrative approach to Christian theology. From an international standpoint, her work is pivotal as a German feminist liberation theology that bridges continents and cultures. But what I want to emphasize, in conclusion, is the value of Soelle's pioneering work in offering a theological alternative to theodicy that addresses large-scale historical evils and personal-political responses to suffering. In forging new directions beyond theism and theodicy, Soelle joins contextual postmodern currents of thought that recognize the historicity, contingency, and class privilege of theological discourse.

Notes

1. I have in mind a diverse group of feminist, liberation, African-American, and post-Holocaust thinkers who take a contextual, practical, anti-theodicy approach to suffering—for instance, Dorothee Soelle, Kathleen Sands, Wendy Farley, Sharon Welch, Delores Williams, Cheryl Kirk-Duggan, Anthony Pinn, Gustavo Gutierrez, Richard Rubenstein, Eliezer Berkovits, and David Blumenthal.

2. In an exchange of letters, Soelle insists that it is not only sinful to directly cause exploitation, by cheating or stealing, but it is also sinful to purchase bananas picked by exploited "third world" workers knowing their economic oppression. Dorothee Soelle, *Theology for Skeptics: Reflections on God* (Minneapolis: Fortress, 1995), 128.

3. For her criticism of postmodern relativism and its ethical impotence, see Dorothee Soelle, "Die Sowohl-als-auch-Falle: Über postmodern Toleranz," in *Mutanfälle: Texte zum Umdenken* (München: Deutscher Taschenbuch Verlag, 1996), 30–33.

4. The typology of moderate and radical postmodernism is developed in Thomas Guarino, "Between Foundations and Nihilism: Is Phronesis the Via Media for Theology?" *Theological Studies* 54 (March 1993): 37. Analogous terminology is employed by Terrence Tilley, who defines "moderate" theological postmodernism as including postliberal and cultural linguistic theologians (indebted to Wittgenstinean philosophy of language), Catholic fundamental theologians (indebted to German critical theory), and liberation theologians (indebted to postcolonial Marxian and feminist thought). Focus on liberatory practice locates Soelle in the latter group. Terrence W. Tilley, *Postmodern Theologies: The Challenge of Religious Diversity* (Maryknoll, N.Y.: Orbis, 1995), vi–x, 115–18.

5. Dorothee Soelle, *Thinking about God: An Introduction to Theology* (Philadelphia: Trinity Press International, 1990), 171–82.

6. Defining the approach of praxis-oriented moderate postmodern theologians, namely Gustavo Gutierrez, James McClendon, and Sharon Welch, Tilley writes: "What joins them is that they leave behind the endless debates of modernity about the foundations of religious belief in true or warranted doctrines. What is key for this postmodern approach are the practices which constituted shared religious life." Tilley, *Postmodern Theologies*, viii.

7. Simone Weil, "Love of God and Affliction," in *Waiting for God* (New York: Harper and Row, 1973), 117–20; Dorothee Soelle, *Suffering* (Philadelphia: Fortress, 1975), 13–15.

8. Soelle, *Suffering*, 105–7. For reflection on the inadequacy of Soelle's position in response to severe affliction known as trauma, see the chapter in this volume by Flora A. Keshgegian, "Witnessing Trauma: Dorothee Soelle's Theology of Suffering in a World of Victimization."

9. Ibid., 36–39.

10. Ibid., 19.

11. Ibid., 42.

12. Ibid., 32.

13. Martin Buber, *I and Thou* (trans. Walter Kaufmann; New York: Simon and Schuster, 1970), 129; for interpretation of Buber's I-You philosophy as a theological alternative to "theism," see Soelle, *Thinking about God*, 183.

14. Soelle, *Thinking about God*, 186-88; Soelle, *Theology for Skeptics: Reflections on God*, 112.

15. Soelle, *Suffering*, 145. It is interesting that in post-Holocaust thought in general there is a major trend toward the rejection of theodicy. See Zachary Braiterman in *(God) After Auschwitz: Tradition and Change in Post-Holocaust Jewish Thought* (Princeton: Princeton University Press, 1998); and Sarah K. Pinnock, *Beyond Theodicy: Jewish and Christian Continental Thinkers Respond to the Holocaust* (Albany, N.Y.: SUNY, 2002).

16. When Soelle responded (in personal correspondence) to my claim that she neglects nonvictims in her post-Holocaust theology, she expressed surprise at this conclusion. She clarified that Christian bystanders, rather than perpetrators or victims, have been her main concern. But judging from her publications, I maintain that her theology emphasizes the perspective of victims and their suffering, not Holocaust bystanders or perpetrators. See Sarah K. Pinnock, "Die Theologie der zweiten Generation nach Auschwitz: Eine kritische Analyse," in

Von Gott reden im Land der Täter: Theologische Stimmen der dritten Generation seit der Shoah (ed. Katharina von Kellenbach, Björn Krondorfer, Norbert Reck; Darmstadt: Wissenschaftliche Buchgesellschaft, 2001), 95–109.

17. Soelle, *Suffering*, 109–19.

18. Ernst Bloch, *Atheism in Christianity: Religion of Exodus and the Kingdom* (New York: Herder and Herder, 1970), 111–15.

19. Soelle, *Theology for Skeptics*, 66.

20. Soelle, *Suffering*, 134.

21. Soelle, *Theology for Skeptics*, 71.

22. Kenneth Surin, *Theology and the Problem of Evil* (Oxford: Blackwell, 1986), 112–24.

23. Rather than call Soelle's response to suffering a "theodicy," as Surin does, I limit the term theodicy to philosophical and theological arguments that defend God's goodness and explain or justify suffering.

24. Gustavo Gutiérrez, *Theology of Liberation* (Maryknoll, N.Y.: Orbis, 1988), xxx.

25. Ada Maria Isasi-Diaz, *En La Lucha/In the Struggle: A Hispanic Women's Liberation Theology* (Minneapolis: Fortress, 1993), 186–88.

26. Soelle, *Thinking about God*, 180–81. The confirmation of meaning found in faith cannot be objectified but is realized and proven in action, a position that Buber presents in *I and Thou*, 159.

27. Soelle, *Thinking about God*, 194.

28. Soelle, *Theology for Skeptics*, 80–82.

29. Soelle, *Suffering*, 91–93.

30. Soelle, *The Silent Cry: Mysticism and Resistance* (trans. Barbara and Martin Rumschedit; Minneapolis: Fortress, 2001), 51. See my book review of *The Silent Cry* in *Union Seminary Quarterly Review* 55, nos.1–2 (2001): 163–68.

31. There are striking parallels with Soelle's work in Wendy Farley, *Tragic Vision and Divine Compassion: A Contemporary Theodicy* (Louisville: Westminster/John Knox, 1990), 115–33; Kathleen Sands, *Escape from Paradise: Evil and Tragedy in Feminist Theology* (Minneapolis: Fortress, 1994), 137–69; and Sharon D. Welch, *A Feminist Ethic of Risk* (Minneapolis: Fortress, 1990), 172–80. A synoptic overview of feminist, anti-theodicy approaches to suffering, which gives due credit to Soelle's seminal importance, is developed in Kristine M. Rankka, *Women and the Value of Suffering: An Aw(e)ful Rowing toward God* (Collegeville, Minn.: Liturgical Press, 1998), 120–34, 215–16, and 222–25. Rankka's conclusion that a spirituality of suffering must have both mystical and political dimensions is in full agreement with Soelle's position.

PART 4
MYSTICISM

10. Dorothee Soelle, Feminism, and Medieval Women Mystics

Christine E. Gudorf

Like many Americans, I first came to know Dorothee Soelle in the late 1970s when she taught at Union Theological Seminary in New York. She came to Union with a reputation as an activist theologian and a socialist Christian, famous for the "Political Night Prayer" movement she had organized in Cologne that had spread to other European cities. Assigned in spring 1978 as her teaching assistant, I was both delighted and intimidated.

Our conversations about feminism began one day early in our semester together when Dorothy plunked down her tray next to mine in the refectory at Union and began to quiz me about American feminism. She asked why so many Union women identified themselves as feminists, why they thought that the cause of women as women was central enough to identify persons. To her it seemed a narrow cause advocated by women of privilege—white, middle-class American women—when there were so many other groups, even in the American context, blacks and farm workers, for example, not to mention other oppressed peoples around the globe, who should be the focus of efforts for justice. Most complaints of white feminists seemed rather petty to her. Furthermore, the direction of some feminist thought she thought completely anti-liberatory, such as Shulamith Firestone's idea that women's full liberation might require the freeing of women from pregnancy and childbirth through new forms of reproduction. She rejected the idea of childbearing and child rearing as a burden, insisting that even in her years as a single mother her children had been a principal source of joy and empowerment, and pointed to women around the world who understood their motherhood as the defining role in their lives. Feminism seemed to her to devalue their choice by denying motherhood as a worthwhile vocation.

There were, of course, some points on which we could agree. Her socialism deplored the American privatization of childcare and the organization of work in ways that destroy family relationships. One interesting aspect of that conversation I have never forgotten was her denial that she had ever felt discriminated against as a woman. Countless Germans, men as well as women, have since insisted that her failure to gain a teaching post in the German university system was the result as much of her sex as of her politics. Perhaps they read the continuing reluctance of the German university system to appoint women to theology faculties back into her case. Or perhaps Dorothee needed to understand her exclusion in terms of the politics she had chosen for herself, rather than in terms of some assigned characteristic. Possibly she, having spent her life championing victims of injustice, was unable to label her treatment unjust for fear that it would obscure the greater injustices done others.

During the course for which I was her teaching assistant, the topic of mysticism arose. It has since remained important in my own life and theology, and since the spring of 1978, I have always connected it with Dorothee. I remember vividly that one day she became frustrated at eliciting little response from the class about religious experience, about experience of God. As we walked out of the classroom, she insisted on the importance of consciousness of experience of God, and wondered what was wrong that the students seemed to have such difficulty articulating their experience. I offered to begin the next class with a brief description of my own, and she immediately responded "Yes! That would be wonderful!" with typical Dorothee enthusiasm. She later recounted my presentation in *The Silent Cry:*

> Accordingly, she told us that as a very young girl in the American Midwest she had spent many hours reading in bed at night, without permission. One winter's night she woke up at four in the morning, went outside, and looked at the stars on a clear frosty night. She had a once in a lifetime feeling of happiness, of being connected with all of life, with God: a feeling of overwhelming clarity, of being sheltered and carried. She saw the stars as she had never seen them before. She described the experience in these words, "Nothing can happen, I am indestructible, I am one with everything." This did not happen again until about ten years later when, in a different context, something similar took place. The new context was a huge demonstration against the Vietnam War. There, too, she knew that she was sheltered, a part of the whole, "indestructible,"

together with the others. Struggling with words and with her own timidity, she brought both experiences together under the rubric of religious experience.[1]

Dorothee's response to my semicoherent account clarified for me how basic such experience was for her theology and praxis. Without it, I am not sure that I would have seen mysticism as foundational for theology/praxis in her subsequent works, until *The Silent Cry*.

The validation of my religious experience then, and the corpus of Dorothee's work since, helped me understand Gustavo Gutierrez's insistence that it is experiencing the gratuitousness of God's love that calls forth from humans not only faith but love for each other and for the rest of creation. Since then I have been convinced that, though I still have never heard Dorothee speak in any direct or elaborated manner of her own experience of God, such experience is, for Dorothee, the source of her extraordinary passion for life, for love, and for justice. Later I came to see Dorothee in earlier figures of women mystics noted for both their passion and the breadth of their interests and achievements. Dorothee the anti-Vietnam protester, the theologian, the poet, the socialist, the Witness for Peace, came to seem very like figures of Hildegard of Bingen, Mechthild of Magdeburg, Catharine of Sienna, and Teresa of Avila, and to share some aspects of the tragic Marguerite Porete. In this brief essay, I will first treat Dorothee's use of mysticism and then turn to feminism in her work.

Mysticism in Soelle's Early Work

Though I was very aware that the experience recounted in Soelle's class was religious, an experience of God, I never would have called it mysticism then, because, like many others, I understood mysticism as something that happened to solitary ascetics who had divorced themselves from the world. Soelle herself then did not speak about "mysticism" as such. Her own Lutheran tradition lacked a tradition of mysticism but retained the powerful conversion experience of Martin Luther in addition to the biblical visions and dreams of God. Though always eclectic in her choice of exemplars, she rarely chose medieval mystics in those days, preferring more clearly prophetic, active figures. Throughout her early work, in books and in lectures, Soelle always told stories, and many of those stories involved elements of mysticism, but virtually all of such accounts were from "secular" figures of recent history, sometimes from folklore or song, but presented as contemporary parallels with revelation in biblical visions. Many of her writings drew on the Bible, especially biblical dreams and visions that she linked to passages from the Gospels and epistles on poverty, community, sharing, and God's demand for justice.

But Soelle made little use of the high mystical tradition in Christianity until recently, probably because, as was clear to readers of *Suffering*, and as she admits in *The Silent Cry*, she rejected self-inflicted suffering, which figures so frequently among the medieval mystics. From the perspective of someone dedicated to the elimination of unnecessary suffering and the creation of communities of justice and solidarity, the infliction of suffering on oneself seemed masochistic and to contribute nothing to the common cause. Furthermore, for Soelle, the God who died on the cross does not want other people to create crosses for themselves—there are already too many crosses constructed by others that need to be destroyed.

But with *The Silent Cry*, Soelle has "come out of the closet" as a mystic in continuity with the late medieval flowering of mysticism. Some readers will inevitably interpret this turn as a result of age; the onset of old age prompts many to an inwardness, a preparation for what is to come. But I suspect that it is more a question of what has been happening in her life for many decades, than of what is ahead, that prompted this turn to medieval mysticism. For mysticism has been more than simply the ideational foundation of her call to liberation on behalf of the poor, for elimination of war, for justice of all kinds. I suspect it also has become the well at which she has renewed her hope and energy.

Soelle has spoken more of resistance than revolution or liberation. One important difference is that resistance is almost always longer-term: It holds out no hope for swift and total victory. In the early 1980s Soelle was invited to my university to give a lecture on resistance and revolution and strongly defended resistance as the more universal praxis. She referred to James Cone's book *The Spirituals and the Blues*, in which he presented both the spirituals and the blues as major forms of black resistance to slavery and Jim Crow.[2] She named many current and past situations in which liberation is and was simply not possible in the near run, but showed how resistance kept alive the dignity of the oppressed, the vision of liberation in the future, while chipping away at the structures of oppression. Her book of poetry, *Revolutionary Patience*, illustrated this same need for understanding the construction of the Kingdom as a long, wearying task built on hope and patience.[3] Resistance can take many forms, some of which are always possible. For Soelle, mysticism is the grounding we must draw on in our everyday resistance to the alienation that surrounds us. Mysticism is what supports us in our everyday struggle for dignity, for relationships with people rather than things, and for defying the forces in our societies that try to isolate and commodify us.

So some forms of mysticism have always been a part of her political activism and theological vision. But the more suffering and injustice we confront, the more we bleed with the oppressed over long decades filled with more oppression than liberation, the more need we have to go back to the well that Gutierrez referred to in *We Drink from Our Own Wells*—the well that provides us access to God, the living water.[4] As our need for sustenance at that well gets greater, the more we must seek out new and more effective disciplines to take us deeper into the well. And that is what I think drove Soelle to the medieval mystics.

Soelle and the Medieval Women Mystics

There is a great variety among the medieval women mystics, and in some ways Soelle shares little with them. Most of them, but not all, were in religious orders, often mother superiors or abbesses. Soelle understandably reveals a deep sympathy for the Beguines, a women's lay movement of small communities of celibate women devoted to spiritual pursuits and work in the world, not only because of their persecution by the church but also because they anticipated her own struggle to be lay Christian in the secular world:

> In an ocean of patriarchal, hierarchically directed injustice, the Beguines created islands of freedom for women. The revolution that occurred there was spiritual. It refused to bow down to the world's secularity in relation to sexuality and property, as well as creating a new way of life that also found new forms of expressing the inner life in language and ritual.[5]

When Soelle writes of the Beguine Marguerite Porete, the author of *The Mirror of Annihilated Simple Souls* who was condemned by the Inquisition and executed in 1310, she explains a number of reasons why Porete was considered dangerous, many of them not limited to her own thirteenth and fourteenth centuries. For Porete was not only a target because the King wanted to "demonstrate his orthodox disposition to Rome by sacrificing a Beguine suspected of heterodoxy; a woman, that is, without the protection of marriage or the head of a religious order."[6] The underlying danger that Porete posed to the church and to the secular government as well was her championing of freedom. Like other mystics, she claimed that "the immediacy of the experience of God is in no need of mediation," undermining the authority of the clergy and of the institutional church as a whole.[7] The entire journey of the soul to God as described by Porete consists of clear steps that begin from but lead away from what she called the "Sainte Eglise la Petit" (the empirical/scholastic church) to the "Saint Eglise la Grande" (the Great Holy Church of the Spirit). The soul begins pursuing the virtues, such as attending masses, listening to sermons, or fasting and praying, but as it ascends to God it becomes freer from the rule of the virtues and is more and more encompassed by love.[8] The soul annihilated by love is focused not on earning God's gifts by works but simply on unity with God for the sheer joy of sharing God's goodness. It is the self that is annihilated and the soul that is set free to union with Love.

This is, of course, the guts of mysticism. Porete's was a solitary journey but paralleled by the journeys of many others before and since. What makes her so memorable today is not only the clarity of her writing but the fact that she, without any official role in the church, claimed the authority to instruct others in the ascent to God. Moreover, she addressed her instruction deliberately to the popular masses, "expressing it in the courtly language, in the literary and social schemas which allowed the author to be understood by the readers, or rather listeners, of those days. In fact, the text is presented in the form of a play, with allegorical characters, the chief ones being Soul and Lady Love."[9]

This is a critical point: Porete did not write to theologians and clerics but to ordinary Christians. When the book was first examined for orthodoxy by a panel consisting of a Friar Minor, a Cistercian, and theologian Godfrey of Fontaine, the Cistercian's approval was without reserve, but Godfrey and the Franciscan, "though expressing their deep admiration, consider that the book should be shown to only a very few persons, for it might be a source of dangerous illusions to those who do not possess an adequate spiritual preparation."[10] In many ways Soelle's work parallels Porete's. Holding no official church or university post in theology in her own country, Soelle claimed the authority to take her vision and her theology directly to the popular masses, not only in her writing but through her lectures and sermons and organizing. There is both freedom and danger in such outsider status. Porete was burned at the stake in Paris at the Place de l'Hotel de Ville when she refused to retract what she had written, having lived out the liberation she claimed in her book. She continued to teach her book even though by 1306 it had been condemned by her bishop and burned on the public square at Valenciennes and its use prohibited under pain of excommunication.[11] Given eighteen months in prison in which to retract before her trial before the Inquisition in Paris, Porete refused in the spirit of her teaching: "This soul replies to nobody, unless she wished to, if he is not of her lineage; for a gentleman would not deign to answer a churl, if he called him or challenged him. This is why whoever calls this soul does not find her, and so her enemies have no reply from her."[12]

In a different age, Soelle has also been disturbing the order and peace of the Sainte Eglise la Petit by teaching a theology based in a mystical union with Love that binds us in solidarity to the suffering of Christ in others through radical political praxis, above and beyond the practices of ordinary religious devotion. She is impatient with the church for not satisfying its members' hunger for bread that will sustain: "I cannot agree with your covert pleading for the institution—as if the bread it baked were edible!"[13] She knows that ordinary people can understand this theology and even arrive at it on their own, and in her work she quotes innumerable peasants and ordinary people who have realized that the real God is the one whose Spirit supports their dignity and sustains their activity to claim that dignity.[14]

Politics and Mysticism

Soelle shares similarities with other medieval female mystics regarding the connection of mysticism and politics. If Marguerite Porete's writings offended the church authorities of the day, other late medieval women mystics, including Catherine of Sienna and Teresa of Avila, challenged the church by interpreting the apostolic role ideally by integrating the contemplative path to the "cell" of self-knowledge with an active life.[15] Refusing to compromise, as did other holy women such as Clare of Assisi, with church authorities who strove to restrict the women to the cloister, Teresa and Catherine troubled the church hierarchy. Even setting aside Catherine's well-known political influence and her engagement in conciliar politics by calling the pope to return to Rome from Avignon, her sanctity combined powerful mystical insight, supernatural powers, intense charitable activity, and evangelical activity.[16] Catherine exemplified the linkage of popular piety and civic patriotism of the late medieval Italian cults; she and other holy figures were popularly regarded as communal protectors who expiated the sins of their community and devoted their lives to the care of the sick and poor. Such saints were increasingly in the late middle ages women and of humble origins.

Teresa of Avila, in addition to her mystical writings, struggled to reform religious life, beginning the Discalced Carmelites to reconnect religious life with the sufferings of the poor and restore popular respect for religious life. Two aspects of her reforms that encountered great opposition concerned admissions to her convents and meditation. She insisted not only on admitting women with a small or even no dowry but also on ending the bans on admitting women (like herself) who had some degree of Jewish descent.

In addition, Teresa, like Catharine, believed that meditation had an important role in religious life and included in her rule regular time for silent meditation at a time when church authorities believed that the minds of women were too weak for meditation, that prayer should be oral recitation of approved devotions, lest weak female minds give rise to hysterical imaginings and heresy. Though much of these women's work, especially their mysticism that encouraged lay piety outside sacerdotal control, was dangerous to the institutional church, Catherine and others were tolerated by both local and papal authorities as useful in combating heresy, especially the heretical groups preaching various kinds of insubordination (democratization) among the laity. So dangerous was the appeal of heresy understood to be at the popular level that St. Dominic embraced the salvation of heretical women as a special Dominican mission.[17]

Leaders of women's religious orders such as Catherine and Teresa have often been presented to Christians through hagiography developed within the institutional church, which sanitized them by disconnecting them from the social and ecclesial context in which they lived and by focusing on the fact of their mystical communion with God rather than on the effects of their mysticism on their societies through the activity it supported. In an age when significant proportions of women could not marry because so many men became priests, monks, apprentices, and journeymen (thus long postponing marriage), or died as soldiers, these religious orders offered women havens where they often were educated, trained in respected skills, accorded status, and enabled to serve the neediest in their societies, as well as supported in seeking union with God. Despite the many dissimilarities that result from historical distance, Soelle shares with such women an experience of God that links one to solidarity with others, propelling one to change the world in which she lives.

Soelle, whose mysticism is very much centred in creation, appreciates the insights of mystics like Julian of Norwich, whom she cites both for her ability to find "the Maker, the Keeper, the Lover" in the hazelnut in the palm of her hand and for insisting that, though Scripture never attributes laughter to Jesus, it pleases him when we laugh.[18] But Soelle never attempted to protect herself from persecution and heresy charges with the strategies that Julian adopted: the disclaimers of authority expected of women, her accounts of needing the assistance of confessors to understand her visions, and her cultivation of approval and protection from powerful men in the church. These strategies are what Soelle referred to when she wrote of Marguerite Porete: "Absent, too, are the formulae of modesty or references to feminine weakness."[19] Soelle, due to the different time in which she wrote and her excellent theological education—in contrast to Hildegard, one of whose disclaimers of authority was that she was barely literate in German and was without Latin, the language of theological scholarship[20]—has more in common with the public, prophetic voice of Catherine of Sienna, who publicly taught and called women to lead the mixed life of contemplation and reformist, charitable activity in the world.

Suffering and Mysticism

Perhaps the most interesting chapter in *The Silent Cry* is the one on suffering. Before this book there is a tension in Soelle's treatment of suffering, one which is partially resolved in it. In *To Work and to Love,* she recounts her visit to a class at a liberal arts college:

> The class was exploring the meaning of human suffering, death and dying. They had read my book on suffering. When I arrived, I felt a certain tension in the room. "What are the boundaries on suffering" was the first question I heard, from a shrill voice that belonged to an attractive, healthy-looking young woman of eighteen. Had she ever experienced genuine suffering in her life, I wondered. "How far should we go in response to suffering?" she queried. . . . Some of the students felt that I demanded they take on all the sufferings of the world. . . . At that moment, the New Testament story came to mind where Peter asks Jesus, "Lord, how often shall my brother sin against me, and I forgive him? As many as seven times?" Jesus replies, "I do not say to you seven times, but seventy times seven" (Matt. 18:21–22). I had no sooner finished telling this story when I was bombarded with indignant responses from several students. "I am not Jesus." "Forget about Jesus." "What do you expect us to be? Do you expect us to be saints?" The debate was superficial, because we never explored the real causes of suffering.[21]

Soelle's question about the student above is significant, because she was not merely asking the young woman whether she had ever suffered but whether she had experienced suffering. These are not the same thing for Soelle, who has written so extensively on contemporary alienation, on numbness to our own suffering, and on the need to experience our own suffering if we are to feel compassion for the suffering of others. For her, the resurrection is the work of Christians overcoming the sin that causes suffering in the world. We are called to the elimination of all unnecessary suffering, and to the supporting in love of those whose suffering is unavoidable. But Soelle saw no gain in creating suffering for oneself in order to share the suffering of Christ and the millions of suffering Jesuses in our world.

Among Latin American liberation theologians, this issue of boundaries between sharing the sufferings of the poor in order to end them and creating more suffering has been the topic of agonized debate. That to accompany the poor meant to live in their midst and share their everyday lives was clear. But did this mean to give up medical and dental care, access to libraries and other privileges of the nonpoor? Gustavo Gutierrez put off for many years knee surgery on his "good" leg (deformed by the need to compensate for his "bad" leg, shortened and severely weakened by a long adolescent bout with polio) and later treatment for severe migraines, because the poor did not have access to such luxuries. Only when first one and then the other totally incapacitated him for parish and theological work did he finally concede to treatment.

Many of the medieval mystics went much further than this, into what Soelle terms an "addiction" to suffering, as Soelle recounts:

> It is said about a recluse from Madgeburg, who, on account of her crippled condition was called Margareta Contracta, that "suffering did not cause her concern; what troubled her was that no suffering could suffice her." Such craving for suffering no longer distinguishes between fruitless, unavoidable, and self-inflicted suffering and that which Paul accepted "for the body of Christ's sake," that is, for the sake of the community that suffered persecution in the Roman Empire. *Compassio* in this sense is not suffering that people bring upon themselves through unparalleled demands of asceticism. It arises in the immediacy of innocent suffering and from solidarity with those who have to bear it. On the other hand, Dolorousness draped in mystical yearnings has nothing to be glossed over. It patently bears the marks of masochistic substitutionary satisfaction. In a horrendous example of such obsession and dependency, Mechthild von Hackborn (1242–1299) scattered glass shards on her bed "for repentance's sake" and then tossed and turned "until her whole body dripped with blood so that she could neither sit nor lie down because of the pain."[22]

In this passage Soelle reveals that she still rejects self-inflicted suffering as "horrendous," but in the chapter, as she develops the distinction between dolorousness and compassion, she does admit their relationship. "If God, too, is one who suffers, then suffering is not simply something bad to which one can surrender or stand up in resistance. . . . The way of suffering that is not just tolerated but freely accepted, the way of the passion, becomes therefore part of the disciple's way of life."[23] The collection of stories in this chapter does not make the distinction between dolorousness (suffering as chosen end) and the free acceptance of suffering any clearer. For example, she terms Heinrich Seuse's "addiction" but praises the suffering of John of the Cross. John, while imprisoned and tortured by his unreformed Carmelite brethren, refused to cover his feet with his two woolen blankets because he was Discalced (barefoot), and allowed his toes to freeze many times over, while Seuse imposed on himself fasting, sleep deprivation, cold, iron chains, self-flagellation, and the wearing of a nail-studded cloak. Both of these examples of suffering seem self-inflicted; the real difference seems to be in the degree of suffering inflicted on the self. The difficulty Soelle has in drawing the line between many cases of compassion and dolorousness brings her very close to admitting that just as "numbness is a metaphor for apathy; agony one for *compassio*," so there are times when the threat of numbness is so great that only the self-infliction of personal agony holds it off.[24] Soelle's reservations about dolorousness—which would be better understood not as simply self-inflicted suffering but as excessive self-inflicted suffering as an end in itself—are understandable and appropriate, for dolorousness seems only valuable as a first step to compassion. This is what I think Soelle intuited in the story of her visit to the liberal arts classroom, when she asked herself if the student who demanded to know the limits one should suffer had ever felt suffering. If we are not in touch with personal suffering, then *compassio* is difficult, if not impossible.

Yet there is perhaps another approach to dolorousness to be found in the medieval mystics to which Soelle pays next to no attention at all. She explains the three steps of classical mysticism—purgation, illumination, and finally union with God—but prefers the path of letting go of the world, the ego, and God—letting go of the known God in favor of the unveiled, naked, and nameless God. But her emphasis remains on union with the Lord of creation, and opening ourselves to that union: "Mystical experience happens when the I steps forth from its self-imposed and imagined limits."[25] She insists that "God alone is enough"; the only way to satisfy our seeking is a coming to rest in God, "a coming home of the homeless being that cannot find its way in the commotion."[26] Yet if we look at the writing of the Beguine Mechthild of Magdeburg (1210–1270), we find both this and another message. Soelle writes of the persecution that Mechthild suffered in her lifetime and appreciates Mechthild's joyous language: "'If I am to do much springing, you yourself must do the singing' is what Mechthild von Magdeburg says to Christ, the leader of the dance. 'Praise-dancing' is her word for what the soul does in anticipation of the bridegrooms' arrival," an example of Mechthild's erotic language for her relationship with Christ.[27]

But the other side of Mechthild's relationship with her divine lover is that union with God brings not only ecstasy but the agony that comes from the realization of God's freedom. Just as union with God is possible as God's free gift, so God also chooses to retreat. Mechthild understands God as absolute Freedom: "I come to you according to my pleasure, when I wish to."[28] As Brun and Burgard write of Mechthild's experience:

> For the soul who, in order to adhere to God has given up everything, has left all, and has taken herself to the desert of God, this experience [of God's withdrawal] is absolutely incomprehensible. Did God not call her? Did she not obey? Does she not follow Him "with the voice of a hungry lion"? . . . [I]t is possible to trace the development of her central experience in this way: from the first shock of this possibility (of God's

withdrawal), through the repetition of the mystical "night," until the tremulous conviction that such is really the case, and that God so wills it, and therefore the soul must bear it. Then, slowly and with indescribable resistance, comes the acceptance of the return of this possibility. Finally, in an almost incomprehensible manner, there comes a desire for this return (of withdrawal), a realization that this possibility corresponds to the most inward will and law of Love, that the soul-in-love will choose this possibility and no other, when God puts it before her. And, at the very end, we find her familiar with this "withdrawal of God," which she now grasps as a mode of the Flowing Light itself: the void of what flows, the uselessness of emanation. This is doubtlessly the centre.[29]

Brun and Burgard interpret Mechthild to be correcting the Platonic formula of the purgative, the illuminative, and the unitive steps in the mystic path and proposing, based on her own experience, to instead say, "It is the nature of Love to flow first in sweetness, then she becomes rich in knowledge, and thirdly she demands and desires to be rejected."[30]

Soelle understands well that joy and suffering are inextricably intertwined, yet she tends to present mysticism in terms of joyous communion, in contrast to the suffering that accompanies the building of the Kingdom in the world: "Mystical jubilation lies hidden in everything, and that is why it is contagious. . . . Mystical joy needs and produces beauty."[31] Mechthild, on the other hand, warns that union with God, while irresistible, joyous, and all-consuming, is limited, that God remains God, not untouchable, but still distinct, still Mystery. The deeper we have penetrated the Mystery, the closer we have arrived, then the more painful is the realization that it is not possible for us to close the last gap.

Soelle's Feminism

Soelle's affinity with the largely female mystics of the middle ages has two aspects that directly relate to her feminism. Soelle, like the medieval female mystics, is not concentrated on women. They wrote for and ministered to all; their concerns were with the spiritual and material needs of all humanity, not just women. Like them, Soelle has addressed herself to all of suffering humanity, and not particularly to women. And yet Soelle, like the medieval female mystics, is feminist in two distinctly different ways. She has taken firm stands against the patriarchal repression of women, insisting that they have direct, unmediated access to God and that their physical, mental, and spiritual integrity must be respected in church and society. And in addition to this advocacy for the equality and dignity of women—but not only for women—Soelle is feminist in her method of doing theology. When in *The Silent Cry* she hails mysticism for being "women-friendly," she not only means that it is open to women but that it accords with the experience of women, that it is "feminine" in the sense of reflecting the socially constructed experience of women. Mysticism is relational, it is intuitive, it involves emotion and feeling, and it is multidimensional in that it involves the whole self and all of its experiences and relationships. This appreciation of the "feminine" is, I think, an important part of what makes Soelle feminist.

At the time that I first encountered Dorothee Soelle, the second wave of American feminism was still very young. Most feminist writing was secular liberal feminism; the first texts in religious feminism were just being written. Most of Soelle's reservations and rejections of feminism were based on secular liberal feminism, emanating as it did from white, middle-class women in the United States who wanted access to the roles previously monopolized by men. Women were defending their ability to be strong, rational, objective decision makers and downplaying the devalued "feminine" characteristics that had for so long been used to exclude them from authority and power.[32]

Some of Soelle's same reservations about early second-wave feminism I discovered within the Latin American liberation theology movement in the late 1970s and through the 1980s as well, specifically a fear that raising the issue of women's oppression would rupture the unity needed among the poor if they were to have a chance for liberation. That is, class unity was necessary, and raising the issue of sexism threatened class unity by pitting women against men among the poor.[33]

Soelle's justice and peace commitments between the late 1960s and today exposed her to many organizations of the poor and oppressed in developing nations. She saw, as did the liberationists in Latin America, that in organizing at the local level it was essential to involve women as well as men, that men's and women's welfare were sometimes different, as were their priorities. Especially in societies in which the roles of men and women were still often very distinct, leadership from both groups had to be deliberately planned; it could not simply be assumed that the most capable men and women would be recognized across gender lines. While there was sometimes conflict between men's and women's interests, perspectives, and priorities, the welfare of the entire community required their integration, which could only be secured through negotiation of conflicting points of view. While many sectors in Latin America and elsewhere in the developing world still use language that distinguishes "feminism" from local women's organizations within the women's movement, with "feminism" referring to U.S. liberal feminism, women's movements exist at many different levels of society today all over the developing world; and because these women's movements, like Soelle, seek the equal dignity and welfare of women with men, they are feminist in goal, if not in name.

At least as strong in Soelle's early suspicions of feminism was her vigorous rejection of the radical feminist position that men were the problem, that reason was male and limiting, and that emotion—feeling—was the superior legacy of women. Like the medieval women mystics who pioneered new "feminine" approaches to God for both men and women, Soelle has always insisted that humanity, made up of men and women, is one, sharing a common human nature. Moreover, her theology, as we have seen above, always integrated the mystical, feeling aspect of experience with the critical, rational capacities of humans. To live out in ourselves God's gratuitous love that we receive in mystical experience entails both so-called "feminine" empathy with the neighbor and so-called "masculine" reason applied to satisfying the neighbor's need.

In another section of *The Silent Cry*, I hear echoes of the arguments Soelle made to me so many years ago against feminism: that it has accepted very masculine, conflictual, and competitive understandings of freedom and autonomy.

> Since the individualism of the Enlightenment, the relation between self and others has been loosened from many body-alienated and ascetic institutions and won more freedom. But the relations between the sexes have not become new and have not been conceived in terms of greater mutuality. Instead, they are seen more as a competition and a struggle for power. Freedom was defined in purely male terms: as the freedom from dependency. Goethe's question about "mutual dependency, this most beautiful condition—how could it be without love?" seems forgotten in the face of sheer self-limitation to individual autonomy. In the "free" societies autonomy related to the individual reigns, as heretofore, as the highest good, defined as self-possession and self-direction. This grants perpetuity to the struggle for power in human relationships and blocks the recognition of the indeed transcendant power, named the sacred power that is being shared.[34]

Here Soelle again complains that feminism, instead of advocating the virtues of (inter)dependency over against notions of autonomy that make solidarity impossible, had capitulated to the masculine emphases of the Enlightenment. This criticism cannot be dismissed lightly. In some ways she points to a tension that separates Anglo feminism from the feminism dominant throughout the developing "two-thirds world." Anglo feminism, especially liberal Anglo feminism, has had a tendency to adopt legal and juridical concepts that predicate equality upon sameness. Women are equal to men when they are treated the same as men. Obviously, women in the United States have made many significant gains by hitching their stars to men's, especially in terms of education, employment, and income. But the concept of equality as sameness has handicapped women's ability to satisfy needs that are specifically female, either biologically or in terms of inherited roles. If equality entails sameness with men, then it will be difficult to make claims for equality that entail support for reproduction (maternity leave, contraception, and abortion) or childcare. On these issues Anglo feminism is still struggling for gains after forty years. In developing countries, on the other hand, campaigns for equality for women tend to begin with the concerns of women as women, beginning with reproduction and childcare and including specifically female work roles, such as close access to potable water and fuel. For them, equality means equal concern for the quality of women's and men's lives, not just sameness with men. In some areas, of course, equal concern will mean sameness of treatment, as in education. But that is not the starting point.

Soelle's feminism is this feminism of the "two-thirds world," which is more open to differences between men and women. For her, the centrality of the erotic in humanity requires difference, otherness. She is neither heterosexist or essentialist in her approach to difference, arguing both that difference of all kinds be recognized where they exist, at multiple levels, and that the biological and social differences of women, as well as the different characterological traits that have come to be known as feminine and masculine, all be respected and cherished as valuable. She fears that a search for equality that leads women toward "masculine ways of being" without engendering an appreciation of "feminine ways of being" may impoverish both spiritual and communal life.

Despite her statement above that relations between the sexes have not moved toward mutuality, Soelle's own marriage to Fulbert Steffensky, with its difficult negotiation of careers rooted on different sides of the Atlantic, in some ways exemplifies a kind of mutuality that many others have forged as well. Mutual dependency must constantly be renegotiated in changing circumstances, and this negotiation is never fully separable from power struggles. More and more couples share childcare and housework, each of whom depend upon each other's support and work as well as shared intimacy. Struggles for justice always involve struggles for power, but not all struggles for power are aimed at domination. Soelle is right to indicate the massive task still necessary to reclaim real eroticism. But it seems to me that she underestimates and undervalues the initial successes that have been achieved. They are limited, but they exist and should be celebrated.

While *The Silent Cry* and, in fact, most of Soelle's recent work continues her dialogue with feminism, it is a minor theme. Soelle is principally addressing postmodern, consumer society and its popular culture, calling for resistance to them. The basic argument in *The Silent Cry* is that mysticism, as direct unchannelled access to God, apart from the hierarchical church, is not only "women-friendly" but is a basic resource for all forms of resistance to injustice, including feminism.[35] Soelle does not want feminism to repeat the mistake of socialism in rejecting religion on the basis of its historical institutional abuse of freedom. Religion is more than simply hierarchical institutions; religious experience in its capacity to support dignity, to connect persons to the love and power of God and to each other in solidarity, is necessary for successful struggle against all forms of oppression. Rational critique is not sufficient to defeat the structures of oppression.

For Soelle, mysticism is creation mysticism, and just as it links us to God, it links us to the world God created. And in this mystical journey, the soul, she says, is feminine, in the sense of being open, receptive, ready to respond and relate. The soul in mysticism is not protected by thick layers of ego-boundary that are more characteristic of social constructions of male identity, but is open to relationship. Because she sees mysticism as so open and useful a tool for feminist struggle, she argues that a feminist hermeneutic of suspicion should not be used to dismiss mysticism or religion in general as good and useful for women in their struggle for liberation:

> The hermeneutic of suspicion has won its place through struggle and has in the past twenty years become commonplace, at least in post-Jewish and post-Christian culture. Today, women can know that all biblical texts are formulated in androcentric language and thereby transmit patriarchal social structures, whether they want to or not. Suspicion is an element that critical consciousness cannot relinquish. But is it enough to enable women and men to put new questions to religious tradition and to give expression to their experience by means of the tradition's language of suffering and hope? Must not another hermeneutic be articulated in a world where hope itself is exiled, where it has, so to speak, no work permit among us? Is suspicion our only lens? Is critical consciousness the only consciousness we have? And is the self-attestation of negativity all we can accomplish?[36]

Soelle responds by proposing suspicion as the appropriate response to domination but points out that the feminist struggle for liberation, or that of the poor around the world, is also, and perhaps even more powerfully, fueled by hunger—hunger for life, dignity, and, especially for "first world" women, spiritual meaning: "Depression and isolation transport men and women into a kind of spiritual anorexia where any kind of nourishment is nauseating. Suspicion can no longer release such people from the constraints of tradition; what drives them on is a yearning to live a different kind of life."[37]

When Soelle addresses feminism, particular theorists are not identified. The hermeneutic of suspicion is most closely connected with New Testament scholar Elisabeth Schüssler Fiorenza. But Schüssler Fiorenza has never stopped her work with critical consciousness or the hermeneutic of suspicion but has been long engaged in a feminist reconstruction of the New Testament community from which contemporary women can take inspiration. Soelle's critique of feminists who reject transcendent experience as another dismissal of the body and thereby dismiss mysticism is best aimed at secular feminists who understand and reject religion as a product of patriarchy. Many religious feminists would appreciate more clarity as to which feminists, or at least to which groups of feminists, Soelle is responding.

There seems to be at least one area involving sacred power and the erotic that Soelle has only begun to explore. In *The Silent Cry* she very briefly takes up the theme of the otherness of the Other in both mysticism and erotic relationships:

> At times I ask myself whether this otherness can be lived without recourse to the language of religion, without "allowing the gardener in." It is not because she might conjure up something we really do not wish for. All mystics know the incomprehensibility of God grows rather than diminishes when God's love comes close to us. But is that not precisely the same with the incomprehensibility of the other? We are not rid of the bitter, the dark, especially when we come to celebrate the power of the erotic by sharing it.[38]

I think that what she is talking about here is what Mechthild called the withdrawal of God. Soelle is recognizing that in our love relationships, no matter how many levels of intimacy we have ascended, no matter how perfect the communion we have achieved, there is an inevitable return of separateness that is intensely painful. Like Mechthild, who suffered the withdrawal of God who was her delight, the breath in her body and the fire in her heart, after years of relatively easy access to God, sometimes we are able to move back and forth between separateness and communion for a time and, like Mechthild, assume that this communion will always be available for us. But it is not so. The Other remains the Other; and even the most devoted of lovers will, at some time, need to build a new relationship at another level, a different kind of communion. Though it is powerfully glorious, communion can only be momentary because the essence of relationship is the presence of *two* people, self and other. They remain two and must remain two if there is to be relationship and not possession of one by the other.

Possession is not stimulating, it is not glorious, and it is not relationship. Persons who are truly possessed are not fully conscious, not fully alive. As Soelle writes, real love involves both communion and the acceptance of otherness on the part of both lovers. The glory in moments of communion must be sufficient both to sustain us in the painful moments of the reemergence of separateness and to motivate us to construct a new path to communion with that other. So it is with self and God, and so it is with self and lover.

But this source of suffering within mysticism itself gets short shrift. Throughout *The Silent Cry,* and again in the concluding conversation between Soelle and Fulbert Steffensky, Soelle distinguishes two different groups of contemporary seekers: those who are willing to embrace the full discipline of mystical experience, and those who seek only the anestheticization of mysticism, escapism in the "miraculous," by selecting pieces of the exotic from many religious traditions, ignoring internal processes, stages, and connections.[39] Soelle and Steffensky agree that "we are all mystics" in the sense that everyone needs access to beauty and vision, an experience of the oneness and wholeness of life. But I think Steffensky's summary of their agreement on mysticism does not take seriously enough either Mechthild's experience of the withdrawal of God or Soelle's short reflection on the incomprehensibility of the Other in erotic love:

> Mysticism is the experience of the oneness and wholeness of life. Therefore mysticism's perception of life, its vision, is also the unrelenting perception of how fragmented life is. Suffering on account of that fragmentation and finding it unbearable is a part of mysticism . . . the long lasting and most dangerous resistance is the one that was born from beauty.[40]

The Silent Cry's principal argument is that communion with God holds out to us joyous experience of oneness and wholeness, of union with creation and Creator, which then must sustain us in facing the hard and painful life of resistance to sin and suffering in the world. We move back and forth between mystic moments of perfect goodness and the life of struggle.

But what if Mechthild is right, if Soelle's brief reflection about the limits of erotic love is on target? Then the mystic experience of God is not so totally different from the life of resistance, from the struggle for truly human erotic relationships, but rather they parallel one another. In both, there are inevitable moments of suffering and pain due to the otherness of the one with whom we are in relationship. The otherness of the Other is at once the source of the joy in communion and the source of the pain when communion cannot be sustained. Most people simply rejoice in the unexpected moments of communion we experience, drawing on them for inspiration and motivation in resisting the dehumanizing elements in our lives. But it is crucial for those committed to resistance, for feminists and for all who struggle against dehumanization—who are Soelle's target audience—to recognize the element of tragedy that exists at the center of human reality.

Just as Soelle argues against seekers who search out the easy path of sensation, the "miraculous," and the exotic in religion to satisfy the numbness and emptiness in their lives, so it is possible and relatively common to enter into the work of resistance naïvely, expecting that commitment to the other, whether victimized women, abused children, or the desperate poor, and identification with their pain, will suffice. It is even more common to expect that when we have committed ourselves in erotic love to another, and received love in return, that a unity is forged that will stand against all odds. But in real lives we periodically face moments when we realize that our most intimate relationships lack the communion we had thought we had achieved. We often feel betrayed by the other when we experience the loss of communion, as if the other had viciously and irresponsibly repudiated us. We had come to depend on this relationship. We need to be reminded that the failure of communion is not always betrayal, or sin, or weakness, though these are common. Separateness also arises from the very nature of otherness, which always stands at the heart of relationship, of love.

All the women medieval mystics understood that, as Soelle points out, joy and suffering are part of the same package. This is true not only in relationship with God but in all love relationships, including the struggle for justice. Solidarity among the oppressed is a form of love. Like other forms of love it must constantly be reconstructed. It is dangerous to assume that solidarity once gained is forged in steel. The solidarity for and among the oppressed that Soelle supports requires constant attention to the otherness of the oppressed. It is too easy for some oppressed people, or those in alliance with them, to speak for other oppressed people, to assume that they know the oppressed and their interests, that they and the oppressed are one. Oppressed persons then become possessions to be manipulated in the struggle.

In struggles for justice, as in erotic relationships, the startling realization that solidarity is lost, that oppressed others are separate and distinct, should alert us to the need to find a new path up the mountain, to forge a new relationship of solidarity. As in the relationship to God, the visions and joys that sustain us come from the ground gained as we move up the mountain, not from achieving the top, which is never fully scaled. Periodically, our path is blocked, and we must reconstruct a new path to move upwards. The ground we gain can support us not only in continuing up that mountain but also in moving up the other mountain journeys in our lives. Individual consciousness, the source of both our yearning for union and our capacity to pursue it, is also the condition for our never fully achieving it, "until we rest in thee." Soelle points us to those moments of private meditation that we all need, that Teresa and Catherine demanded for their nuns. Furthermore, Soelle together with the medieval mystics in their writings invite us to use those moments to remember the joyous moments of union that are ends in themselves, and to draw on them in constructing new paths to union with God, with other individuals and groups, and with creation as a whole. The part of the message that is missing is the warning of the limit that lies, not only in the world of sin, suffering, and resistance, but in the relationship with the divine itself.

Notes

1. Dorothee Soelle, *The Silent Cry: Mysticism and Resistance* (trans. Barbara and Martin Rumscheidt; Minneapolis: Fortress, 2001), 195.

2. James Cone, *The Spirituals and the Blues: An Interpretation* (New York: Seabury, 1972).

3. See, for example, Dorothee Soelle, "The Long March," in *Revolutionary Patience* (Maryknoll, N.Y.: Orbis, 1977), 56–57.

4. Gustavo Gutierrez, *We Drink from Our Own Wells: The Spiritual Journey of a People* (trans. Matthew J. O'Connell; Maryknoll, N.Y.: Orbis, 1984).

5. Soelle, *Silent Cry,* 166.

6. Ibid. 122.

7. Ibid.

8. Marguerite Porete, *The Mirror of Simple Souls,* in Emilie Zum Brunn and Georgette Epiney-Burgard, eds., *Women Mystics in Medieval Europe* (trans. Sheila Hughes; New York: Paragon House, 1989), 172–73.

9. Brunn and Epiney-Burgard, *Women Mystics,* 151.

10. Ibid., 145.

11. According to Porete, in one who has not become free through union with the divine, "my body is full of weakness and my soul full of fear," while the one who has followed the path of Love to freedom "is strong and great, entirely free and disencumbered of everything, for God sanctifies him." Porete, *Mirror of Simple Souls,* in Brunn and Epiney-Burgard, *Women Mystics,* 174–75.

12. Brunn and Burgard, *Women Mystics,* 146.

13. Soelle, "Afterward," in *Silent Cry,* 301.

14. For example, see her quote from the Nicaraguan peasant women in *To Work and to Love,* with Shirley Cloyes (Philadelphia: Fortress, 1984), 43, which was taken from Ernesto Cardinal's *The Gospel in Solentiname* (trans. Donald M. Walsh; Maryknoll, N.Y.: Orbis, 1976), 209.

15. Denise L. Despres, "Ecstatic Reading and Missionary Mysticism: The Orchard of Syon," in *Prophets Abroad: The Reception of Continental Holy Women in Late Medieval England* (ed. Rosalyn Voaden; Rochester, N.Y.: D. S. Brewer, 1996).

16. See Despres, "Ecstatic Reading," and Donald Weinstein and Rudolph M. Bell, *Saints and Society: The Two Worlds of the Christendom: 1000–1700* (Chicago: University of Chicago Press, 1982), 167–68.

17. Despres, "Ecstatic Reading," citing Michael Goodich, "The Contours of Female Piety in Late Medieval Hagiography," *Church History* 50 (1981): 20–32.

18. Soelle, *Silent Cry,* 100, 180–81.

19. Ibid., 100.

20. Hildegard of Bingen, "Letter to Bernard of Clairvaux," in Brun and Epiney-Burgard, *Women Mystics,* 19–20.

21. Soelle, *To Work and to Love,* 42–43.

22. Soelle, *Silent Cry,* 139.

23. Ibid., 138.

24. Ibid., 150.

25. Ibid., 27.

26. Ibid., 37.

27. Ibid., 182–83.

28. Mechthild von Magdeburg, *Flowing Light of the Godhead,* vol. 2, 25.

29. Brunn and Epiney-Burgard, *Women Mystics,* 48–49.

30. Mechthild, *Flowing Light of the Godhead,* vol. 6, 20.

31. Soelle, *Silent Cry,* 186–87.

32. As religious, specifically Christian and Jewish feminism in the United States and Europe developed, it met many of Soelle's objections, incorporating relatively quickly racial and class analysis of women's oppression, and gradually opening to the very different situations of women in developing nations. Soelle herself had some role in pushing religious feminism in this direction, but figures such as Rosemary Ruether, Beverly Wildung Harrison, Elisabeth Schüssler Fiorenza, Judith Plaskow, and many others led the way in opting for feminist theology as a liberation theology that must include liberation for all oppressed groups, recognizing the cross-cutting lines of oppression.

33. I suspect that in both Soelle and many Latin American liberationists the Marxist legacy was one source of this tendency. Though Marxist tradition recognized the oppression of women, it isolated the root of this oppression in the institution of private property. The solution, according to Marxism, was the combination of socialist revolution (ending private ownership of the means of production) and women's reentry into production, which according to some theorists was supposed to be accompanied by the socializing of traditional domestic work, though this never took place in socialist systems. From the perspective of Marxist-inspired movements, to end the oppression of the poor through socializing the means of production (land and industry), would liberate women (and other oppressed groups) as well. From the perspective of second-wave U.S. feminism, the Marxist solution to women's oppression was inadequate in that it failed to deal with the problematic ideological understandings of female bodies, sexuality, reproduction, and many more, which though they may have originally arisen in conjunction with private property, had taken on a life of their own.

34. Soelle, *Silent Cry,* 127.

35. Ibid., 46.

36. Ibid., 47.

37. Ibid., 48.

38. Ibid., 130.

39. Soelle, "Afterward," in *Silent Cry,* 301.

40. Ibid., 302.

11. Conversations with Meister Eckhart and Dorothee Soelle

Nancy Hawkins

Dorothee Soelle's consuming admiration and love of the mystics, and in particular the work of the thirteenth-century Roman Catholic mystical theologian Meister Eckhart, had their beginning early on in her life when she attended a lecture in Frieburg, Germany. From that moment on, Eckhart's theology would play a significant role in her theological reflection.[1] Of all the mystics, it is Meister Eckhart who receives the greatest attention from Soelle. She has been in thoughtful conversation with him for over thirty years. At times she quotes his work directly, while in other instances she nuances and interprets the thought of the mystic for her own purposes. Eckhart's theology contains numerous elements, which resonate with Soelle's insistence that the essence of God is not independence, otherness, and domination; rather, God is relational, immanently transcendent, and compassionate. Soelle recognizes that Eckhart's mysticism addresses the suffering question in an entirely different manner than contemporary theodicy, which Soelle finds inadequate and even oppressive. Eckhart's stimulating mystical phrase "to live without a why," combined with his thoughts on the Martha and Mary passage in Luke, offers Soelle a model for living the life of an activist while being detached from its results. Soelle also finds in Eckhart's mystical theology a way to unburden the name of God from the authoritarian images cast upon it by organized religion. Recently the work of Eckhart has given direction to Soelle's plea that mysticism become democratized and understood as resistance. The work of Meister Eckhart continually accompanies Soelle on her theological journey.

Soelle's retrieval of Meister Eckhart is significant because it demonstrates her willingness to engage other faith traditions, affirms the importance of using multiple sources for one's theology, and shows that she recognizes a political dimension within Eckhart's theology. Ordinarily, Eckhart's work is not understood within the framework of political theology; in understanding his work in this way, Soelle brings to light new possibilities of interpretation. She also opens the door to a significant debate as to whether Eckhart was a political figure for his time and whether his theology had a direct impact on the vast social change taking place in Germany during the thirteenth century. Some will say that Eckhart showed no political inclinations, while others believe his mystical theology is politically charged. The final section of this essay offers the reader a possible approach to this question by suggesting that Eckhart's work be viewed as both politically sensitive and spiritually focused. It also evaluates Soelle's desire to democratize mysticism while offering the mystical journey as a means to political resistance.

Why Mysticism?

For Soelle, the mystical tradition presents a form of religion born out of relationship rather than out of submission and obedience. Mysticism is, as Soelle states, "an experience that bursts the existing boundaries of human understanding, feeling, and reflection."[2] The mystical experience originates not from within the defined limits of organized religion but from within the experience of the human soul. The gift of mystical union is given to human beings independent of specific religious institutions and specific religious structures. It occurs in all religions and, most especially, is meant for all people of faith. Soelle's goal, with regard to mysticism, is to democratize the ideal of mysticism and cleanse it from what she views as a "false elitism." In her own words, *"Wir Sind all Mystiker!"* (We are all mystics!)[3] Most likely such words would appeal to the Meister himself, who tried to make his theology and his mystical understanding of God available to the masses, and in particular to specific groups of women such as the Beguines.[4] Eckhart's style of theology and preaching were innovative and challenging. As Eckhart scholar Bernard McGinn points out:

> Powerful new forms of mystical speech came to birth in Eckhart, his contemporaries, and his followers, and it is worth investigating the terms of their own making that shed light on what was distinctive, daring, even dangerous in their thinking.[5]

Meister Eckhart lived and theologized in an era when society was undergoing vast change and a new surge of religious enthusiasm was emerging. What had previously taken place in the Latin countries was now taking hold in Flanders, the Netherlands, and Northern Germany. In truth it was the beginning of the end of the medieval religious world. Tremendous growth was taking place in the towns and cities, especially in Cologne, Germany, where Eckhart resided for more than a decade. Until the thirteenth century, the highest form of the religious life had been the cloister or the solitude of the hermitage. It was during Eckhart's lifetime that laypeople, while remaining in the world, wished to embrace a mode of life suited to their piety. Numerous groups sprang up that desired to follow the evangelical counsel of poverty and imitate the life of Christ.[6] There was a significant rise in mystical activity and writing during this period. Many scholars attribute this to the newly born spiritual needs of women, both lay and religious. Along with the rise in mysticism, a new theological reality began in the thirteenth century, that of the vernacular theological tradition. Meister Eckhart's preaching in the vernacular is one of the most significant witnesses to the new "democratizing" trends in mystical teaching evident in this century. Eckhart was an innovator in his use of the vernacular and is considered by some to be one of the creators of modern German. Preaching and writing in the vernacular made theology and spirituality available to the common person. Bernard McGinn explains:

> Eckhart preached the possibility of a radical new awareness of God, in rich and often difficult terms, not to the clerical elite of the schools, but to women and men of every walk of life. Finding one's ground in the depths of the Godhead did not require adopting traditional religious ways of life, especially not one that involved fleeing from the world.[7]

Dorothee Soelle believes that Eckhart's use of the vernacular is a truly subversive act. No longer would theological teaching be solely reserved for the upper classes and clerics. She points out that the Papal Bull of condemnation issued by Pope John XXII in 1329 against selected excerpts from Eckhart's writings specifically mentions that Eckhart presented many things as dogma that were designed to cloud the true faith in the hearts of many. It appears that preaching and teaching in the vernacular was considered extremely threatening to the institutional church.[8] Vernacular theology organizes and presents itself in a different way than scholastic and monastic theology. It tends to express itself in a sermonic form while employing treatises, letters, hagiography, and even poetry. Many Eckhart scholars, including McGinn, believe that the greatest contribution of medieval vernacular theology came in the area of mysticism.

It is no wonder that Dorothee Soelle champions the vision and thought of Meister Eckhart. This medievalist was able to respond to the changing needs of his time, he saw mystical union as a possibility for all, and he undertook the challenge of spiritually guiding those who were outside the hierarchical sphere. Eckhart, whom Soelle believes is the greatest German mystic, made God accessible to all human beings. In doing so he brings to Soelle's life something that she is missing, something she believes was stolen from humanity before she was ever born. This is evident in her latest book, in which she writes that what drew her to mysticism was the dream of finding a form of spirituality that is lacking in German Protestantism:

> What I was seeking had to be less dogmatic, less cerebral and encased in words, and less centered on men. It had to be related to experience in a twofold sense of the word: how love for God came about and what consequences it has for life.[9]

Perhaps what Soelle seeks is what draws so many to the mystics: a desire to yield one's soul in joy to God. This act is based not on God's exhortation that the soul "obey" but on the love between the soul and God. The gift of mystical union is freely offered to everyone; this reality supports Soelle's insistence that all people who seek this path are called to be mystics.

Eckhart's Mysticism and Suffering

For Soelle, the mystical question as it relates to suffering is quite different from the theodicy question, "which looks at whether God wants to punish the sufferers or whether he has forgotten them or whether he loves them in spite of their suffering, or precisely because of it."[10] Mysticism offers a path by which one can face suffering and possibly transform suffering into inner joy. Soelle is drawn to a mystical understanding of suffering because she believes this addresses the suffering question in a much different fashion than what she calls Christian masochism and Christian apathy. Christian masochism encourages an irrational desire for suffering as well as the belief that such suffering makes one spiritually superior to others. Those who embrace Christian apathy deny the very existence of suffering and choose to distance themselves from it. On the other hand, mystical theology speaks in terms of the soul "giving itself over" to the suffering that is a natural part of life. The mystical approach is not one of averting or avoiding suffering but rather one that implies one can be with suffering in the fullest possible way.

Soelle champions the mystical approach to suffering because mysticism is based on the belief that God is continually present to those who suffer, offering them consolation in their time of need, while taking their sufferings into God's very essence. This idea resonates with Soelle's belief that our God is a God who suffers with humanity. Her belief is supported by Meister Eckhart's writings, especially his *Book of Divine Consolation*, the longest of his German works. This mystical text offers specific examples of Eckhart's conviction that God suffers with humanity. The following quotations illustrate this belief:

> If God is with me in my suffering, what more or else do I want? If I think rightly, I want nothing else and I want nothing more than God. . . . I say: That God is with us in suffering means that he himself suffers with us. Indeed, anyone who sees the truth knows that what I say is true. God suffers with man, he truly does, he suffers in his own fashion, sooner and far more than the man who suffers for love of him. Now I say, if God himself is willing to suffer, then I ought fittingly to suffer, for if I think rightly, I want what God wants.[11]

Eckhart has confidence that God is present to human beings in their suffering, and as divine presence God suffers with them. For Eckhart, the one who suffers literally "finds" God in the very act of suffering. The result of such unification with the Divine is great consolation. Both Soelle and Eckhart formulate a theological connection between suffering and consolation.

The only way for the soul to open itself to the love of God is to become detached. The idea of detachment is a mystical virtue that Eckhart calls *Abgeschiedenheit*. Without detachment there is no inner room for the presence of God to come to birth in the soul. The Meister is convinced that if one is to become "equal" with God, insofar as a human being can have equality with God, this must occur through detachment. Drawing upon Eckhart's wisdom, Soelle writes in *The Strength of the Weak* that what one should try to learn from the mystics is to leave the self, to make the self empty, open, and ready; for only if one is empty (and detached) can God fill us.[12] Soelle understands that it is only through detachment that interior freedom is achieved, for without detachment, and ultimately without abandonment, the soul remains closed and cannot conceive the Word of God. Soelle formulates a connection between mysticism and suffering in that she has come to realize that mysticism presents a love of God that is ultimately more powerful than any suffering one can experience. She knows that the love of God is stronger than any kind of affliction. Soelle writes that the mystics have described how a person could become free and open, so that God is born within the depths of His soul; they have pointed out that a person in suffering can become "calm" rather than apathetic, and that the capacity for love is strongest where it grows out of suffering.[13]

Soelle's statement reflects Eckhart's controversial doctrine of the birth (German, *Geburt*) of the Son (or Word) of God in the soul that lies at the very heart of Eckhart's mystical theology. Eckhart's "birthing mysticism" is connected with his new teaching on the ground *(grunt)* of the soul. As McGinn explains, Eckhart seeks to create an indistinct identity between the soul and God. While Eckhart is not alone in stating that the human person is capable of attaining indistinction with God, his mysticism takes the idea of union with God to new depths never explored previously. Eckhart's understanding of union includes no difference at all between God and human beings. "God's ground and the soul's ground is one ground."[14] Soelle maintains a connection between God's presence in the soul and one's ability to embrace suffering. It is the mystical concept of the birth of the Son in the soul that provides the avenue for her to declare that one's suffering can be united to God.

According to Eckhart, the birth of the Son in the soul is the work of God and cannot be accomplished without the soul's cooperation. It is the function of the soul to prepare itself for God's action; it must make ready a "place" in which the birth can occur. An open space must be created within the human soul. This requires the soul to rid itself of that which is not God. The mystical concept of creating an open space in the soul is exemplified by Eckhart in the statement "So therefore let us pray to God that we may be free of God."[15] Soelle has a great affinity for this statement and uses it as a reference for her work on suffering and God language. It describes for her what is necessary if human beings are to free themselves from any belief, concept, or word that creates a barrier between the soul and God. Likewise, it is only when the soul has "rid itself of God" and the self is annihilated that Eckhart is able to declare, "The eye in which I see God is the same eye in which God sees me. My eye and God's eye are one eye and one seeing, one knowing and one loving."[16] It is here, in the paradoxical, mystical moment of emptiness and presence, that it is possible for human pain to become God's pain, and God's pain to appear in human pain. This is the moment Soelle yearns for in her work on suffering. It is also the moment that the soul comes to learn the mystical name for God: You Silent Cry.

Soelle believes that mystical prayer has the potential to transform the aloneness and despair of suffering. It is through prayer that the soul can move from an isolated place of mute powerlessness to a place of solidarity where suffering is accepted, learned from, and eventually channeled into action, even joy. Soelle describes what is possible when suffering is transformed through prayer.

> Suffering makes one more sensitive to the pain of the world. It can teach us to put forth a greater love for everything that exists. . . . What

is essential is whether we carry out the act of suffering or are acted upon, indifferent as stones. What matters is whether the suffering becomes our passion, in the deep double sense of that word.[17]

Thus, suffering approached in the context of mystical prayer stands in opposition to the model of apathy, illusion, and suppression that characterizes how many individuals choose to deal with it.

Soelle is convinced that mystical suffering, which is given expression through prayerful lamentation and is faced in union with God, has the potential to become a source of political action and societal change. This is possible because the language of mystical prayer is explosive language. In stating this, Soelle refers to the fact that mystical language operates outside the confines of church dogma. It embraces images from nature, from poetry, and from other religions. The one who is immersed in the experience of mystical language awakens to the possibility of expression, communication, and ultimate solidarity with others. It becomes clear through the writings of Eckhart that as one experiences mystical union, one is related to the entire created order. One becomes a cocreator with God. Those like Soelle who embrace the inward mystical journey eventually find themselves involved with the outward journey into the world. Now all actions, including suffering, are more than exercises in living; they are activities of the spirit in the world.

To Live without a Why

The phrase *sunder warumbe* (translated "without a why") lies at the heart of Meister Eckhart's mystical theology. For Soelle, this phrase is an indispensable guide for anyone who wishes to comprehend his theology and the mystical lifestyle. For the mystic lives in the spirit of *sunder warumbe*. According to Soelle, this phrase is Eckhart's description of essential being and the innermost ground of life itself. It encompasses her understanding of how one is to live life in relationship to God and the entire created order.

The notion of *sunder warumbe* is very much connected to an element of the German mystical tradition called *Gelassenheit*, translated as "releasement." The root of *Gelassenheit* means to let go, to relinquish or abandon. The soul in *Gelassenheit* must rid itself of all things that prevent the birth of God in it. As Soelle explains, "What does it mean, this 'without a why' in which we should live and in which life itself lives? It is the absence of all-purpose, every quid pro quo, every tit for tat, and all domination that makes life itself a servant. Whenever we are torn between being and doing, feeling and acting, we no longer live *sunder warumbe*."[18] To live "without a why" means to live without intentions, goals, purposes, or power.

In his Sermon 5b, Eckhart explains that any life that is lived "without a why" lives out of its own ground and finds its origins in its own being. Such a life is not concerned with why it acts but with the purity of how it is acting.

> If anyone went on for a thousand years asking of life: "why are you living?" life, if it could answer, would only say: "I live so that I may live." That is because life lives out of its own ground and springs from its own source, and so it lives without asking why it is itself living.[19]

The soul that is able to live without a why has no need to justify its existence; it simply appreciates the fact that it is alive. To live "without a why" is to live and love as God lives and loves. It is to go about accomplishing one's deeds without needing justification and recognition.

Soelle, the political theologian and activist, builds on this phrase of Eckhart when she states that human beings must do many things in life without any why. In *The Window of Vulnerability,* she writes, "There is an inner strength of being-at-peace that cannot make the goal orientation of action the measure of all things. All nonviolent action in a violent world participates, in this sense, in the 'without a why' of the rose."[20] Here she is referring to the mystical poetry of Angelus Silesius (Johannes Scheffler, 1624–1677) who most scholars believe borrowed Eckhart's *sunder warumbe* for his beautiful metaphor of the mystical rose:

Without Why
The rose is without any why, it blooms because it blooms,
It does not look at itself, and does not ask if it is seen.[21]

Even though there is a difference between the mystical rose and the human being with regard to freedom and free will, the metaphor of the rose still holds. Living one's life in the manner of the mystical rose, which blooms because it blooms, eliminates the need to witness firsthand the fruits of one's actions. Soelle insists that actions done for the sake of the act itself are powerful and worthwhile. One's praxis need not be recognized nor praised in order for one's deeds to effect change, for transformation to take place. No doubt the activist Soelle is personally challenged by Eckhart's phrase, because what activist does not seek to know that his or her action has made a difference and has borne fruit? But the reality of life is that most of us do not see the fruit of our labors, at least not in the beginning. Soelle recognizes that a life lived under the mantle of *sunder warumbe* eliminates the tension and contradiction between actions directed toward immediate results and the purity of creation that realizes itself in the simple act of blooming.

But is it possible to reconcile this mystical concept of *sunder warumbe* with political resistance and a passion for justice? Is it possible for feminists, for example, to embrace such an idea when it seems to rely on dependence and surrender, two factors that often defeat a woman's sense of self? Soelle does not shy away from these questions. She does not view *sunder warumbe* as an impediment to justice or feminism. To live "without a why" is not to cease acting, resisting, or questioning. It simply renders the one who acts honest. It forces those acting to ask why they act and what they expect in return for their actions. Soelle is convinced that there is no true liberation without the subjective experience of doing what you have to do without asking about success.

While on first appearance the idea of *sunder warumbe* seems to counter action and resistance, in reality it supports those who act on behalf of justice. It reinforces the idea that political action must emanate from the inner ground of the self. To live "without a why" is to live for the sake of living and to act for the sake of acting. A political theology done from a sense of *sunder warumbe* does not evaluate political action based on others' approval. Rather, it clarifies how one should translate faith into action, and it offers an inner serenity that does not make the goal orientation of action the true measure of success.

When Dorothee Soelle looks at the mystical theology of Meister Eckhart, she sees a theologian who effectively combines contemplative prayer and action. An example can be found in Eckhart's Sermon 86, based on the story of the sisters Martha and Mary from Luke's gospel. While many biblical scholars and theologians have stressed the fact that Mary chooses "the better part" by sitting in quiet adoration at Jesus' feet, Eckhart views Mary in terms of spiritual immaturity. For him, Martha, the active realist, has the developed spiritual life. He writes:

> We harbor the suspicion that dear Mary was sitting there more for enjoyment than for spiritual profit. Therefore Martha said, "Lord, please tell her to get up," because she feared that she would remain stuck in this pleasant feeling and would progress no further. . . . Why did he [Jesus] name Martha twice? He wanted to indicate that Martha possessed completely everything of temporal and eternal value that a creature should have.[22]

Soelle views Eckhart's interpretation of this passage as a radical new reading. She believes his explanation reflects the spirit of the growing women's movement of the late middle ages. It is, for her, an affirmation that people need not choose between mystical contemplation and action.

Soelle does not divide the world into doers and dreamers, into the contemplative, self-reflecting Marys on one side and the pragmatic, busy Marthas on the other side. She recognizes that activity and prayer need not be opposites; they are in fact two sides of the same desire to serve the Lord. What must be rejected is the need to position the Marys of the world against the Marthas. Mysticism offers a unity of these two "ways." Soelle builds on Eckhart's observation that the true contemplative one is aware of her or his surroundings and chooses to minister therein.

Here, Soelle's political reading of Eckhart is influenced by the writings of Matthew Fox. She willingly admits that his ideas have impacted her thinking.[23] Fox declares that "Eckhart resists contemplation as a passive gazing at. Knowing for Eckhart is a 'participation in being' and not a 'gazing at' being. His is an effort at getting persons to give birth, to become, to beget, and to create. Eckhart, like Marx, is action oriented."[24] Fox is convinced that there are distinct political overtones to Eckhart's theology. He points out in *Breakthrough*, his work on Eckhart's creation spirituality, that "Hegel admits an indebtedness to Eckhart. Likewise, Marxist scholars like Erich Fromm and Ernst Bloch invoke Eckhart as a forerunner of the spirit of Karl Marx."[25] Soelle, a Marxist herself, gravitates toward this observation. Whether a political and/or Marxist reading of Eckhart is correct is a matter of dispute and shall be taken up later in this chapter. For the moment it is sufficient to state that Soelle is not alone in her political interpretation of Eckhart. She views his writings as affirmations of her conviction that the true Christian must be one who prays and acts.

"I Pray to God to Rid Me of God"

In many of her writings on God, Soelle quotes a line from Sermon 52 by Meister Eckhart that reads, "So therefore let us pray to God that we may be freed of God."[26] Soelle reconstructs these words to read, "I pray to God to rid me of God." Soelle views this statement born of Eckhart's mysticism as a petition by its author for liberation from all things that limit God. The mystic's words affect Soelle's basic concerns regarding the theology of God and God language. She believes that traditional Christian theology focuses its efforts on promoting one dominant attribute of God to the detriment of other equally important attributes. Therefore, she searches for ways to expand how God is spoken of and conceived. Any mystical theology that "liberates" the image of God from the constraints of one particular attribute is most welcome.

When Eckhart begs to be "rid of God," he is operating out of the long and rich tradition of Christian apophatic theology. This form of theology affirms that the highest form of knowing is to venture into the unknown. It is as if one knows and loves God more profoundly when one has no God to love, when one has rid oneself of the very desire to know and love. Eckhart's mystical theology makes a distinction between "God" (*deuss, Gott*) and what he refers to as the

"Godhead" *(deitas, Gottheit)*. When Eckhart refers to "God," he means the divine being insofar as it can be named and known by the human mind. "God" is the cause of all creatures; "God" is the name used to signify the relationship of "God" to the world of which "God" is the creator. On the other hand, the "Godhead" signifies the hidden being of God, which recedes behind every name. The statement "So let us pray to God that we may be freed of God" is a powerful plea by Eckhart for the soul to "free itself" from created notions of God in order that the true being of the "Godhead" might be experienced. It seems that Eckhart is all too aware that human beings desire to "capture" and hold on to specific notions of divinity. By using negative theology Eckhart enters into the wilderness of the "Godhead" and searches for a God who will never be entirely found.

Soelle willingly embraces the challenge of Meister Eckhart's mystical theology: to rid oneself of God. She recognizes that the word *God* has the potential to lead believers further from God because it is burdened by the language of those in authority who associate God with power. According to Soelle, theology must provide an alternative "God thinking" that asks the power question anew and frees it from the authoritarian model of thinking about the "wholly other" God as ruler.[27] Theology must carry out Eckhart's leave-taking from God; it must venture beyond ideas and concepts that try to define God.

What must one become "rid" of in order to formulate a theology of God freed from the burden of authority? For Soelle, the believer must be free of assumptions and preconceived notions of divinity. One must take the lead from Eckhart's mysticism that does not stress defining God but accepting God as nondefinable. Theology must free itself from the prison of language that is too small for God. We see this emphasis in Eckhart's Sermon 53, in which he writes:

> We should learn not to give any name to God, lest we imagine that in so doing, we have praised and exalted him as we should; for God is "above names" and ineffable. . . . Now pay attention: God is nameless, because no one can say anything or understand anything about him.[28]

Eckhart has a profound appreciation that God is beyond all names. This inspires Soelle to turn to the language of the mystics and to their personal experiences in order to offset God language based on the concepts of obedience and authority, specifically the image of God as father, begetter, ruler, and manager of history.

There are many linguistic aspects of mysticism that foster nonpatriarchal God language. For example, the primary form of communication between the Beloved and the soul takes place in dialogue form, fostering a natural give and take between the soul and God. Mystical theology emphasizes nothingness over attainment and gratification and views God as the ground of the individual, not as a patriarchal figure imposing his will upon the faithful. Because the mystical lifestyle is personalistic and experiential, it exists outside the confines of organized religion and is not bound by institutional rules and regulations. Such a lifestyle offers greater creativity of expression. From within such structures new nonpatriarchal images of God can emerge. What is especially significant about mystical language is its poetic expressivity, with its freedom to narrate instead of philosophize. Soelle recognizes "that a stylistic mode of rhetorical tradition appears in most texts of occidental and oriental mysticism, such as intensification, exaggeration (hyperbole), negation, antithesis, and paradox."[29] Such diversity in linguistic style allows for the flow of sentiment between the mystic and God. Such expression is based on communication and the power of being-in-relationship.

Mystical theology offers Soelle creative and liberating ways to envision the relationship between the believer and God. There are a variety of possibilities of mystical names for God, such as ground of our being, water of life, spring of all goodness, whispered stillness, fertile desert, source of all grace, fountainhead, and of course Soelle's favorite name for the mystical God: You Silent Cry. All of these names have diverse but powerful effects on our understanding of God. Mystical theology refuses to canonize one particular attribute or description of God. This appeals to theologians such as Soelle who search for liberating names for God. Eckhart's mystical theology in particular helps the believer comprehend how the various attributes of God must be viewed as only partial understandings. The Meister's words encourage Soelle to state that "a God who does not exceed God is not a God. God imprisoned in a certain language, limited by certain definitions, known by certain names that have established certain socio-cultural forms of control, is not a God but becomes instead a religious ideology."[30]

Eckhart and Political Mysticism

It is impossible for Dorothee Soelle to separate her understanding of mysticism from her commitment to the sociopolitical aspects of life. For her, mysticism has always had political overtones. Soelle is correct when she states in *The Silent Cry* that "there has been very little examination of the relationship between mystical experience and social and political behavior."[31] This is because many in the past viewed mystical experience as a private matter between the soul and God. They failed to see any ramifications for one's life in society. Soelle sees a significant connection between mysticism and social responsibility. She also points out that many mystics were, and continue to be, the reformers of their day. She specifically highlights Teresa of Avila, the Carmelite reformer; Thomas Muntzer, the leader of peasants; and Daniel Berrigan, the Jesuit peace activist. Soelle believes that in their own way the mystics of the past practiced what we today would call "political resistance." The mystics of our own time carry this mantle forward. Soelle looks at the idea of resistance from the perspective of a first-world theologian. In this light, resistance is how human beings who are members of the "white bourgeoisie" participate in liberation struggles. There can be no liberation without the subjective experience of resistance: of doing what you have to do without asking about success. Resistance is the ability to issue a radical *no* to those individuals and structures that belittle and oppress others. For Soelle, the journey toward wholeness and liberation must end in resistance.

And it is prayer that prepares human beings to accept their responsibility for the world and to embrace resistance. For Soelle, to pray is to revolt. It is to embark on the mystical journey, or as some state it, the mystic way. This idea may not sit well with those who view prayer as an individualistic act between the believer and God, but for Soelle, prayer must never be seen as a solitary act. Soelle views the mystical journey as a necessity because the soul is continually pressured to conform to the ways of the "world," and only by pursuing the leap of faith beyond the self can the soul retain its spiritual balance. The inward spiritual journey provides what is needed for spiritual maturity. For Soelle, the mystical journey begins with the *via positiva* of amazement, moves through the *via negativa* of letting go, and concludes with the *via transformativa* of resistance.

For as much as Soelle relies on Eckhart for her understanding of mysticism, she differs from him in her understanding of the mystical journey. Both she and Matthew Fox not only stress the importance of the mystical movement toward God but emphasize the return journey of mysticism, a return that leads ultimately to political resistance. For Eckhart, the mystical journey reaches its high point when the soul progresses to total immersion with God. This union with God involves transformation, purification, and ecstasy. It is at this point that the soul sees God in God's own being. Eckhart's many descriptions of the soul's journey into God speak of the soul as becoming oblivious to temporal realities as it becomes immersed in divinity. His mystical theology stresses a movement away from involvement with the created order so that one may experience profound union with God.[32]

For Soelle, the journey to give oneself over to God is in actuality a journey back into the concrete historical situation where people are continually changing, making decisions, and suffering. Out of the wonder of the mystical experience is born the desire to resist and change those elements of life that are unjust and oppressive. The soul is not meant to live in the perpetual bliss of union with God but is to embark on a return journey into the world. For mysticism to truly become resistance, the journey back into the world is a necessity.

In Soelle's model of the mystical way, inner transformation occurs only when one "resists" that which keeps one from God. Transformation is the fruit of resistance. Soelle rejects the idea that the mystical journey is solely an experience of individualization, an experience that removes one from the larger world community. As she explains, "The last step in this process is to leave God. I take this to mean, in religious terms, that we have to leave the Lord in order to find God in our brothers and sisters."[33] At this point the goal of the mystical journey is realized. Human beings become cocreators united in love with God and participators in God's ongoing creation.

It is clear that Soelle and Eckhart emphasize different aspects of the mystical journey. While both are concerned with inner transformation and purification, Soelle takes a distinctive turn as she stresses the importance of the journey back into one's lived experience. Her interpretation of the mystical journey reflects her political hermeneutic as well as the demands of contextual theology. Eckhart, on the other hand, stresses a withdrawal from the temporal order so that total union with God can be achieved. Both interpretations of the mystical journey are valid and informative. Both reflect human experience and need. In actuality they balance each other and together provide numerous insights into the soul's journey to God.

Assessing the Conversation

After exploring Dorothee Soelle's reliance upon and use of Eckhart's theology for her own work, one needs to ask: Is Soelle's retrieval of Eckhart a distortion of his work or rather a valuable contribution to contemporary theology? I applaud Soelle's use of Meister Eckhart's theology. She is able to find various themes in his theology that resonate with her understanding of God, suffering, and social action. Those who have contributed to our theological past (such as Eckhart) lay their work before us as a testimony to the significant questions of their time. If their work is to be taken seriously, it must be understood not only in the context in which it was written but also in the context of today's questions. Soelle honors Meister Eckhart in her appropriation of his theology. She grasps the fact that many of his insights transcend time and speak to those of us living and theologizing in the twenty-first century. Soelle is willing to enter into conversation with a theologian of a different faith and time than her own. This willingness to engage Eckhart expands her theological perspectives and adds a distinctive spiritual element to her work.

As mentioned in the introduction to this essay, Eckhart enthusiasts and experts are not in agreement as to whether this influential teacher and preacher should be viewed as a political figure. There are those like Soelle and Fox who believe there is ample evidence to do so, while others such as Bernard McGinn disagree. McGinn writes:

> Eckhart's writings show no interest in the politics of his day, and surprisingly little in directly social or economic concerns. He was far from being an advocate of social revolution. . . . The Meister's teaching regarding inner transformation has no direct relation to one's social or economic status.[34]

I believe, however, that it is possible to view Eckhart in a manner that unites the two distinct views of Soelle and McGinn. Eckhart's choice to teach and preach new understandings of God in the vernacular to those outside the ecclesiastical sphere had to have had political implications, especially with regard to the Beguine women who were eventually disbanded and condemned by the Catholic Church. These lay women were especially threatening to the church because they discovered a way to live the gospel message outside monastic confines at a time when the church was increasingly corrupt. Most likely they were recipients of Eckhart's preaching and perhaps personal spiritual direction. Eckhart's preaching challenged the artificial boundary established between the ordained representatives of the church and "ordinary" people. We know this is so because the Papal Bull accusing Eckhart of heresy highlights the fact that he preached to an uneducated crowd.[35] By addressing and befriending the emerging laity of his day, Eckhart obviously threatened many clergy and monastics, who assumed that the masses were unable to participate in "higher" forms of religiosity. He also threatened those in the academic establishment by offering new and creative ways to conceive God and interpret theological axioms.

The question that has become essential for me is this: Did Eckhart *intend* to become a controversial political figure for his time, and did he *intend* his theology to be viewed as subversive? I think not. From my reading of Eckhart I conclude that he did not overtly decide to be a political figure. What he did desire was to put forth new theological possibilities for union with God, and he wanted those possibilities to be available to all. I believe McGinn is correct in stating that Eckhart's theology rises above the economic and social concerns of his day and is not dependent on them. However, I think one is very naïve to think that Eckhart did not know the social issues of his day or have an opinion on them. In this regard, I agree with Soelle. For my mind, Eckhart manages to be both political and apolitical at the same time. He is definitely a spiritual innovator whose writings threatened the institutional church. At the same time, he is a man of prayer who clings to his God above all others. There is a complexity to the man and to his theology that is impossible to fully unpack.

In many ways the life of Eckhart reminds me of Dietrich Bonhoeffer, the twentieth-century German moral theologian, who also died before he was fully able to explain the many nuances of his later works. The "disciples" of both Eckhart and Bonhoeffer would carry forth their theology after their death. But even those who knew the master were not always in agreement as to what he intended.

In my view, Eckhart's theology is best served when Soelle uses it as a stepping-off point for new insights into her own work. In the 1970s, Eckhart's theology impacted Soelle's belief that God can indeed suffer with humanity; in the 1980s his writing inspired Soelle to look for new names for God in order to counter the patriarchal image of a powerful divine Father God, and at the turn of the twentieth century Eckhart's work impels Soelle to devote her energies to exploring how political theology and mysticism can go hand in hand. Eckhart's theological and spiritual insights have assisted Soelle in countless ways as she develops her own distinctive political theology.

For instance, Soelle offers much to consider when she explores how at the core of mystical experience a person can find a basis for social action. Soelle's choice of "You Silent Cry" as the mystical name for God is a prophetic move that has profound implications for the theology of suffering, as well as for a theology of God. Her exploration and use of Eckhart's "to live without a why" is a unique contribution that she brings to the world of political theology and is one of the most creative appropriations of his work. We find in Soelle, the Marxist and feminist Christian, a woman who recognizes the dangers of activist burnout. She sees in mystical theology a path not only for personal renewal but also for an honest corrective to a life lived in frantic activity.

A significant concern of Soelle is her desire to democratize mysticism. Eckhart also shares this concern. In her latest book Soelle states that we are all called to be mystics. Some might think that she is going a bit too far in her reduction of mysticism to a democratic ideal. Many people do not believe they are called to mystical union with their God. The well-known mystics have been idealized and portrayed as somewhat "out of reach," even though they were ordinary women and men. By stating that we are all called to be mystics, Soelle is trying to combat any idea that the mystical life is only meant for a select few. There is strong support in Christianity, both biblically and in the tradition, for declaring that every human being has the capacity to enter into a deep and personal relationship with God. Union with God is not reserved for a special few, and the call to this mystical union transcends any limitations based on age, gender, race, or class. I therefore support Soelle's declaration that mysticism is indeed democratic in its ability to be available to all and to reach beyond defined boundaries.

Just as Soelle is open to critique by those who resist her casting Eckhart as a political figure, she is also critiqued for applying her political hermeneutic to mysticism. Is Soelle thrusting mysticism into the political arena in order to "prove" that mysticism and resistance go hand in hand, or has she discovered a side to mystical theology that was always there but that lay covered? I do not believe it is empirically possible to "prove" that mysticism is inherently political, but it is possible to observe and chronicle how a mystical prayer life leads people toward greater personal and spiritual freedom. It is that freedom born of prayer that empowers ordinary people to stand against and resist repressive political systems, to challenge religious doctrines that ignore lived human experience, and to align themselves with the outcast of society. Such resistance is viewed as dangerous by those who wield political or ecclesial power. In the sense that Meister Eckhart's theology encourages believers to embark on a mystical journey toward personal freedom and think outside the ecclesiastical boundaries of their day, his is a dangerous theology and he is a dangerous man. Soelle understands this aspect of Eckhart's theology, and she successfully appropriates it to enhance her political theology.

When Dorothee Soelle declares mysticism a force for social change, she is remaining true to her task as a political theologian. She is also presenting her readers with new and stimulating ideas about mysticism as prayerful union with God. Soelle adds to her understanding of the mystical life the insights she has gained from her study and contemplation of Meister Eckhart's theology. His work has been a lifelong beacon guiding her distinguished career. The final product of Soelle's work is an understanding of mysticism that is both political and imbued with the spirit of Meister Eckhart. There lies within Soelle's theology a fruitful tension between the call to active political resistance and the call to the "letting go" of mystical prayer. I believe it is the mystical theology of Eckhart that fuels this creative tension and impels Soelle to offer it to the theological community for our consideration.

Notes

1. Dorothee Soelle, interview by Nancy Hawkins, New York, N.Y., 20 May 1997.

2. Dorothee Soelle, "Mysticism, Liberation and the Names of God," *Christianity and Crisis* 41, no. 11 (22 June 1981): 179.

3. Dorothee Soelle, *The Silent Cry: Mysticism and Resistance* (Minneapolis: Fortress, 2001), 302.

4. One of the dominant mystical groups that existed in the Rhineland Valley of Eckhart's era was the Beguines. They were celibate laywomen who took private vows, dedicated themselves to simplicity of life, wore religious habits, and formed small quasi-cloistered houses called Beguinages. Considering that the Beguines tended to cluster near

Dominican priories, and that Eckhart was a prior and vicar of houses of nuns in Strassburg and Cologne, is it likely that Eckhart had considerable contact with this group of women.

5. Bernard McGinn, *The Mystical Thought of Meister Eckhart: The Man from Whom God Hid Nothing* (New York: Crossroad, 2001), 37.

6. Jeanne Ancelet-Hustache, *Meister Eckhart and the Rhineland Mystics* (New York: Harper Torch Books, 1957), 13.

7. Bernard McGinn, ed., *Meister Eckhart and the Beguine Mystics* (New York: Continuum, 1994), 8–9. McGinn further explains that the movement into the vernacular implied a different and wider audience than that addressed by traditional monastic and scholastic theology.

8. The entire text of the Papal Bull *"In agro dominico"* can be found in *Meister Eckhart: The Essential Sermons, Commentaries, Treatises, and Defense* (trans. and intro. Edmund College, O.S.A., and Bernard McGinn; New York: Paulist, 1981), 77–81.

9. Soelle, *Silent Cry*, 2.

10. Dorothee Soelle, *Suffering* (Philadelphia: Fortress, 1975), 95.

11. *Meister Eckhart: The Essential Sermons*, 232–33.

12. Dorothee Soelle, *The Strength of the Weak: Toward a Christian Feminist Identity* (Philadelphia: Westminster, 1984), 105.

13. Soelle, *Suffering*, 93.

14. McGinn, *Mystical Thought of Meister Eckhart*, 47.

15. *Meister Eckhart: The Essential Sermons*, Sermon 52, 200.

16. Bernard McGinn, ed., with Frank Tobin and Elvira Borgstadt, *Meister Eckhart: Teacher and Preacher* (New York: Paulist, 1986), Sermon 12, 270.

17. Soelle, *Suffering*, 125.

18. Soelle, *Silent Cry*, 60.

19. *Meister Eckhart: The Essential Sermons*, Sermon 5b, 184.

20. Dorothee Soelle, *The Window of Vulnerability: A Political Spirituality* (Minneapolis: Fortress, 1990), 40.

21. Angelus Silesius, *Cherubinischer Wandersman* (selected trans. by Maria M. Bohm; New York: Peter Lang, 1997), 104.

22. McGinn, *Meister Eckhart: Teacher and Preacher*, 339–40.

23. Dorothee Soelle, interview by Nancy Hawkins, New York, N.Y., 20 May 1997. In her new book Soelle admits to being inspired by the writings of Matthew Fox, see *Silent Cry*, 88.

24. Matthew Fox, "Meister Eckhart and Karl Marx: The Mystic as Political Theologian," in *Understanding Mysticism* (ed. Richard Woods; New York: Image Books, 1980), 543.

25. Matthew Fox, *Breakthrough: Meister Eckhart's Creation Spirituality in New Translation* (New York: Image Books, 1980).

26. *Meister Eckhart: The Essential Sermons*, 200.

27. Dorothee Soelle, *Theology for Skeptics: Reflections on God* (Minneapolis: Fortress, 1995), 46–47.

28. *Meister Eckhart: The Essential Sermons*, Sermon 53, 205.

29. Soelle, *Silent Cry*, 92.

30. Soelle, *Theology for Skeptics*, 38.

31. Soelle, *Silent Cry*, 3.

32. It is important to note that scholars are not in agreement when it comes to describing Eckhart's stages of the mystical journey. Robert Forman points out that Eckhart himself left us at least seventeen separate phases the mystic might undergo in the journey toward God.

See Robert K. C. Forman, *Meister Eckhart: Mystic as Theologian* (Rockport, Mass.: Element, Inc., 1991), 53–59.

33. Soelle, *Strength of the Weak,* 105.

34. Bernard McGinn as quoted in Forman, *Meister Eckhart: Mystic as Theologian,* 33.

35. In the Papal Bull *In agro dominico,* we read, "He presented many things as dogma that were designed to cloud the true faith in the hearts of many, things which he put forth especially before the uneducated crowds in his sermons and that he also admitted into his writings." *Meister Eckhart: The Essential Sermons,* 77.

12. Dorothee Soelle: Mystic/Activist

Anne Llewellyn Barstow

Soelle is known as a Marxist spokesperson and a Christian theologian. While we ponder the tensions implied in those two commitments, we are challenged by a second conundrum: that she lives a life of admirable political activism while writing ever more deeply about the relationship of the soul and God. The woman who took to the streets in Germany in the early 1980s in order to protest the nuclear missiles buildup, and who was arrested and arraigned, is the same person who speaks eloquently of our need for transcendence and a passion for the infinite.

The connections between spirituality and activism have long engaged those of us who find our political work growing out of, indeed guided by, our religious beliefs. That not only our ethics but also our necessity to act come from religion is a fact that marks our lives. The connections are not always clear, the direction sometimes confusing, but we remain impelled to witness to justice and to work for change because of our religious experience. For some of us this has become even a call, an imperative that we do not fully understand. When I learned that Soelle had written a book about mysticism and resistance, I turned to it for guidance.[1] Drawing on *The Silent Cry* and earlier writings, this essay will examine Soelle's claims that today religion must incorporate mysticism or die, and that spirituality must lead to world-changing action or be judged barren.

༄༅

Finding herself in a milieu of cynicism, fear, and doubt, Soelle resolutely sets out the ground of her Christian belief. Although the church repeatedly disappoints and even bores her, and worse, betrays her on crucial issues such as the arms race, still it is absolutely essential to her. Nowhere else does she find the depth of meaning that she needs in order to live authentically in these times: In Christianity nothing is meaningless. Here she escapes from the superficiality and cynicism of secularism; here—at least in radical religion—she finds the community in which she can express her passionate longing for transcendence, her hunger for God.

The need for community is a major part of what keeps Soelle in the church. By offering community, the church helps to overcome the extreme individualism of Western society. Because it believes in the forgiveness of sins, it can incorporate both victim and perpetrator into its society. When it is true to itself, it breaks down walls between classes, races, genders.[2]

For Soelle, religion as business as usual is blasphemy; she scorns the security-hungry bourgeois church that will not take risks, will not speak up to the government. Although she does not mention Bonhoeffer on this point, she is saying something very like the question he put in 1934. Bonhoeffer asked, "How does peace come about? Through a system of political treaties? Through arming so strongly that one 'guarantees peace?' Through none of these, because all of them confuse peace with safety. Peace must be dared. Peace is the opposite of security. To demand guarantees is to mistrust, and this mistrust in turn brings forth war."[3] Soelle knows the price that individuals and the church must sometimes pay in order to oppose the state during a time of war: being shunned, possibly imprisoned, even put to death. She maintains, however, that the only way the world will respect the church is if it takes this risk.

It is only radical religion that speaks to Soelle. She found this religion in the writings of Kierkegaard when she was a young student and has been guided by it ever since. When she was struggling with the post-World War II fatalism of her peers, she found hope in Kierkegaard's call for us to go beyond what is. His insistence on having a passion for the unconditional spoke to her seriousness; his insistence on transcending the ordinary encouraged her to strike out in new theological directions. One way Soelle expresses Kierkegaard's point for our time is by challenging us to "imagine peace when all one hears is war."[4] In other words, we must dare to stand for peace when the majority does not believe in it. It was Kierkegaard's leap of faith that captured the young Dorothee, and she realized that it is only suffering (or an anxiety so deep it hurts) that can push us into taking that leap. Only when we are "in extremis," when our world is desperate, will we let go of what gives us security (complacent religion) and blaze a new trail. This "letting go" would strongly influence her life and thought in later years.

For Soelle, the activating energy that enables us to take this daring step is the presence of the Holy Spirit. She delights in quoting Luther to the effect that the Holy Spirit is not a skeptic. Rather, the Spirit is a force that pushes us until we open our eyes and see the truth. The Spirit gives us the strength to look truth in the face. For me, this has meant staring into the uncomfortable truth about the civilian casualties that our bombers create, or facing the fact that in some countries people are starving in order that our agribusiness may have bigger profits. These acknowledgments have been so painful that they have forced me to let go of some of my complacency, to rethink some of my patriotism and religious faith.

From this basis, we cannot be surprised that Soelle developed theological concepts filled with personal immediacy, movement, and change. She insists on the need for personal involvement. This is Soelle's understanding of incarnation, that it is God-in-Jesus involving himself in the suffering and injustice of the world. As we must do also, for God creates through us and only through us. Thus, we must be active, daring if necessary, in order to do God's work.[5]

Besides involvement, Soelle's theology is filled with process, challenge, risk. These qualities shape her conclusion about grace: that it is more than justification; rather, it is what heals and changes us. If we do not change, we have settled for cheap grace. The challenge here, I believe, is to accept being changed. How much do we really want to change? If offered a world of peace tomorrow, could we accept the upheaval in our lives that this would cause? Do we truly want to be liberated from militarism, if that means giving up the comfortable world as we know it? In my long life I have struggled with what seemed like too much demand to change. My basic beliefs about race, gender, sexuality, the church, world religions, and American imperialism have all been turned on their heads. I took my place in white society for granted; I was so brainwashed by patriarchal thinking that I did not even realize that as a woman I was oppressed. Like many of my generation I have been overwhelmed by so much change; in order to protect myself, I resisted it. Soelle's realism helps me by identifying this tumult as the Holy Spirit working in my life. She accepts the "mess" that living truthfully creates, the painful price we must pay in order to challenge the status quo. Here Soelle forces us back to her initial paradigm of suffering as the engine that drives all theological work. Only when we acknowledge the misery of poverty, the injustice of oppression, the starvation of our own souls, only then are we able to receive grace. Only then are we ready to begin the struggle for liberation, our own and others'.[6]

The crucifixion is fundamental for Soelle. Although she has written little about the resurrection, she places the cross at the center of her understanding of how God works in and through us. Yes, she sees the pitfall of overidentification with Jesus' suffering, especially for women, who are already urged too much by society to suffer for others. Still, she maintains that for the Christian, a willingness to stand for what one believes, even to the point of suffering for it, is inescapable. And so, inspired by Martin Luther King, she prays, "Lord, help me to understand the mystery of your cross. Help me to love your cross, and give me the power, the grace, to take it upon myself as you offer it to me." She reports that this prayer has enabled her to take on the risks that today's kind of witnessing demands. She is available to God, who now can become visible through her.[7] Since the ultimate Christian symbol of struggle is the cross, it is through the cross that Christians must live. For this deeply realistic twentieth-century theologian, putting aside the cross is not an option.

Soelle had already hammered out her basic beliefs by the 1970s. In 1979 two events occurred that tested her theology and marked her life thereafter: NATO's decision to place Intercontinental Ballistic Missiles on German soil, and the Sandinista Revolution in Nicaragua. As she lives in Hamburg, the first crisis was more immediate to her life. It meant not only that Germans were complicit in pointing a preemptive nuclear strike at Eastern Europe but that they in turn had made themselves potential victims of retaliation. It meant also that Germany must now invest more of its national budget into arms and less into services for its people.

That the German government had not said no to NATO meant to Soelle that she, an individual citizen, must do so. She gladly joined with those whose task was calling all Germans to their responsibility. In *Of War and Love* and *The Arms Race Kills Even without War,* she declared that civil disobedience is an obligation. Far from being an option or worse, an embarrassment, it is our duty. How, she asked, can we teach ourselves to say no when even the churches (mainly the churches!) do not oppose the arms race, and talk of war? In sermons, radio talks, and speeches she attacked militarism. She called the NATO plan a preparation for nuclear holocaust, mass murder, and suicide. She pointed out how accepting the arms buildup eventually makes it seem normal, how it conditions us for death. Mindful of the connections between militarism and totalitarianism, she warned of what the remilitarizing of German society could do.

For Soelle, the question was religious: If we have faith, we can dare to "let go" of the security of weapons; we can render ourselves vulnerable, even as Jesus did, refusing to bear arms. In meditations such as "God Lives Unprotected," she made the case for nonviolence, no matter how risky or even foolish it may seem.[8] She concluded that we must disarm even unilaterally, and not try a cheap bargain in which one side keeps x-many weapons, while the other holds on to y-many. We must demand a real peace based on disarmament, not the uneasy truce based on treaties and bargaining. We must demand the truth about the numbers and kinds of weapons we now live in the shadow of, and we must admit to the world that we are capable of destroying it.

She spoke about disarmament at peace rallies, at the protest against U.S. Secretary of State Haig's visit, to a Christian women's congress. While constantly urging Germans to take up resistance against their government, she did not fail to do so herself. Arrested and tried in court, she was fined. She declared that the movement for peace and justice is "the most important religious movement of our time." Yet she admitted that it was often a silent movement, one without the words that a theologian needs. Despite the partial success of this nonviolent resistance to nuclear weapons, Soelle was well aware of the fragile nature of the peace movement, a movement "so powerless that it has no language."[9] This silence impressed her and, as we shall see, led to some of her deepest insights about mysticism.

As the nuclear arms crisis in Europe occurred, another upheaval took place, this one in Central America—the Sandinista uprising that overthrew the U.S.-backed government of Nicaragua. This Marxist revolution with its connections to the new liberation theology in Latin America had a profound effect on many Christians, including Soelle. She visited Nicaragua in 1983, 1987, and 1990, teaching at the Baptist Seminary in Managua, becoming a friend of the Minister of Culture, Fr. Ernesto Cardenal, and serving as an observer in the crucial election of 1990, when the Sandinistas were voted out. While sharing in the hardships of the Nicaraguan people during the Contra War, she further developed her convictions about the injustice of "third world" poverty and the greed of the developed nations.

A seminal event was her visit in 1983 to the island of Solentiname, where Cardenal had built a community with peasant artisans. Of her journey there she wrote, "Solentiname is for me like a holy place, like Jerusalem or Mecca."[10] The artists' paintings, done in "primitive" style with religious themes in which the followers of Jesus are portrayed as Nicaraguan peasants, became icons of the Revolution. The Sandinistas' identification with the poor seemed to her the only honest position for a government to take. She admired their work for the education and health care of the poor, and especially commended their attempt to give dignity to the poor. While Soelle's rapture was shared by many of us at that time, her wise phrase *"Für eine Zeit"* was guarantee that she kept her wits about her. Soelle was realistic about what the Sandinistas could and could not accomplish, given the overwhelming power of the United States against them. Solentiname could be celebrated, "for a time."

It was of course the connections between social justice and religion that most captivated her. The God of the Peasants' Mass was a simple, hard-working Jesus who sweated like the rest. Middle-class converts to the Sandinista cause became revolutionaries "in order to be Christians," (so that they could still call themselves Christians), a necessity Soelle understood all too well, and some of them were killed for their idealism. Soelle observed that at last Marxists were willing to respect Christians, at least of the radical kind, because they were willing to die for the revolution.

The fact that there were three priests in the Cabinet, and that some parish priests joined the revolution in order to live out their new "preferential option for the poor," convinced Soelle that her dream of Christian socialism had been justified. Here it was, being lived out before her eyes. She responded hungrily to the optimism in the air. When the writer Gioconda Belli said that hopelessness was a luxury that Nicaraguans could not afford, Soelle knew that she had found the place where she belonged. She was moved to proclaim, "What has happened there . . . is irreversible."[11] We know of course that this was not true, that there have been bitter reverses, that much of the revolutionary dream was lost. I was with Soelle as an observer at the 1990 election when the Sandinistas were voted out of office. For us both this was the end not only of our dream for Nicaragua but for Christian socialism in the world. There was no comfort for us. The defeat was perhaps even more bitter for me because I am a citizen of the country whose power crushed the revolution. Still, it left Soelle inconsolable, too.

I believe, however, that we were right in an important way. One part of the revolution, in the radicalized church at least, has not and will not vanish. It is the empowerment of some of the laity, of those willing to accept a greater awareness of what being a radical Christian means. In the base community congregations, uneducated rural people had explained to their priests what crucial biblical texts meant. People who were risking their lives for political liberty were supremely prepared to interpret the more radical parts of the Bible. I believe that even today, over a decade after the revolution ended in defeat and after almost every base community has closed, Nicaragua continues to have a civil society more active, more responsible for itself, than it had before. To be able to dream, even once in one's life, is absolutely essential to the freedom of the spirit.

Soelle expanded her contacts with liberation theology on a lecture tour of Argentina, Chile, Brazil, and Peru; she also traveled to El Salvador, where she interviewed prisoners and was moved by the mourning for Archbishop Romero and the four North American church women.[12] In Brazil she met poor people, women especially, who like their Nicaraguan counterparts had learned to think about religion for themselves and were speaking out. In Argentina she interviewed members of the Mothers of the Plaza, whose long resistance to state terrorism profoundly impressed her. She visited Bolivia, where her daughter Caroline, a doctor, lives. Caroline introduced her to the mammoth marches that peasants took in order to defend their rights to land, forests, water. She dedicated *Stations of the Cross* to Caroline, "who does much of which I can only dream, who lives much while I trail behind, laden with words. . . ."[13]

In many ways, the suffering, indeed the long crucifixion of Latin America under the exploitation of transnational corporations and its own ruling class, affected her theology. While in Latin America, she enlarged her understanding of the role of suffering in the divine economy. Suffering became her basis for activism. Resistance became the very fulfillment of faith; as she put it, "To commit civil disobedience is to be obedient to God."[14]

Most activists can recall the moment when they realized that they must go beyond what they had done so far as citizens. For me it was the day when an officer at the U.S. embassy in Nicaragua lied to a group of us from Witness for Peace. We had just come from the war zone, where we had seen the brutal suffering of civilians caught in the crossfire of the Contra war. When we asked him what he could tell us about civilian killings, he replied that he knew nothing. Yet we knew that the Contra war was being run out of the U.S. embassy, the very building in which we were sitting. Being lied to by my own government angered me to the point that I was ready to commit civil disobedience, a step I had previously not been able to take. From that time on, I was prepared to seek arrest, to break one law in order to honor the higher law of truth telling. In a moving recollection, Soelle tells how she knew that she was called to activism: On a Good Friday in Washington, she stood outside the White House with a few other mourners, holding a memorial vigil for Oscar Romero. The crowds of people hurrying by ignored them. The memory of his murder, of all the torture and murder of the past decade in El Salvador, brought a new reality to her traditional sorrow of the memory of the crucifixion. Later that day she went into a large church to hear a concert of religious music. Despite her lifelong love of music, the hollowness of that emotionless service chilled her heart. She reported that "at the end of that day I knew quite clearly where I belonged: on the street, not in the solemn church with its thin music . . . I belonged with that unrespected group that was . . . making the connections between [Good Friday] and present-day suffering."[15] From that time on, public witness was a form of theologizing for her. For both of us, the U.S.-sponsored suffering of Central American civilians was the turning point.

Soelle knew that what pushes us from ethics ("doing good") into transcendence is suffering. What she had not fully understood was how to connect the mystical strain within religion with resistance to injustice. When she finally published her book about mysticism and resistance, she explained that she did not want to live her life going back and forth between two planes of reality, the mystical and the active. Her book is the story of how she brought the two together.

Soelle identifies the five "places of mystical experience" as nature, eroticism, suffering, community, and joy. She approaches each one from her definition of mysticism as a longing for God, completed by God's need for us. Wanting to democratize mysticism, she chooses places (experiences) that are available to all. Insisting that God's love is actualized within us as a healing force, she focuses on places that need reconciling. The mystic approaches nature, for example, by acknowledging her dependency on it, confessing her abuse of it, and opening herself to a new, protective way of relating to it—all the while maintaining in tension the awe that one feels for the Creator. In community she finds the place where God works through us, often in ways that surprise us, for God needs community in order to enact justice. For the mystic, community has an additional purpose: It is the place where the living and the dead come together to demand justice, where we call out the names of the martyrs so that their memory energizes us. Her discussion of suffering perhaps illustrates best her belief that faith must be conscious of its historical setting. Here, because she is a Christian, she can open herself to the worst atrocities of our times—war, holocaust, nuclear annihilation—and not be overcome by the pain, for she knows that "agony is better than numbness." Following Simone Weil, she finds the suffering of Christ "useful" in that it enables Christianity to seek a super-natural use for suffering. In all of these areas Soelle describes a two-way action between the believer and God.

Two areas of Soelle's economy of mysticism, however, seem not to share in the reciprocal, dialogic nature of the others. Her discussion of eroticism, highly nuanced, describes a one-way street: In the relationship between humans, there cannot be the sharing and mutuality necessary for sacred sexuality, nor is this association part of our life with God. We have no access through sexuality to sacred power. The need to dominate impedes the presence of the holy. Our very attempt to come close to another is so threatening that it is self-defeating. Far from finding God in the intensity of human sexual sharing, Soelle finds that sexuality keeps God away. Perhaps she has a kind of perfectionism about eroti-cism: Because it never produces what she wants—total wholeness and union—she rejects what it does provide, the lessening of barriers between persons, a glimpse of ecstasy. I believe that Soelle's realism fails her here, for she does not find a way out of this dilemma. Similarly with her discussion of joy: In it God seems not to be present in the ecstatic moments of life. Where then for Soelle is religious ecstasy to be found?

In 1993 she had complained that she did not understand the joy of the poor, or their certainty that God is with them.[16] Nor could she fathom how they derive power from this joy. For all the strength of her empathy for the poor, she could not translate their pain into something positive. And yet the poor of Latin America, whom she had listened to so carefully, clearly understood something that she did not: [Their] "hope, pain, and perseverance ... put me to shame and [yet] make me strong."[17] Finally, she wrote, as if in exasperation at herself, that "what I do not understand is the mystery of God." It was in her accepting of some of these mysteries that she discovered what she had been missing. For example, in the conclusion of her discussion of eroticism, she seems finally willing to allow shared sexuality to remain a mystery, for "the other" to remain partly unknown. Perhaps in future she will pursue further the presence of God's mystery in human sexuality.

Very different from these mysteries that bring strength to the oppressed is the "letting go" of a mystic such as Marguerite Porete, the fourteenth-century Flemish Beguine burned at the stake in 1310 for heresy. One of my favorite mystics, whom I treasure for her clarity of will, she occupies an important place in Soelle's discussion of desire and eroticism. In moving beyond the pursuit of virtue, Marguerite transcends her need of church, good works, or even human love. When challenged by an inquisitional court, she is able to make no resistance, to refuse to take an oath, to do nothing to save herself. She wants only God. Soelle is correct to show that living in the immediate presence of God enables one to make a heroic death; what she does not spell out is what this kind of resistance to injustice would mean on a large scale. When done by a group, we call it mass suicide, and we deplore it. Here I lose the thread that Soelle is weaving.

It is of course not surprising that Soelle turned to mysticism, or that the mysticism that she writes about is different from traditional forms. Already inspired by the intensity of passionate caring that she found in radical religion, she could champion the mystic's undivided consciousness and injunction to be wholly present. Already devoted to the connectedness of all things, all people, she embraced the mystic's ideal of selfless unity with reality, a connectedness that fosters harmony among all beings. Long a proponent of a simple lifestyle with fewer possessions, she equated that with mystical asceticism, saying that asceticism for today consists of being free of a dependency on things. Totally convinced of the need to relate to others and to work together for the common good, she accepts the community that comes when the old ego barriers are broken down. What is gone from Soelle's mysticism is the mortification of the body and the intense individualism of traditional hermetic practice. What she must have from mysticism, and surely the reason she turned to it, is that it understands the deep contradictions in our human condition. Because it teaches the ego to let go, it is that part of religion that is able to reconcile opposites and permit opposed parties to coexist. *That* is the mystery of God that she needed in order to fully understand the hopefulness of the poor.

A word from the mystical canon that she seldom mentions is *silence*. Yet on one occasion her use of it illumines the connection between mysticism and political action. In describing the silent vigils for peace that German young people make, she comments that simply by standing there, "they make God visible."[18] Acknowledging that they lack a vocabulary for peace, acknowledging their vulnerability, even weakness, in the face of the state's nuclear weapons, not hiding in churches but facing the scorn and indifference of the crowds, they maintain a silence that speaks volumes. It is a new form of piety, a silence that speaks of God's presence, just as the Spanish term *presente* summons the martyrs in the Liberation Mass.

I would argue that it is this reversal of expectations, offering silence instead of violent resistance, that takes us into transcendence. Another reversal is Soelle's understanding of the way the pacifist may incorporate the aggressor. When the pacifist is not able to accept/love his own weakness (thus admitting vulnerability), he both fears the aggressor's power and even envies it. He may thus soon act like an aggressor himself. Or out of fear he may submit. Only by admitting this "aggressor within" and thus identifying with the "aggressors without" could Soelle finally overcome her fear of the perpetrators of violence in her own life, of the riot police, for example, whom she had to face when she took part in demonstrations. She saw that it is through our fear that the aggressors control us; it is by facing our fear that we can begin to affect them. The more that Gandhi accepted the humanity of his opponents, the stronger became his spiritual power.[19] When much of our strength goes to defending ourselves from others, we do not have enough energy left to do the work of creating alternatives to violence. Only when we stop caring about winning, stop insisting on being right, and start accepting/loving "the other" can we model what nonviolence is.

Soelle observes that there are three powers that mysticism frees us from: ego, covetousness, and violence. Of these, violence is the hardest to escape. The punishments for it are harsh: One may experience physical harm or loss of freedom when one comes up against it, and thus we fear it. At this point she turns to Thoreau, who saw that if he clung to his freedom he would become enslaved to it. Besides, he concluded that anyone *not* in jail when the nation condoned the enslavement of Africans was, as we say, "part of the problem." And so he actually sought a jail sentence (he had refused to pay his poll tax, to protest the Mexican War and slavery) and was disappointed to be bailed out after only one night. He had freed himself of the need to be seen as law abiding; he did not fear the scorn of conventional folks. He established the concept of being a "prisoner of conscience," of performing what Soelle calls "prison mysticism," and many including Soelle have followed him in acts of civil disobedience, forcing the government to arrest them. In prison some of these witnesses truly see the aggressor as human just as they are: friendships are formed across the line between prisoner and guard, and among prisoners. These acts turn the world upside down: The peace lovers become the lawbreakers in order to witness to a higher or better law. It requires a certain leap of faith, a certain leaving behind of conventional wisdom, to accept jail witness as an obligation. Soelle crossed that line.

Resistance of course has its own rationale, separate from religion. It is however inevitably tied into spiritual life for Soelle, as we have seen, and the relationship is a two-way street. By opposing inaction and converting neutral action into good, resistance saves religion from its worst sin, that of inertia and acceptance of wrong. In turn, by being allied with religion, it can save itself from destructive action. She says little about this last except to point out that resistance needs roots in order not to stray from the good. Religion, she believes, can give resistance the wisdom of tradition. And it does so in a way that overcomes the political tendency to be overly rational; it roots action in a suprarational motivation. Finally, mysticism can enable resistance to bear witness to the dead, can stand in for those absent, thus connecting what might be only ephemeral politics with the witness of the ages in its struggle for justice.

For all the richness of the connections that Soelle makes in it, however, *The Silent Cry* does not reveal Soelle's own encounter with the mystery of God. Perhaps for her the silence itself is the encounter; perhaps Soelle the poet and ethicist does not have words for this deep treasure. In insisting that faith and action must not be separated, she seems to give herself more to action than to sharing her faith. While I trust this form of active contemplation, I long to know more. For example, I want to know Soelle's thoughts about the altered states of consciousness that mysticism often awards to those hungry for God. Surely this alteration is a form of change that she has thought about! When I remember that my only experience of trance occurred in the midst of a huge, intense political protest for Central American human rights, I affirm Soelle's wisdom in keeping the mystical and resistance together; they are together for me. Yet she gives no clue as to how she is changed by similar experiences. I have long pondered what to do with my feelings of grief and anger that I bring home from trips to Central America. Political protest alone does not assuage them. Finally I joined thousands of protesters against the Military School of the Americas at Fort Benning, Georgia. Over 70,000 Latin American soldiers have been trained there, many of whom have returned to their own countries to kill their own citizens. Each year at the School of the Americas we hold a memorial service for the dead civilians of Latin America, killed by this armed violence. Just as Soelle described in writing about the mystic's need for community with the dead, so do we invoke the presence of the dead; as the names of thousands of dead Central Americans are sung out, we shout *"Presente!"* One year, hours of calling out *"Presente!"* brought me into a different psychological state than I had ever been in. I was suddenly outside myself, no longer standing in a crowd of thousands outside a military base. I had crossed a psychological line; I was with the dead, they were with me. It was a powerful gift, an unforgettable feeling of God-with-me. It further strengthened my commitment to the cause I was working for. Just as the mystic longs for God with all her heart, so I longed for justice; perhaps in our time these longings may be the same. I want to know in what ways Soelle is touched and changed by the actions she takes.

Most important for Soelle, mysticism insists on the oneness of all beings. Thus, in war there can be no humiliation, no winners, no losers. No unconditional surrender, no death penalty, no sanctions, no punishment in order to "rub it in." Next must come the healing. After the last World War, certainly the churches did not speak up sufficiently for peace, educate for peace, or offer to suffer for peace. They did not offer a vigorous alternative to the militarizing of the world. Not until the end of the 1980s did the German Lutheran Church take up its call to peacemaking, when it organized the prayer cells that became the core of the amazing nonviolent resistance to Soviet control over East Germany. Soelle points out that it then truly became "the church," and became the model for similar nonviolent resistance across Eastern Europe. What could have been a terrible blood bath became the "Velvet Revolution." And in the negotiations for Communist withdrawal, the Lutheran Church served as the bridge.

This historic event proved Soelle correct when she called for building "democratic cells" of resistance to injustice rather than building missile systems.[20] It was exactly such cells, nurtured in the church but now out in the streets, standing up against the Communist police, that overthrew the East German government.

When we consider the many examples of this kind of nonviolent peacemaking—South Africa, the Philippines, the elections that ended civil wars in El Salvador and Nicaragua, even the overthrow of Milosevic in Yugoslavia, and more—we realize that there is already a witness to the power of nonviolence. Yet in the end Soelle chooses to emphasize the weakness of the peace movement, not its strength. In doing so she reaches the heart of the ambiguities faced by the mystic-activist. She concludes, "Our religiously grounded resistance is still so weak, so experientially impoverished, so little practiced that we can hardly think of it."[21] What Gandhi and King worked out in the first sixty years of the twentieth century is what Soelle is urging us to take up now, in these perilous first years of the twenty-first: that our weakness is our strength. She knows that nonviolent resistance is a high-risk venture. Yet reminding us that one must believe that love is stronger than hate, Soelle challenges us to put down our weapons and pursue peace through every possible nonviolent way.

Notes

1. Dorothee Soelle, *The Silent Cry: Mysticism and Resistance* (trans. Barbara and Martin Rumscheidt; Minneapolis: Fortress, 2001).

2. Soelle, *The Window of Vulnerability: A Political Spirituality* (trans. Linda Maloney; Minneapolis: Fortress, 1990).

3. Dietrich Bonhoeffer, *No Rusty Swords* (trans. Edwin H. Robinson and John Bowden; New York: Harper and Row, 1965), 80–81.

4. Dorothee Soelle, *The Arms Race Kills Even without War* (trans. Gerhard Elston; Philadelphia: Fortress, 1983).

5. Dorothee Soelle, *Of Love and War* (trans. Rita and Robert Kimber; Maryknoll, N.Y.: Orbis, 1983), 10–11.

6. Dorothee Soelle, *Thinking about God: An Introduction to Theology* (trans. John Bowden; Philadelphia: Trinity Press International, 1990), ch. 8.

7. Soelle, *Thinking about God,* 128–29.

8. Soelle, *Of Love and War,* 91–98.

9. Soelle, *Silent Cry,* 76.

10. Dorothee Soelle and Peter Frey, *Revolution Ohne Todesstrafe: Zwei Berichte Aus Nicaragua* (Zurich: Pendo Verlag, 1984), 83. "Solentiname ist für mich so etwas wie ein heiliger Ort, wie Jerusalem oder Mekka. Ich werde die Erde küssen, denk ich, noch im Flugzeug, es muss doch irgendwo auf diesem Planeten ein Stück Land geben, zu dem ich sagen kann: Hier. Jetzt. Zieh deine Schuhe aus. Der Ort, wo du stehst, ist heiliges Land. Hier haben ein paar Menschen, Kunstler und campesinos ein Stuck Leben realisiert, für eine Zeit."

11. Dorothee Soelle, *Stations of the Cross: A Latin American Pilgrimage* (trans. Joyce Irwin; Minneapolis: Fortress, 1993), 135.

12. Soelle, *Stations of the Cross.*

13. Ibid., vii.

14. Dorothee Soelle and Fulbert Steffensky, *Not Just Yes and Amen: Christians with a Cause* (Philadelphia: Fortress Press, 1985), 94.

15. Soelle, *Of Love and War,* 91–92.

16. Soelle, *Stations of the Cross,* 91–92.

17. Dorothee Soelle, *On Earth as in Heaven: A Liberation Spirituality of Sharing* (trans. Marc Batko; Louisville: Westminster/John Knox, 1993), 7.

18. Soelle, *Silent Cry,* 76.

19. Ibid., 259–61.

20. Ibid., 276.

21. Ibid., 6.

PART 5

THEOLOGICAL
LIBERATION

13. The Feminist Liberation Theology of Dorothee Soelle

Rosemary Radford Ruether

Dorothee Soelle is, in my view, one of the foremost Christian theologians of the late twentieth century.[1] She and I have long found our perspectives on theology and social criticism highly compatible. In the mid-1980s, she and I, together with Elisabeth Schüssler Fiorenza, engaged in a weekend dialogue at the Grail in Loveland, Ohio, on the general topics of feminism, social justice, and theology. Dorothee recounts that she expected to be less in tune with my views than those of Elisabeth, a fellow German. Because of my stance as an American feminist, she expected me to have a view of gender dichotomy that was different from her own, perhaps lacking class and race analysis. To her surprise she found that this was not the case and that our views were very similar.

I don't remember the topics we discussed in detail. We ranged across many issues of theology, society, church, and women. One minor topic that stands out because it became a debate between myself and Elisabeth was pay for housework. Elisabeth had already developed an advocacy for pay for housework. I had not thought about this issue but came to disagree with it in the course of discussion. I argued that housework was the remnant of a preindustrial realm of unpaid subsistence labor that people did for themselves. Pay for housework would commodify housework and make it part of the labor market. Also, where would the pay come from? It could only come primarily from the husband, who would be redefined as the employer of the wife. I preferred an equal sharing of housework by husband and wife or all members of the household, rather than converting it into a realm of paid labor. Dorothee also had not thought much about this issue but came to agree more with my view.

Dorothee Soelle and I have been traveling parallel to each other in our theological and social critique for many years, only occasionally interconnecting but finding ourselves on very similar paths. In April of 1996, Dorothee and I had an opportunity to engage in dialogue at a women's conference in Northern Germany with a focus on feminism and ecology. At that time I had a chance to visit her in her home in Hamburg. She was then working on her new book on mysticism. She mentioned the prejudice against the mystical tradition that was typical of the Protestant neo-orthodoxy of her early studies, but how she herself had found it necessary to break with this view. For her, mysticism and social action were not in contradiction but were necessary allies. Only with experiential communion with God can we sustain a struggle for justice.[2]

Dorothy and I also did a joint lecture and dialogue in the chapel of the Pacific School of Religion in Berkeley, California, in the fall of 1998, when I was teaching there and she was visiting for lectures. On another occasion we came together for a shared discussion in Evanston, Illinois. In these discussions we continually found points of convergence in our views despite our different contexts and relatively rare meetings. We share a common critique of the United States as a dangerous neo-colonial and militaristic power that is causing great harm in the world. Our occasional miscommunication in such dialogues come primarily from our different social locations and experiences, as a German and an American. Dorothee sometimes seems to find it difficult to understand that Americans such as myself are as critical of this "American evil" as she is, but my critique comes out of passionate concern for my country, not a despising of it, just as she is vehemently critical of the German treatment of the Jews because she loves Germany.

One global issue we have not shared is concern for the Israeli mistreatment of the Palestinians. Dorothee, by contrast, finds it impossible to speak out on this issue. As a German, her feelings of guilt toward the Holocaust seem to make her feel she can't speak about evils being done by Jews. Palestinian Christian friends of mine have tried to engage her on this issue to no avail.[3] I have never tried to confront her on this issue, but I feel disappointed when "German guilt" toward Jews becomes a barrier to concern for another people who are being victimized. Perhaps this reflects somewhat different sensibilities toward victimized people. While I believe in standing with victimized people, I am also sensible to the way that suffering can make people desire revenge, rather than becoming loving and caring people. Once in power, such former sufferers can feel an entitlement to take out their desire for vengeance on others who had nothing to do with their former suffering. Jewish friends of mine have seen that kind pattern of the "battered batterer" in the Israeli relation to the Palestinians.[4]

Dorothee Soelle has found a fuller reception in the North American theological world than in the Germany university system and for years taught at Union Theological Seminary in New York City. I have never discussed her relationship to German universities, so I don't know that history in detail. I have been told by friends at Union that the German university system has never recognized her as a scholar or given her an adequate position. But at the same time, Dorothee was less concerned with her academic career than with the integrity of her context. She refused to move to New York with a full-time position so that she could continue to spend a major part of the year in Germany. She has been very concerned not to "become" American but to retain her roots in her own German context.

My own career trajectory has been different. I taught briefly at a Catholic school, Immaculate Heart College, in the early 1960s as I finished my doctorate, but I was told with great regret that they could not continue to hire me because of my writings criticizing the Catholic teaching on birth control. That alerted me to the reality that I should not seek a teaching career in Catholic institutions, although I have continued to maintain a presence in Catholic institutions through lectures and occasional courses. I presently do some teaching in the Sophia Center of Holy Names College in Oakland, California. But my main work has been at Protestant seminaries, teaching for ten years at the Howard University School of Religion in Washington, then for twenty-seven years as the Georgia Harkness professor at Garrett-Evangelical Theological Seminary, and now in a quasi-emeritus status as the Carpenter chair in feminist theology at the Graduate Theological Union in Berkeley, California. I have been well received at these institutions.

Despite her extensive work in the United States, Dorothee has been concerned to continue to think theologically and socially from her context as a German of the Left. Moreover, it would be more than a decade after she began her published writing before Soelle would explicitly own feminism as one of the social contexts for her theological reflection. Some of the German feminist women to whom I have spoken still do not think of her as a feminist theologian.[5] However, I disagree with this view. I believe she has integrated a significant gender analysis into what remains a liberation theology steeped in Marxist class critique.

The theological worlds in which Soelle was trained did not dispose her to be sympathetic to feminism. The German theology of Barth repelled feminism as contrary to a Christian anthropology of hierarchically ordered I-Thou relations,[6] or else, in the case of Bultmann, tended to ignore it altogether. The German Left of the 1960s also was unreceptive to feminism. Socialists decried any attention to women apart from the "worker's struggle" as bourgeois and reactionary.[7] But Soelle's late embrace of feminism perhaps owed less to these influences than to the primacy of her preoccupation with the meaning of the experience of the Holocaust and Nazism for Christians, especially in Germany.

These preoccupations biased Soelle against American feminism in the 1970s, which she tended to assume lacked roots in "class struggle." But her dialogue with feminist women at Union Theological Seminary brought her to realize that her theology had always been implicitly feminist. The questions she had been asking as a political theologian were along the same lines as the critique and reconstruction of theology being undertaken by feminism.[8] But Soelle had to develop her journey to liberation theology before she could allow herself to add "feminist" to her self-understanding as a liberation theologian of the German Left.

In her developed theology in the 1980s, Soelle would speak of herself as working out of three interconnected social contexts: as a German, as a Protestant Christian, and as a woman.[9] As a German born in 1929, Soelle took and continues to take the Holocaust as the primary question for German theology after World War II. In her view, no German can do theology authentically if he or she does not take the Holocaust seriously as a radical challenge to German national culture.[10] How could this event have happened with the acquiescence of most Germans in a land steeped in Christianity?

The Holocaust for Soelle is not simply a past German event. She also connects it with the threats to life on earth from the postwar global capitalist economic "order." An economic system that provides an affluent life for a first-world elite while condemning the majority of people in the third world to living death through desperate poverty and violence has emerged as the world system of global oppression. The rivalry between East and West, communism and capitalism, a struggle over what economic and ideological system would govern the world, has also spawned a system of global militarism capable of exterminating all life on earth. This threatened future holocaust of the whole planet through nuclear war must be the context for theological reflection in the late twentieth and twenty-first centuries. Theology must cease to think of doing theology as an end in itself; rather, as in Latin American liberation theology, theology must be seen as a "second step" to be done in and through reflection on political praxis.[11]

In Cologne in the late 1960s, Soelle was part of a group of engaged Christians who developed a monthly "political night prayer." The worship services consisted of a reading of important recent news and the analysis of its social justice implications concerning Christians. This political reading and analysis was then followed by appropriate scriptural readings that sought to bring the light of the Bible to these political events. There was then a brief sermon that brought the political events and the light of Scripture into interaction, followed by prayer and a discussion of "what we are to do." At the time this kind of dynamic interconnection of the Bible, theology, and politics was seen as very radical, challenging both the political order and the apolitical tradition of theology. Soelle's political theology was shaped by this practice of socially engaged prayer.[12]

Soelle began her political theology in the context of a critique of Bultmann. Bultmann's existentialist hermeneutics had been very important to Soelle's theological development. Existentialist theological method had allowed her to situate the categories of Christian theology in the context of real human experiences in a concrete way, freeing herself from Barth's rebuke of the older liberal correlation of theology with experience. But Bultmann's view of sin and grace remained resolutely individualistic. He refused to allow a political dimension to enter or to see social systems as places of sin and grace.[13] Bultmann's project of demythologizing remained limited by this individualism. He sought to overcome past mythic worldviews but refused to own problems of social ideology that might be stated in nonmythic form, whether in Scripture or in contemporary social thought.

Soelle wished to take the insights of existentialist hermeneutics of the gospel further and to add ideological critique of ancient and modern cultures to demythologizing. She believed that the existentialist "call to decision" in response to the gospel should be situated in the context of political resistance to the oppression of groups by other groups. As she saw it, sin, politically interpreted, must mean a critique of the real contradictions of society. This also demands a critique of the ideologies that blind us to these contradictions, making them appear normal, natural, and the will of God, disposing us to accept unquestioningly the lies of the dominant society.

Forgiveness is not simply a transaction between God and the individual soul that has come to recognize its sinfulness. Politically interpreted, forgiveness means concrete acts of repentance expressed through social struggle to overcome oppression and to create a more just world.[14] This political interpretation of sin and grace led Soelle to critique both orthodox and liberal theologies, including Barthian neo-orthodoxy and Bultmannian existentialism, in regard to the ideological elements in their theologies that disposed them to refuse any real engagement in questions of social justice.

Soelle's theological method thus came to be characterized by a systematic ideological critique of both orthodox and liberal theology in Germany and the enunciation of an alternative feminist liberation theology. This method is found scattered through her writings of the 1980s and 1990s but is found laid out most systematically in her introduction to theology, *Thinking about God,* developed from lectures of the late 1980s.[15]

Ideology critique for Soelle means a denunciation of the orthodox idea of God and of human nature or of the "human predicament," and the demonstration of the ways in which the view of both God and "man" in German Protestant orthodoxy and neoorthodoxy sustained an unjust, violent world and allowed Christians to ignore and tacitly support systematized evil without ever naming it as "sin." Because of its privatization of the religious questions in terms of the individual self, because of its splitting of church from state, individual from society, liberal theology in Germany, from Schleiermacher to Bultmann, failed to challenge these orthodox patterns, despite its apparent greater openness to the modern world, its acceptance of the autonomous authority of modern science, and its use of historical criticism of the Bible.

Reflection on this analysis of Protestant orthodoxy from a feminist perspective brought a new dimension to her critique. Gender critique illuminated for Soelle the particular ways that this concept of God was part of a gendered system of male power over females. Soelle has denounced what she has called the "phallocentric" Christian imagery for God as Lord, Sovereign Power, and patriarchal Father. This view of God, imaged primarily in terms of power, as "all-powerful," rather than in terms of justice or love, is the theological identity myth of powerful males, supported by a church led by ruling-class males.[16] This idea of God not only supports the patriarchal family and church but also undergirds economic and political systems of empire, from the Pax Romana to the Pax Americana.

Such a concept of God allowed Germans to exterminate the Jews in the name of obedience to authority. It continued to justify the Holocaust and obedience to the directives of the Nazi state after the war by claiming that God's all-governing providence would not have allowed such things to happen unless they expressed the "will of God." For Soelle, this "God Almighty" is an idol, a false god. Worship of this idol must be rejected in order to discover the "powerless God of love" who speaks through Jesus Christ.[17]

One cannot reject the false God of the rulers without also deconstructing the classical dualism of transcendence and immanence. When Karl Barth loudly proclaimed his "No" to liberalism, he did so by renewing a concept of God as "wholly other," far removed from this world in a transcendent realm inaccessible to human experience. The Christian traditions of mysticism that cultivated experiences of communion with God were rejected as false human efforts to "possess God."[18] For neoorthodoxy, God's saving word must always be seen as coming to humans "from above." We humans, women especially, are always called to submit to a divine will that we can never fully understand. This split between the divine and the human virtually denies divine immanence. The result is a Protestant orthodoxy whose spirituality is fixated on the themes of human sin, powerlessness, and the call to submission. In this spirituality the created world is left devoid of the presence of God.

Theologians of the 1960s, such as Harvey Cox, celebrated the connection between this supposedly biblical view of divine transcendence and the secularization of the "world."[19] But what was not recognized was the impact of this driving out of any sense of the sacredness of creation by a "wholly other" God. All created things are handed over to human use and disposal, which concretely means handing over all created things to the market forces of a technocratic economic order and its military reinforcement. The ideology of secularity disconnects human society and the earth from the presence of God. Humans need no longer be restrained in their rapacious use of all "things," including human beings who are reduced to commodifiable objects, without any sense of a Creator God to whom we are accountable for our use of the earth.[20]

The underside and presupposition of this view of God as disconnected and all-powerful male will, ruling over creation from outside, is a belittled human being who is called to become acceptable to this God by endlessly acknowledging her or his worthlessness and powerlessness. The human being stands before God always as the convicted sinner, whose sins have been paid for by Christ's blood on the cross and who thereby is atoned for and accepted by God. But this atonement is presented in a way that does not free the human for joy and love of God and one another but rather reinforces human guilt and unacceptability.[21]

In this theology of "forensic justification," any human "works" are demonized as the greatest sins. What is seen as the wrongheaded tendency to do "works" that detract from God's grace includes works of spiritual cultivation and political struggle. Humans are never allowed to feel joy in the living presence of a God whose grace wells up in our well-being. Nor should we hope that society can be in any way changed for the better by our efforts. The belief of liberation theologies that the world can be brought closer to the reign of God through alleviating poverty, lessening racism or sexism, or preventing the threat of a nuclear holocaust is denounced by Christian orthodoxy as "works righteousness."

For Soelle, this theology of divine transcendence and impotent human sinfulness nicely supports a "do-nothing" Christian practice in which "redemption" rules out both action and contemplation. Christians gather week after week in their churches to reiterate the rhetoric of sin and salvation without changing anything, indeed being warned against imagining that they should try to change anything, either within themselves or in the world around them. This theological stance carries over into secular society in cultural attitudes of awestruck submission to a rapacious market system, supported by expanding militarism and causing increasing violation of the earth. The neoliberal market economy with its destructive consequences is defined as a manifestation of the "natural law" whose operations are implacable and unchangeable and to which we can only submit. No alternative system of economic life is possible.[22]

In the 1990s, the old Christian orthodoxy and these new secular military and market orthodoxies were merging in right-wing Christian movements, particularly in the United States. After Jimmy Carter's presidency it became common for presidents and politicians to claim to be "born again." Politicized Christianity in the United States is expressed in the simultaneous claim that America is God's elect nation and "religion has nothing to do with politics"; that salvation has only to do with the individual soul and life after death and nothing to do with making a more just society. The global "free market" is assumed to be identical with both "democracy" and God's laws for creation. This kind of New Right Christianity Soelle dubbed "Christofascism."[23]

Far from not taking sin seriously, as orthodox Christians often claim, feminist liberation theologians take sin far more seriously than do the established churches. Soelle reinterprets the traditional Christian description of the sinful self as one that is enclosed in its egoism and passivity and out of touch with God. This alienated human reality is seen as having three dimensions: an inward personal dimension, a structural systemic dimension, and an ideological dimension. Soelle thinks of the alienated individual as more often victim than aggressor, although there are individuals who hold great power and engage in real decisions and actions that erect and erect again the world of exploitation and militarism.

But most individuals are collaborators with evil more than active decision makers. Some belong to what she calls the *kaputter typ* ("broken-down type") who have died inside and lost any sense of how to relate to others or to themselves.[24] Others are the self-satisfied bourgeois who simply go along as cogs in a machine of rapacious exploitation, gaining their little bits of profit from it without questioning the evil workings of the larger reality in which they live, much as "good Germans" went along with Nazism and then later justified themselves as "just doing what they were told" and as having "not known what was happening."[25]

Soelle faults the Christian churches as playing a major part in shaping this ethic of collaboration, confusing obedience to authorities with obedience to God. Unquestioning compliance with orders itself became a virtue, without raising questions about the meaning and purpose of what was ordered. Questioning, dissent, rebellion against authority, these were seen as the essence of sin. The primal sin of Adam (or, more particularly, that of Eve) was disobedience to authority and rebellion against God's commands, even if those commands made no sense. The way to show one's repentance for sin is through redoubled submission to authority. Christians are taught not to question authority to discern whether or not it is of God.[26]

Personal inner deadness and lack of relationship as well as the religious and secular ideologies that sacralize submission to authorities both have their source in this system of dominating power. Systems of oppression spring from and collectivize human arrogance, greed, fear, and hate. These negative tendencies have their roots in human persons but go far beyond this bad side of individuals. They are organized and institutionalized as collective systems of death that hold humans themselves in bondage. Soelle sees sin in its collective form as a demonic counterworld to God's creation. This is the anti-creation of the "man-eating ogre" that masquerades as God's creation and claims God as its Lord but that is actually counter to all that is truly of God. Like the death camps of Nazism, it masks its evil reality with false slogans, such as "Work makes free" (Arbeit macht frei), over its gates.[27]

Authentic theology, for Soelle, begins in pain; it begins in painful recognition of the hurt to oneself and to others caused by this violent world and one's own collaboration with it.[28] God's gracious presence stirs up dissent from the official ideologies of the dominant world that try to sacralize it as God's will and the natural order, calling "good Christians" and citizens to bow before it. Theology speaks God's word only when it expresses this dissent and unmasks the false idols. Sinful collaboration with evil can never be known in the abstract but only as one dissents from this system and begins to recognize its effects on oneself and others. Breaking free from obedience to "this world" and disbelieving in its "god" are the first gifts of grace. Naming this system as evil and disobeying its commands are the first acts of conversion. In this sense Eve is the first liberator. Dissent from the orders of a patriarchal God, asking questions about whether the orders make sense, is the beginning of conversion. It was appropriately led by a woman who received these orders only secondarily from her husband but who was held particularly guilty for questioning them.[29]

When the patriarchal Cosmocrator has been unmasked as an idol, and the extent of the church's role in making this idol its god has been revealed, the dissenter may become permanently estranged from Christianity. The dissenters assume that these ideological notions of God and "man" are the actual Christian message. In Soelle's view, many Marxists, feminists, and other dissenters have entered this first stage of critique of false Christianity. They have rejected the patriarchal God of sexism, racism, and class hierarchy. They have experienced themselves being ejected from the patriarchal church as unbelievers. But they have not known any prophetic community within the Christian world that welcomes them as daughters and sons of God whose very dissent is an integral part of a journey of faith toward authentic life.

For Soelle, this dissent against the idols falsely embraced by the church is not apostasy, but it is the first step toward knowing who Jesus Christ really is, who God really is. But the church has done such a good job of confusing Christ with Caesar and God with Satan that most people find it difficult to go on to the next step of liberated and liberating faith. Without prophetic Christian communities where *kerygma, diakonia,* and *koinonia* (message, service, and community) are constituted on the ground of prophetic faith, feminists and other dissenters fall into alienated skepticism toward the gospel or catch glimpses of a liberating view but lack a community to sustain them in their journey. This is what the church should be, but mostly has failed to be.[30]

Soelle's "theology for skeptics" declares that it is only by passing through a rejection of the patriarchal God of the rulers that we are able for the first time to glimpse the real Jesus Christ.[31] We find him as the powerless Jewish prophet who announced the good news of God's favor to the poor, who declared the setting at liberty of those who are oppressed to the marginalized and despised people of his day. This Jesus also called the mighty of religion and state to repent of their oppressive power and to enter the reign of God in humble solidarity with the lowly victims of their power. This Jesus did not come to suffer and die. His mission in life was not to masochistically offer his blood to a sadistic God to pay for our sins.[32] Rather, he came to liberate us into a new community of joyful life.

Jesus did not die on the cross as a sadomasochistic transaction between himself and an all-powerful God to pay for sins that humans are unable to remedy. Rather, Jesus died on the cross because the mighty of religion and state did not accept his call to repentance and solidarity with the poor—they sought to shore up their system of power and its ideological justifications by silencing the voice of the prophet. His resurrection means that they did not succeed in silencing him. He rose and continues to rise wherever prophets arise, breaking through the system of lies and death and offering a glimpse of the true God of life who stands against the systems of worldly power.[33] The cross is not a payment for sin or a required sacrifice for our redemption, but it is the risk that Jesus and all prophets take when they unmask the idols of death and announce the good news that God is with those who struggle for justice and communicate loving life.[34] The risk is that the powerful will once again try to kill them to silence their message. The promise is that the prophets will rise again, the word of hope will be remembered and announced once again, stirring up new life.

For Soelle, human beings are not powerless, worthless wretches but free beings made in the image of God and called to be cocreators with God in redeeming creation from sin. Jesus is our representative, not as an otherworldly divine figure who has nothing in common with us but as one who expressed what we are called to be as humans. We, like him, are called to be courageous strugglers against evil, tellers of truth to power, healers and joyful livers of life to the full who infectiously communicate well-being to one another. This is who Jesus was, and this is who Jesus calls us to be, as healed women and men.

Soelle reinterprets ideas of God in relation to humans and creation, and ideas of who we are called to be in relation to God and our fellow earth creatures in the light of this vision of who Jesus is. She rejects the alienated dualism that defines divine transcendence as detached otherness and sovereign power from beyond. This critique of transcendence as alienated otherness clears the way for an alternative understanding of God's relation to us as "transcendent immanence." God is totally immanent, not in the sense of sacralizing "what is" qua systems of unjust power, but rather as life-giving presence that sustains us in our struggle for abundant life. God is the one "in whom we live and move and have our being." But God's immanence is also radically transcendent, not in the sense of being far away, detached, and unavailable, but in the sense of being radically free of entrapment in our systems of death and our ideologies of domination. God's transcendent immanence is the liberating grace that continually frees us from our blindedness to lies and our collaboration with evil.[35] For Soelle, God is the power of life as loving interrelationship who is present through those created realities in the times and places where such renewed life is happening.

Soelle deconstructs and reconstructs our calling as Christians, as humans. We are not called to be masochistic self-negaters; rather, we are called to fulfillment and well-being.[36] But we have to discover what true well-being is. We have been offered a false well-being as prosperity and security purchased at the expense of impoverishment and violence to others. Making profit at the expense of others means living with a suppressed guilt that makes us hostile to others. It impels us to continually seek to dominate them and to repress their protests lest they unmask our thievery and take away our stolen goods. The world economic system, defended by global militarism, has been constructed on this wrongful profit and repression of protest. This system threatens to undo creation itself and to turn the whole earth back to nothingness.

True well-being is found when this false "success ethic" is renounced and we learn to live more and more freed from it. Then we can begin to taste the joys of true well-being lived in mutual service and shared life. When life is lived in solidarity with others in shared well-being, every act of sustaining life becomes a sacrament of God's presence, whether that be bread broken between friends, sexual pleasure given and received between lovers, the tilling of the ground to bring forth fruit, the creation of a beautiful artifact, or the act of giving birth to a baby.[37] God does not call us into a kingdom of God beyond this world in some distant place called "heaven." Rather, God calls us to the fulfilling of the promise of life on earth, when "God's will is done on earth as it is in heaven." God's will done on earth is the work of justice in love done among all earth creatures, not just in relation to humans.[38] It is this will of God done on earth that is the "kingdom come," and not some flight to a distant realm outside the earth.

For Soelle, there is an essential dualism that divides the world, but it is not the dualism of a platonic Christianity that divides mind and body, heaven and earth, spirit and matter, nor a dualism that divides a sinful, impotent human from an all-powerful God. Rather, it is the dualism between death-dealing dominating power and life-giving love. The God revealed in Christ is life-giving love. This is also the essential nature of human beings and all creation. Humans are called to liberate and heal one another and creation as cocreators with God.

Soelle rejects any essential difference between women and men in this task of liberation and life-giving love. Women have no superior capacity for love. They, too, can be deluded by and become collaborators with dominating power. Yet for her there are differences of social location between most men and women, as well as between the affluent and the marginalized. Because women as a gender group have been marginalized by dominating power and have been socialized to identify with love and relationality, Soelle hopes that women may be readier to break with lies and power systems and to align themselves with the struggle for justice and love.

But the struggle is finally about both men and women and must be lived out by both men and women. It is not primarily a struggle of women against men, but a struggle of both men and women together for life on earth. The good news of the gospel, when it is freed from patriarchal distortion, is that God in Christ is with us and in us in this struggle. This is Soelle's essential message, reiterated in volume after volume, lecture after lecture, and in her lived practice of daily life over more than four decades. It is a message that must be heard all the more urgently in the Christofascist world ruled by born-again Christians, such as George W. Bush, and his holy crusade against "terrorism."

I had not spoken to Dorothee in the last two years before her death, but I cannot imagine that she was not even more sharply critical of American official behavior after September 11, 2001, than she was before. The rampant militarism that has been unleashed in response to this event, the dualizing of the world into "good guys" and "bad guys," and the assumption that whoever is not with us is against us would confirm her worst suspicions of American global power. I hope she knew that Americans such as myself are equally alarmed and critical of this American presence in the world.

Notes

1. This essay is based on my account of the theology of Dorothee Soelle in Rosemary Radford Ruether, *Women and Redemption: A Theological History* (Minneapolis: Fortress, 1998), 182–90, revised and updated. Revised and reprinted with permission.

2. This book has now appeared as Dorothee Soelle, *The Silent Cry: Mysticism and Resistance* (trans. Barbara and Martin Rumscheidt; Minneapolis: Fortress, 2001). Translation of *Mystik und Widerstand: Du stilles Geschrei* (Hamburg: Hoffman and Campe, 1997).

3. I learned this fact in oral communication with Jean Zaru, Christian leader in Ramallah, Palestine.

4. I see the abuse of the Palestinians as coming primarily from a colonial relation of Israelis to Palestinians as people they wish to displace and whose land they want to take, but justified and made emotionally vehement through the "battered batterer" syndrome. For my general work on the Palestinian issue, see *The Wrath of Jonah: The Crisis of Religious Nationalism in the Israeli-Palestinian Conflict,* with Herman Ruether, second edition (Minneapolis: Fortress, 2002). Rachel Adler, a leading Jewish feminist, was the first person I heard analyzing the Israeli treatment of Palestinians in terms of a "battered batterer" syndrome (personal conversation).

5. This was the view of Dorothee Soelle expressed to me by some women who attended a women's conference in northern Germany on ecology and feminism, where Soelle and I both spoke in 1996.

6. On Karl Barth's famous view of male and female as "A" and "B," see his *Church Dogmatics: The Doctrine of Creation* 3.4, (ed. G. W. Bromiley and T. F. Torrance; Edinburgh: T. and T. Clark, 1961), 169–70.

7. For this inability of men of the Left to embrace feminism, see particularly Margaret Randall, *The Gathering Rage: The Failure of Twentieth Century Revolutions to Develop a Feminist Agenda* (New York: Monthly Review Press, 1992).

8. See Dorothee Soelle, *The Strength of the Weak: Toward a Christian Feminist Identity* (Philadelphia: Westminster, 1984), 96–117; see also Soelle, *The Window of Vulnerability: A Political Spirituality* (Minneapolis: Fortress, 1990), 61–74; *Thinking about God: An Introduction to Theology* (Philadelphia: Trinity Press International, 1990), 68–76; and her new preface to her *Creative Disobedience* (Cleveland: Pilgrim, 1995), xvi–xxi.

9. See *Creative Disobedience,* ix.

10. Ibid., x.

11. Soelle explores the systems of militarism and global poverty in several books; see particularly *Of War and Love* (Maryknoll, N.Y.: Orbis, 1983); *Window of Vulnerability,* ix–xii, 3–11, and 42–49. See also her *Stations of the Cross: A Latin American Pilgrimage* (Minneapolis: Fortress, 1993); and *The Arms Race Kills Even without War* (Philadelphia: Fortress, l983).

12. Dorothee Soelle, *Political Theology* (Philadelphia: Fortress, 1974), vii–viii, xx.

13. For Soelle's evaluation of Bultmann, including her report of his letter to her in response to her writings on political theology in which he repudiated the idea of corporate sin, see *Window of Vulnerability,* 122–32.

14. Soelle, *Political Theology,* 83–107.

15. Soelle, *Thinking about God,* especially 7–41; also *Window of Vulnerability,* 105–16.

16. See Soelle, *Strength of the Weak*, 96–97; *Window of Vulnerability*, 85-92; and *Thinking about God*, 171–95.

17. Soelle's first book, *Christ the Representative* (Philadelphia: Fortress, 1967), translation of *Stellvertretung* (Stuttgart: Kreuz Verlag, 1965), developed her Christology, based on Bonhoeffer's view of Christ as the powerless One in whom we encounter the powerless God against oppressive power. For additional expressions of Soelle's view of Christ, see *Thinking about God*, 102–19; and *Theology for Skeptics: Reflections on God* (Minneapolis: Fortress, 1995), 85–98.

18. Soelle refers often to the mystical tradition as one from which we can draw an alternative understanding of God and the human person in communion; see her *Strength of the Weak*, 86–90, 103–5. In her 1997 book on mysticism, *Mystik und Widerstand*, she shows the particular contributions of women to mysticism, such as Marguerite Porete, Hildegard of Bingen, Julian of Norwich, Hadewich of Brabant, Methtild of Magdeburg, and Teresa of Avila.

19. Harvey Cox, *The Secular City* (New York: Macmillan, 1965). See Dorothee Soelle, *Truth Is Concrete* (trans. Dinah Livingstone; London: Burns and Oates, 1969), 14.

20. Soelle's major book on creation is *To Work and to Love: A Theology of Creation*, with Shirley A. Cloyes (Philadelphia: Fortress, 1984).

21. Soelle's protests against this belittlement of the human in Protestant theology are found scattered throughout her writings. See, for example, *Creative Disobedience*, 30–40; and *To Work and to Love*, 7–8, 43–46.

22. Soelle's protests against both the religious and the secular forms of a psychology of helplessness before power are found in many places in her writings; see her *Strength of the Weak*, 95–96; *Of War and Love*, 97–98; and *Political Theology*, 89–91. For a fuller development of the ideology of the market economy as "natural law" and the impossibility of any alternative, with a theological critique, see Cynthia D. Moe-Lobeda, *Healing a Broken World: Globalization and God* (Minneapolis: Fortress, 2002).

23. Soelle's major essay on Christofascism is in *Window of Vulnerability*, 133–41; see also *To Work and to Love*, 165–67.

24. See Soelle, *To Work and to Love*, 46–47.

25. Soelle often analyzes what she sees as the "bourgeois" personality, closed to real relationships. See *Strength of the Weak*, 24–30; also *To Work and to Love*, 31-32.

26. See Soelle, *Creative Disobedience*, 7–22.

27. This was the slogan over the gates of Auschwitz. For Soelle's image of the world power system as a "Man-eating ogre," see *Of War and Love*, 3–4.

28. For Soelle's views of suffering, see her book *Suffering* (Philadelphia: Fortress, 1975), especially pages 61–86 and 121–50; also *Strength of the Weak*, 90–92; and *Thinking about God*, 54–67.

29. See Soelle, *Strength of the Weak*, 118–31.

30. For Soelle's theology of the church, see *Thinking about God*, 136–54, where she discusses it in terms of word, service, and community. She suggests that one can often better find these realities of church outside the institutional church, among peace and justice movements; see, for example, *Truth Is Concrete*, 101–9.

31. Soelle, *Theology for Skeptics*, 85–98.

32. On Soelle's theology of the cross, see *Suffering*, 9–32; also *Thinking about God*, 120–21; and *Theology for Skeptics*, 99–108.

33. For Soelle's understanding of the resurrection, see *Thinking about God*, 132–36; also *Truth Is Concrete*, 43–60; and *Strength of the Weak*, 71–76.

34. On the cross and the mandate for Christians to suffer, see Soelle, *Suffering*, 145–50 and 162–74.

35. On Soelle's critique of the immanence/transcendence dualism, see her *Theology for Skeptics*, 37–50; also *Thinking about God*, 189–95; and *To Work and to Love*, 13–14.

36. For Soelle's theology of redemption as fulfillment, see her *Creative Disobedience*, 41–48; also *Window of Vulnerability*, 12–22.

37. Soelle celebrates holistic sex as a part of redemption; see *To Work and to Love*, 115–40.

38. In her book on ecofeminist reflection on the Bible, Soelle draws out the connection between feminism and ecology that had been latent in her earlier defense of creation; see Dorothee Soelle, *On Earth as in Heaven* (Louisville: Westminster/John Knox, 1996).

14. Crossing Over
Dorothee Soelle and the Transcendence of God

Carter Heyward

Dorothee Soelle's most challenging and potentially transformative contribution to the social and religious histories of Western Europe and the Americas has been her insistence that God's transcendence is the depth and pervasiveness of God's immanence. For Soelle, it is not simply that a wholly other God makes himself [*sic*] immanent in Jesus Christ, but rather that God is not, and has never been, wholly other—never a deity above and beyond the world. The Christ-event, to borrow Rudolf Bultmann's existentialist term, is, for Soelle, a historical moment, both in time as we measure it and eternal (outside of human chronology). Christ is that moment, in our life together on earth, in which someone "represents" for us, and to us, what God is doing in history and what we humans are doing in history to the extent that we are loving our neighbors, our friends, and our enemies as we do ourselves.[1] Jesus, the brother from Nazareth, was such a "someone," and so, too, is each lover of God and the world. Hence, the God who was in Jesus Christ is the God who is always with us in the world, Christians and others alike, insofar as we love one another. This chapter explores the implications of Soelle's understanding of God—the radicality of her *theology*—for the Christian church, especially today, at the opening of a new century, in the most affluent countries of the West, which is much of Western Europe, Canada, and certainly the United States of America.

What would it mean for Christians in the North to love and worship the Spirit whom Dorothee Soelle experiences as God? How would our personal lives, loves, and work change? Moreover, how would the social fabric of our lives as nations, cultures, and world be transformed? Even now, what difference to our politics and social order does it make which "god" we worship? These are some of the questions that have been stirred among Western Christians by the theology of one of Europe's most important theologians.

An Introductory Question

I met Dorothee Soelle in 1976, shortly after the publication of my first book, which was about the "irregular" ordination in 1974 of women priests in the Episcopal Church, an event in which I had participated.[2] A close mutual friend, Beverly Harrison, had invited Dorothee and me to dinner because she knew we had a lot in common. All three of us were women fed up with the business as usual of both church and academy. Bev figured also that, as theologians, Dorothee and I would likely have some special shared interests. I had read *Christ the Representative,* Dorothee's first book translated into English, and Bev had loaned Dorothee my book.

Hardly had the door closed behind me and Bev managed to introduce us, when Dorothee Soelle put a question to me: "How can a woman who is seriously interested in justice also be interested in being ordained a priest?" This caught me almost speechless, but I managed to utter something like, "Well, that's a good question." And it was. It was also a question not forgotten, one that has helped navigate my professional commitments in large part because I have never been able to sit easily with the "fit" between a passion for justice and the priesthood of the Episcopal Church.

Even further reaching have been the implications of Dorothee's question for how she, I, and many other Christian feminist, womanist, and liberation theologians negotiate the tensions between our social and political commitments as women and men of faith, on the one hand, and our participation in organized religion, on the other. Soelle's question raised for me then and still does a significant incongruity between her understanding of God (Christ, church, world, and everything else) and the major doctrines professed by Protestant, Roman Catholic, and Orthodox churches.

Dorothee Soelle is not the only Christian whose experiences and understandings of God and all things sacred are a difficult fit with ecclesiastical indoctrination. There are millions of other Christians throughout the world living in tension with, and often outright opposition to, the official teachings of their churches. This is why Soelle is such an important resource for Christians at the turn of the twenty-first century. She provides a theological language that reflects the actual lived experiences of countless men, women, and children whose spiritualities and politics are trivialized or rejected by those who see themselves to be guardians of Christian orthodoxy. Hence, her question to me about my having been ordained a priest was not so much a question about my personal integrity (though this is always of some theological interest to Soelle) as it was a window into the heart of Dorothee Soelle's own spiritual struggle and theological interest: namely, the tension she herself has always experienced between God's ongoing presence with us in history and how the church historically has distanced God from us by objectifying "him" as an omnipotent Being essentially above and beyond us (an image of God, Soelle would assume, and I would agree, that is reflected in most understandings of the priesthood).

The difference between Dorothee's and my "locations" in relation to organized religion is that while I have spent much of my professional life working within the church, at least in part to help change it, Dorothee became indifferent to organized religion very early in her life and turned her attention to the larger world as an arena for theological work. Looking back now, I'd say that Dorothee's disengagement from organized religion freed her to become truly a liberation theologian for and among Christians in Europe and the Americas.

What I did not realize in 1976, of course, is that, in spite of our different relationships with the organized church, Dorothee Soelle would become one of my primary theological mentors as well as one of my dearest friends. I would discover that Soelle's experiences and understandings of God are often very close to my own. Again and again, the study of Soelle's work would sharpen, clarify, and sometimes challenge in wonderfully constructive ways my theological assumptions. My engagement with her theology would become a wellspring for my own life's work as a theologian and, I would hope, as a "feminist liberation priest." As mentor, friend, and sister theologian, Dorothee's politics and friendship, her love and work, have strengthened immeasurably for me the journey we have shared for close to thirty years.

Transcendence as "Crossing Over"

"Every theological statement has to be at the same time a political one."[3] In a sentence, Dorothee Soelle sums up the coinherence of politics and theology. These are different words, each with its own social and personal frame of reference, that point to the same lived human experience: "theology," "politics." There can be no separation between the theological statement and the political one, because the God to whom a theological statement refers is utterly immersed and involved in the human world of politics, where our sociality, our connectedness to one another, gets lived.

Experientially, it is in relation to one another that we find the God who is in the "crossing over"—or "transcendence"—that occurs between and among us.[4] Drawing on the philosophical dialectic of Hegel, and with Martin Buber,

Soelle's God is between and among us rather than either above and beyond our embodied social and personal experiences or simply within ourselves, our communities, societies, nations, etc.[5] In other words, God is with us, but not simply as a Spirit within us or as one to whom we lift up our hearts in prayer. God is the living, active, breathing dynamic of love that we experience in relation to one another—in enemy love as well as neighbor love—or God is not at all. This conviction underlies Dorothee Soelle's interest in the "death of God." Soelle wrestled with Nietzsche's conviction that any notion of "God" in an enlightened world is absurd. Moreover, her assessment of God's "death" occurred in the early 1960s, the same time the "death of God" theological movement was stirring interest among liberal Christian academics in the United States.

Like her North American counterparts, Soelle's perception of God's demise had roots in Bonhoeffer's insistence that God is not a *deus ex machina* but rather one that is hanging on the cross.[6] For Solle the theologian, like Bonhoeffer the political prisoner, every theological statement is inherently ethical, reflecting a standard by which we ought to be living together as groups and individuals. As Bonhoeffer had concluded late in his young life (he was martyred by the Nazis in 1945 at age thirty-nine) that only a suffering God can help us, Soelle reached the same conclusion early in her work as a public theologian, also in her thirties, that the notion of an omnipotent God is absurd. Such a God is truly dead.

To read Soelle as a theologian is to cross over into her political and ethical commitments and be challenged to transcend ourselves: not primarily to protect ourselves but rather to risk solidarity with the "other." Soelle is not talking about "feeling good" about others. She in fact is disdainful of what she sees to be the psychologizing preoccupation of the modern person who has been shaped by capitalism's individualism. Soelle is interested in what we do, not so much how we feel. She wants us to get down and grub with the God whom we meet not merely in, but moreover with, our friends and our enemies, those closest to us and those furthest away from us on many different levels. Soelle charges us to love one another by working for justice, struggling to create a world in which all persons are respected and valued. This, for Soelle, is what it means to love God. Otherwise, we are merely propping up an idol onto a pedestal and imagining that we are worshiping the God whom Jesus loved and, in a special way, embodied and represents to us. (This, of course, was the basis of her objection to the priesthood, which she views as a prop that holds an idol in place that is either destructive or irrelevant to the love of God).

From her earliest theological work, Soelle presents a number of tensions in which she finds God—and, in God's image, human life well lived, human life lived ethically—in the crossing over from ourselves to the well-being of others, a politic that reflects our involvement with the God who is in this crossing over, the one who is in fact the Spirit of this transcendence of self-interest. This essay will look at four of these tensions that tell us something about how, from the outset of her professional labors, Dorothee Soelle was thinking about God. Understanding how she saw God in these tensions, and what kind of God she saw, should suggest why, over the years, the organized church has not let its dogmatics get too close to Dorothee Soelle. As importantly, it may help us see more clearly why so many Christians, like Dorothee Soelle, have such a hard time with, and within, organized religion. It is because neither we nor Dorothee Soelle can swallow the "god" most commonly handed out to us by the guardians of Christian tradition. As the late public theologian Sister Corita Kent suggested in her artwork, God is for many Christians "a big Bayer aspirin." For Dorothee Soelle, to the contrary, God has always been more like a headache, pulsing through us, our lifeblood, connecting us to one another— and seldom without tension. Yet it is in these tensions, which characterize real life for real people, Soelle has always insisted, that God lives and breathes and brings us to life and joy, headaches and heartaches notwithstanding.

Crossing Over: Personal Identity and the (Social) Identity of God

A basic tension in Soelle's theology all the way through her work has been between her interest in "personal identity" and the more radically political, social praxis that provides the context for the self's more classically existential, and Soelle would add, bourgeois question of personal identity. From her first book *Christ the Representative* through her most recent *The Silent Cry,* spanning three decades, this tension has been foundational to Soelle's theological musings. *The Silent Cry,* subtitled *Mysticism and Resistance,* can be read as Soelle's attempt not to remove, or ease, the tension between self and society, individual and community, but rather to make peace with it. This she does by making a strong theological case for its inevitability due to the inextricability of self from society and therefore of the personal from the political. By the time she wrote *The Silent Cry,* Dorothee Soelle had recognized that she is not only a liberation theologian, she is also a mystic, a "crossing over" in her personal identity that we will explore later in this essay.

Earlier in her life, Soelle worked primarily as a philosophical theologian with strong social and political convictions. *Christ the Representative,* which she casts as "An Essay in Theology after the 'Death of God,'" is a product of the young philosopher's trying to explain theologically the redemptive workings of Christ. (By "Christ," Soelle always means both the historical figure Jesus of Nazareth and his ongoing and eternal christic—liberating, healing—presence.)

In this early book, Soelle chooses the concept of "identity" to help explain both our interest in Christ and who, she believes, this Christ was and is for us.

The 1960s was a period of social unrest in Western Europe as it was also in the United States. During this time, Soelle seemed fascinated with the question of how "personal identity" had become in the modern West an occupation of individual self-absorption, where in earlier European and North American periods, there had been less inclination or even ability to imagine oneself outside the context of community. Soelle's answer to her own question was that the industrial revolution in the Northern hemispheres, from the mid-nineteenth century into the twentieth, followed by the wars during the first two-thirds of the twentieth century, had left modern man [*sic*][7] feeling insecure, "interchangeable" and "replaceable" in her words. Soelle not only accepts this but moreover identifies with it in *Christ the Representative*. The modern person, overwhelmed by insecurity, wants to know who he or she is in the midst of a society that seems to have swallowed up the uniqueness of each individual. This existential crisis, the basis of Kierkegaard's struggle and later a driving force behind Bultmann, Tillich, and other existentialist theologians influenced by the early Frankfurt School, provided Soelle with a christological lens: How can Christ illuminate our questions of personal identity as we try to find out who in the world we are?

Because *Christ the Representative* is a philosophically dense book, the radicality of its theological implications can be missed—and are by any reader who imagines that Dorothee Soelle is simply recasting an orthodox Christology in which Christ is fully human and fully divine. For almost two millennia, churchleaders, especially Europeans, have insisted that Christians should not fall into believing that the essential differences between humanity and divinity were lost in Jesus Christ. In fact, Christian orthodoxy might be defined as a commitment to the otherness of God, a pledge implicit in conciliar creeds, a confession that people of faith should never confuse ourselves with God. It is *in tension with* this confession that Dororothee Soelle has worked as a theologian throughout her life.

Not that she is tempted to confuse herself, other humans, or our alienation from one another with God. Working self-consciously as a German appalled by the fascist evil unleashed in her homeland earlier in the twentieth century, Soelle is quick to condemn any groups inclined to make idols of themselves, their culture, race, gender, nation, or religion, people who cannot be self-critical. But she is just as critical of our even more pervasive tendency toward passivity in the face of social evil, a massive failure of moral nerve that she believes is a product of our *apatheia*, our "freedom from suffering or inability to suffer."[8]

It is this "Christian apathy," Soelle contends, that prevents our realizing how profoundly involved in the life of God we actually are—God in us, and we in

God. The spiritual fact of the matter, for Dorothee Soelle, is that our hands *are* God's hands in the world and our voices are the voices of God. This is not meant by Soelle to be interpreted merely as metaphor or simply as poetry, though as one of modern Christianity's most talented poets, Soelle herself is bound to realize that poetry, metaphor, simile, and other linguistic "representations" often point us as close as we can get, through words and images, to God.

One of the ways Soelle has been dismissed by those theologians who either do not understand her work or understand it very well and are upset by it is that she is "merely" a poet. What these critics fail to recognize is the extent to which it is precisely the poetic license that Dorothee Soelle brings to theology that enables her to speak of divine and human activity in ways that ring so deeply true to so many Christians who believe that "justice making" is not "merely" human work but is also the work of the Spirit.

What for many Christians is exciting about Soelle's theology, even in her early work, is that she is always speaking simultaneously of divine and human life in ways that challenge many of our experiences and understandings of both God and humankind. She is much less concerned that we will "confuse" God and humankind than that we will forget humankind and, thereby, God.

By the question of "personal identity," therefore, Soelle is not simply interested in the human quest for personal meaning that had intrigued Kirkegaard and so many of her liberal, bourgeois theological contemporaries. This human identity quest is a springboard for Soelle into questions about the identity of the God who is "represented" to us in the person and ongoing presence of Jesus Christ.

Rejecting what she interprets as the individualistic quests of many of the nineteenth-century theologians who found God "inside" themselves and other people, Soelle works theologically as a Marxist and, on the basis of Hegel's dialectic, proceeds to explore "identity" as an experience of ourselves that is taking shape in the context of a society in which we are whoever we are in relation to everyone else. No one stands alone. Our personal identities are social, historical consequences, having everything to do with our work, our love, and our interdependencies as persons in relation.

Moreover, Soelle insists, the relational crucible of identity is true not only for humans but also for God. In the modern period of industrial advancement and sophisticated machineries of work and communication, Soelle suggests that the identities of both humanity and divinity are threatened by dynamics that are rendering as obsolete our understandings of either ourselves or God as in any basic sense "autonomous" and "independent." In this historical and social context, "Christ," for Dorothee Soelle, "is not only our representative before God, he likewise is God's representative among [us]."[9] To be identified as a representative is to be standing for one who is absent and irreplaceable, yet representable and able to be mediated. Soelle is probably wrestling here with her own experience of the absence of the omnipotent God in whom she as a liberal Christian, or at least her ancestors, had once believed, as well as her own personal experience of "absence" in relation to such a God, an experience she assumes is shared by other liberal and radical Christians.

The point here, however, is not whether Soelle is projecting an accurate psychological view of her own and others' personal experiences of themselves and God in the modern world. The point is that Soelle understands, and presents, personal identity—whether human or divine—as a relational category and not an individual attribute. There is no such thing as simply an individual, no autonomous being, neither human nor divine. God and humanity, every human group and every human person, is interdependent—and thereby able to be represented to one another by someone who is able to stand in for each of us, God and humanity (collectively and each person), in relation to each other and to all others. This someone, Dorothee Soelle suggests, is Christ, someone who represents an absent God to a post-theistic world, and who also represents us, in the fullness of our human yearnings and activities, to a God who is in fact living but for the most part hidden to us.[10] Not that God intends to hide from us, but rather that we are so distracted by modernism's gimmicks—such as the illusion that we are, or should be, autonomous individuals—that we cannot find God.

"Christ is not a replacement for the dead God. He is the representative of the living God, of the God who like man [sic] is irreplaceable yet representable."[11] Soelle continues, "For God has not yet declared himself [sic] fully within the world, nor handed over his cause in such a way that he has become superfluous. *Identity is still to come.* Otherwise Christ merely replaced the dead God of the past. In fact, Jesus of Nazareth has kept the future open for God by 'running ahead of him,' and this is precisely Christ's function right down to the present—to be God's forerunner."[12]

Not only does "identity," for Soelle, not refer to the individual self; it also does not refer to a fixed state of being. Identity is not static. It is being formed. Identity—God's identity and our own—is still to come. Although Soelle does not identify herself as a "process theologian" and thereby as a beneficiary of the philosophical tradition of Alfred North Whitehead, her understanding of God has much kinship with process theology. Even in this early philosophical essay, Soelle's God is transcending, or crossing over: from omnipotence to weakness, from presence to absence, from the "identity" of being known as God to the "nonidentity" of being unrecognized and unknown—absent from traditional Christian understandings of "God." Indeed, the traditional God, our "father above in a starry sky," is dead. His omnipotent "identity" is no longer meaningful. Because of Christ, we can "regard [God's] absence as a possible mode of his being-for-us."[13]

Thus, for Dorothee Soelle in the mid-1960s, God's identity is being re-formed for us through Jesus' experiences of neighbor love, including enemy love, and suffering, poverty, and other forms of weakness on the material plane. What we thought we knew about God's identity, and our own as people of God, is crossing over into something startlingly different than what we assumed. And neither God's identity nor our own, as human beings, can be clear to us in this historical moment, because who God is for us today, and who we can be as people of God, remains at least partly hidden. These were some of Dorothee Soelle's assumptions forty years ago, as she wrestled philosophically with the question of our personal identity as people of God in what Bonhoeffer, twenty years earlier, had named a "world come of age."[14]

Crossing Over: Creativity and Liberation

Like most other creative theologians, Soelle's theology cannot be read very systematically, as if God and the world are moving along a linear time line that began once upon a time at creation and will end someday when we are liberated fully into the realm of God. Following her presentation of a philosophical Christology in *Christ the Representative,* Dorothee Soelle turned to the question of how we are to live together in this modern world in which there is no God Almighty to tell us what to do. In the mid-1960s, she had chosen a popular concept—"identity"—to examine our relationship with an absent God. Several years later she chose "obedience," another timely concept of interest to contemporary Western Christians, to explore a foundation of Christian ethics. In the early 1970s, Soelle's first book specifically on ethics was published in English as *Beyond Mere Obedience.* More than twenty years later, the book was published again in English under a new title, *Creative Disobedience,* and with a new preface by the author in which she states the questions that sparked it in the first place and that continue to bear down on us: "What does it mean to be a Christian in these times? Is it the tradition of obedience or the tradition of resistance we are choosing? Is there anything that goes beyond mere obedience in the Christian faith?"[15]

Her answer is a resounding yes! In fact, Soelle offers a stinging rebuke and rejection of obedience as a basis of Christian life. Like Frederick D. Maurice, the nineteenth-century Anglican proponent of justice work as Christian work, Soelle insists that obedience has no good place in the moral lexicon of women and men who genuinely love God and the world. "Why do people worship a God whose supreme quality is power, not justice; whose interest lies in subjection, not mutuality; who fears equality?" she asks her reader. Soelle's critique of the cherished Christian notion of obedience is thoroughgoing and definitive. In place of obedience, she offers a concept better understood perhaps in its

German rendering—*Phantasie*—than in its translation as "imagination." For Dorothee Soelle, "phantasy" (an English word coined by her translators) is intended to convey the joining of imagination with a sense of personal freedom and passion for God. "[It] is a form of freedom which anyone can achieve during her lifetime. It comes into being like every other virtue as the result of our encounter with the world." And she continues, "Phantasy bursts all boundaries" when it comes to letting ourselves imagine what is possible in the realm of that justice which is neighbor love.[16]

In her critique of obedience and search for an alternative basis for Christian ethics, Soelle is writing quite consciously out of her German heritage and her religious upbringing in the reformed tradition. Both are for her contexts of shame. Here, as throughout her theological work, the Holocaust looms as backdrop not only of the evil unleashed by the Nazis but also of the Christian church's failure, in the main, to prevent it. Dorothee Soelle is ashamed to be German—and, in the historical context of a feckless church, she is ashamed to be Christian as well. And lest her non-German readers think for a second that this shame belongs, or should belong, to Germany alone, Soelle is clear that, especially in the latter part of the twentieth century, other nations—especially the United States—share the blame for the great social, and increasingly global, evils of oppression, genocide, and the unfettered greed of advanced capitalism.

Moreover, having written *Beyond Mere Obedience* in the late 1960s, Soelle acknowledges retrospectively, in the 1995 preface to its republication, that her rejection of obedience as a Christian virtue had roots also in her having been a "hidden feminist," a woman whose gender consciousness would be raised largely through her relationships with colleagues and students at Union Seminary in the 1970s and 1980s. In conversation with Dorothee several years after the 1995 publication of *Creative Disobedience*, she told me she had learned from her feminist friends that "the patriarchal God is too small. He lacks transcendence. He cannot be simply 'I am.' She is also 'I will be who I will be,' a God who knows that autonomy is no virtue, and neither is obedience."[17]

What is most theologically challenging, and interesting to me, about Solle's work on obedience is that she winds up employing a quality usually associated with creativity—phantasy or imagination—as a foundational moral basis for the social, economic, and political work of liberation. Soelle is able to do this because she does not think systematically, in a linear or hierarchical fashion. Her mind does not plod from past to present to future, nor grow from smaller to larger, nor move in a direct line from self to society. Creation does not come "first" and liberation "last" in the realm of God. The person does not precede society. For Soelle, everything is here and now together in God.

Though a relentless critic of existentialism's individualism, she is herself existential, concerned with the immediacy of the present and our significance, here and now, in relation to those pasts and futures that are connected to what we are doing, and who we are, in our present time and place.[18] There is, for Soelle (as for Tillich, Bultmann, and other existential theologians), in every creative act also a liberating significance and vice versa. For Soelle, increasingly, this is not so much an interesting philosophical or even simply theological tenet, but more importantly a compelling spiritual truth. In her later work, she would begin to use the word *mystic* as a way of exploring the coinherence of what may appear to be different forces and the multiple, overlapping meanings of various personal, historical, political, and social events and processes. So just as obedience is a source of terrible theology, bad child psychology, and horrible politics within and beyond the church, so, too, is phantasy a root of a spirituality of liberation that has many meanings for how we relate to children and other adults, both those closest to us and those far away, as individuals and in groups.

Soelle's understanding of imagination cannot be understood merely in personal or interpersonal terms as primarily psychological work—though it may have this component. For Soelle, like Martin Buber, morality is an essentially social and therefore political process of struggling for right relation, an ongoing movement in which divine creativity and the liberating work of the Spirit are one and the same sacred process.[19]

Though as someone always interested in Christology, I had found *Christ the Representative* challenging and instructive when I read it in the mid-1970s. My reading of *Beyond Mere Obedience* a month or so later—like Dorothee's and my first meeting at Beverly Harrison's house—would be for me one of many creative, liberating encounters with Dorothee Soelle. Whereas in the former book Soelle had become one of my theological teachers, in the latter she became a spiritual soul mate, theological companion, and political ally. I would catch a glimpse in this book of what has become brilliantly evident through the years: that everything Dorothee Soelle says about God's acting in history she also affirms about our human possibilities as historical actors, persons born into the world in order to help change it—to participate with and through God in the ongoing creation, liberation, and blessing of the world. Furthermore, everything Soelle says about us at our best, she affirms also about God.

Jesus, whose phantasy she cherishes, and Christ "the representataive" are, for Dorothee Soelle, two images of the same historical person and eternal Spirit. And this Jesus Christ does indeed represent both God and humankind, simultaneously. Parting company with Christian orthodoxy, however, Soelle would insist that Jesus Christ does not represent God by being omnipotent, omniscient, without sin, etc., nor does Jesus represent human beings by being limited, vulnerable, etc. For Dorothee Soelle, there is no omnipotent God. No God Almighty. No Father above it all.[20] The one and only God of the universe, who is represented by Jesus, is vulnerable and limited in what she or he can do in the world and still be a loving God. For Soelle, God cannot be both loving and almighty in this world. God is like us—we truly are in her image—able to love only through our vulnerability and able thereby to embody a sacred power that is completely countercultural to the dominant social and political forces that rule the world. Thus, Jesus Christ is divine as well as human precisely in representing our vulnerability to suffering and, in solidarity with one another, our willingness to pick up our crosses and follow. This moves us into the central realm of transcendence in Soelle's theology.

Crossing Over: Suffering and Acceptance

By the early 1970s, Soelle had been shaken at her spiritual and political core by the Vietnam War, which she understood as primarily an "American" (United States) assault against the people of Vietnam. Dorothee Soelle did not understand this as a war of liberation. Like many of us in the United States and elsewhere, Soelle interpreted "Vietnam" not really as a struggle against world domination by Communists but more truthfully—in the actual context of military strength and economic power—as a struggle *toward* world domination by the United States of America. In her introduction to *Suffering*, published in German in 1973, she states, "I am writing out of the bitterness of those who, in the midst of new American bombing and demonstrations against it, ask themselves, 'Why isn't our outcry doing any good? What's the use of protesting?'" And she continues, "Why [can't] we show Christians who go to church every Sunday where it is that the crucifixion is happening today?"[21] By the time I met Dorothee in New York, the last U.S. soldiers had been emergency air-lifted out of Saigon in 1975, signaling the United States' defeat by the North Vietnamese, an outcome doubtlessly the result, in no small part, of the demonstrations, outcries, and prayers of people like Dorothee Soelle against the Vietnam War. The ending of this war would be one of few apparent victories for peace movements around the world during the last half of the twentieth century.

Beginning in the early 1970s—signaled by her work in *Suffering*—Dorothee Soelle would turn her attention, as a theologian, explicitly to justice work and peace work at home and abroad. Her theological rubric for understanding divine and human life and activity in this social and political context would be "suffering." Soelle would become one of the earliest, and remain one of few, European and North American white Christian theologians for whom not only human suffering but also God's is synonymous with God's own being in history. For Soelle, suffering is, in Paul Tillich's words, our Ground of Being.

But it is not "suffering" simply in the sense of experiencing pain that is most compelling to Soelle. She understands human (and divine) openness, or vulnerability, to suffering as the opposite of human and divine "apathy" (from the Greek *apatheia,* which means "nonsuffering"). It is Christian apathy—in relation to the Holocaust, Vietnam, and other evil events and processes in history—that is most appalling to this woman in her work as a Christian theologian in the late twentieth century.[22] She views apathy as a defense mechanism for people who experience ourselves primarily as individuals; and she understands our attachment to individualism as a product—and necessity—of advanced capitalism.

It is, to me, a sign of Dorothee Soelle's integrity as a theologian that she always seems to be thinking and writing herself theologically toward new arenas, or deeper levels, of activity on behalf of God and humanity, as she understands them. *Suffering* is no exception. While this particular book was born in Soelle's anger and despair about Vietnam, by the time it was published in the United States and began to be read outside of Germany, the focus of much of the most radical Christian activism in the United States and Europe had shifted to (primarily white) women's struggles for justice and also to the popular struggles for liberation from economic and political oppression in Latin America. Over the next thirty years, Soelle would be touched and transformed by feminist and Latin American liberation theological movements. For her and many other Christian women in the United States and Europe, these two theological movements shared a view of the vulnerability and suffering of humans in God's image—and of God in human image.

Interestingly, from her earliest encounters with Christian feminists in the United States and Europe, Dorothee's relationship with many Christian feminists has been mutually challenging. The role of suffering in Christian life seems to me to have been pivotal to these debates. While almost all Christian feminists, like Dorothee Soelle, recognize the centrality of suffering to human and divine life, many Christian feminists (myself included until I stopped numbing myself with alcohol some years back) have balked at "accepting" suffering as, in any sense, creative or liberating for ourselves or anyone else. Many Christian feminists, in this way, have confused "acceptance" with "resignation."[23] For Soelle there has not been this confusion.

Like other feminists, Soelle rejects what she terms "Christian masochism" and its corollary, "Christian sadism."[24] This she does for much the same reason she has rejected "obedience" as a Christian virtue—as attitudes that reflect authoritarianism, a lack of mutuality, cruelty, stupidity, and usually violent relationships. But Soelle sees the "acceptance" of suffering as a very different moral quality. For her, the acceptance of suffering is essential to the struggle for liberation from suffering. Her understanding of suffering and its acceptance is not unlike that of many Buddhists and also of participants in Alcoholics Anonymous and other "Twelve Step" programs, in which the acceptance of suffering is decidedly *not* the psychological end of the matter. Acceptance is rather a person's recognition of reality that empowers her to deal with it—including joining the struggle against it! There is all the difference in the world, for Dorothee Soelle, between acceptance of suffering and resignation to it.

Here, too, we see how Soelle is imaging transcendence—God is the Spirit of transformation crossing over among us. She is deeply involved in questions of personal identity and social responsibility. He is our wellspring of creativity and the constant source of our liberation. God is not only with us in our suffering—she herself is suffering. God is not only with us in our acceptance of this suffering—he accepts his own suffering. God is not only with us in our revolutionary movements of resistance, nonviolence, and liberation from suffering. She is our revolutionary Spirit, our liberator, our God, the one who is ever crossing over among us, from generation to generation, culture to culture, creatively weaving our tapestries of liberation, even as we, by her help, are giving birth to Jesus Christ again and again, bringing hope into the world.

Crossing Over: Mysticism and Resistance

It has been almost thirty years since Dorothee Soelle wrote *Suffering.* Since then she has written at least fifteen books that have been translated into English (in one or two cases, written in English). During this period, her theological work has consistently reflected her passion for justice and peace and her solidarity with those who struggle toward these divine goals and ours as well, when we are most fully embodying the Spirit of God. Everything she has written over the decades has been generated by her engagement with brothers and sisters in the struggle for bread and justice in Nicaragua, Guatemala, Chile, Cuba, and elsewhere in Latin America especially, as well as among peace activists in Europe and the Americas.

As Dorothee Soelle has become more deeply involved in these radical social movements, her theology has become increasingly narrative and poetic, reflecting her experiences of a God who lives and dies, laughs and cries among us— and who can best, maybe only, be imaged creatively through story and poetry. Increasingly over the years, Dorothee has been impatient with dispassionate theology, church dogmatics, and individualism as a component of "capitalist spirituality," a term coined by her colleague and friend Beverly Harrison.[25] As Soelle's theological work has become more narrative and poetic, God has become for her much less hidden. For Soelle, God has become over the last three decades increasingly apparent in the everyday work, poetry, music, and stories of the people who struggle for bread and justice.

When Dorothee was in her sixties, she became critically ill, and for about a month she lay near death. I was snowed in at a faculty retreat in suburban Boston when a phone call from Germany came to Bev Harrison and me from her husband Fulbert Steffensky, telling us that Dorothee had fallen into a coma and asking for our prayers and those of their other colleagues and friends here in the United States. To our great joy, after weeks of uncertainty, Dorothee pulled out of the coma. She began her new lease on life with the writing and publication of *The Silent Cry: Mysticism and Resistance,* the book she considers to be her most important, because in its pages she draws together theologically her life's work—her single passion, that is, for God and justice. All of the themes raised much earlier in her professional life—themes like identity, obedience, and suffering—would be illuminated (perhaps as much for her as for the rest of us, her readers) as she locates roots of her passion for justice in the mystical traditions of both East and West. As always, here, too, Soelle is a critical thinker. She does not accept "mysticism" as an inward journey taken by and on behalf of the self. The mystical journey "leads into a healing that is at the same time resistance."[26] The journey begins with our amazement, intimations of creativity and compassion that we touch together. Drawing from insights of Meister Eckhart and her own contemporary Matthew Fox, Soelle rejects the Neo-Platonic asceticism that begins with the fall of humans from paradise. She is attracted by Fox's image of "original blessing," rather than "original sin," as the origin of our yearning for God.[27]

Soelle, however, pushes further than either Matthew Fox or most other contemporary Christian mystics for whom the vision of God is awesome and, thereby, healing. For Dorothee Soelle, "it is not enough to describe this amazement as an experience of bliss alone. Amazement also has its bleak side of terror and hopelessness that renders one mute."[28] This may be a point at which Soelle's tensions with some of her sister feminists was located earlier in her life, which makes it a little disappointing that she doesn't seem to recognize in her most recent work how close to her own work on mysticism and resistance some other Christian feminists are today.[29]

Because she has always been a mystic, long before she realized it, Soelle sees more clearly than most Christians not only the inevitability of suffering if we are involved in God's Spirit but, moreover, the creative character of this "terror and hopelessness" that "render us mute." Soelle knows, sees, and believes that the creative spiritual journey does indeed involve a "letting go"—especially, she contends, of "our growing dependency on consumerisms." To be truly involved in the work of liberation, Christians must undergo a "purification," a *via negativa,* in which we let go of "possessions, violence, and ego."[30] Only in this way can we sustain the energy and movement to be agents of social transformation.

Only in this way can the mystic really be a resister with staying power and vision. And only in this way, amazed and terrorized, missing God and praising God, is the resister a mystic with faith in a living Spirit rather than a dead tradition. Soelle is planting theological seeds here for a Christian life that transcends popular understandings of both "spirituality" and "politics"—and that transcends most Christian understandings of both divine and human life.

The Silent Cry is an expression of a stunning theology of social change and personal transformation that go hand in hand or not at all. Through its pages, Dorothee Soelle emerges, more vividly than ever, as a theologian of radical coinherence of God and humankind, and moreover a theologian who is stretching as she goes to show how the rest of creation—the other-than-human-creatures—are involved no less than humans with, and in, the sacred Spirit.

Given her special interests in nonviolence and ecology, which are spelled out in *The Silent Cry,* and in the context of the global crisis exacerbated so terribly by September 11, 2001, and its aftermath, we can only imagine how far reaching Dorothee Soelle's spirituality might be when we next meet her. In the meantime, I can thank her for asking me that question so many years ago, "Why would anyone seriously interested in justice want to be a priest?" I have never cared much about the priesthood or the institutional church except as means of helping build the realm of God which is the realm of justice-love, justice and compassion, justice and peace on earth, justice as the well-being of all creatures and creation. With Dorothee, I am confident that every human being—every priest and painter, pastor and plumber, prophet and poet, politician and parent, every person of every sexual, cultural, and religious persuasion—is put here to participate in the building of that sacred realm. No wordsmith in the Western world, anywhere or anytime, has worked more beautifully on behalf of this vision than Dorothee Soelle.

Notes

1. Dorothee Soelle, *Christ the Representative: An Essay in Theology after 'The Death of God'* (London: SCM, 1967); trans. of *Stellvertretung—Ein Kapitel Theologie nach dem 'Tode Gottes'* (Stuttgart: Kreuz Verlag, 1965).

2. Carter Heyward, *A Priest Forever* 2d ed.; (Cleveland: Pilgrim, 1999). In the new foreword to this book, I respond to Dorothee's concerns.

3. Dorothee Soelle, *Against the Wind: Memoir of a Radical Christian* (Minneapolis: Fortress, 1999), 38; trans. of *Gegenwind: Erinnerungen* (Hamburg: Hoffmann und Campe Verlag, 1995).

4. See my essay "Crossing Over: On Transcendence," in Carter Heyward, *Our Passion for Justice: Images of Power, Sexuality, and Liberation* (Cleveland: Pilgrim, 1984), 243–47.

5. Martin Buber, *I and Thou* (trans. Ronald Gregor Smith; New York: Macmillan, 1958).

6. Dietrich Bonhoeffer, *Letters and Papers from Prison* (ed. Eberhard Bethge; New York: Macmillan, 1972), 361.

7. Soelle's use of masculine pronouns for humankind and God doesn't give way to more inclusive language, in German and English, until her later work (early to mid-1980s on), especially after teaching at Union Theological Seminary in New York where feminist theology was being born among women faculty and student colleagues in the 1970s and 1980s.

8. Dorothee Soelle, *Suffering* (trans. Everett R. Kalin; Philadelphia: Fortress, 1975), 36. "Apathy is a form of the inability to suffer. It is understood as a social condition in which people are so dominated by the goal of avoiding suffering that it becomes a goal to avoid human relationships and contacts altogether."

9. Soelle, *Christ the Representative,* 130.

10. Ibid., 131.

11. Ibid., 134.

12. Ibid., 134 (emphasis added).

13. Ibid., 131.

14. Bonhoeffer, *Letters and Papers from Prison,* 362.

15. Dorothee Soelle, *Creative Disobedience* (trans. Lawrence W. Denef; Cleveland: Pilgrim, 1995). Translation of *Phantasie und Gehorsam: Uberlegungen zu einer kunftigen christlichen Ethik* (Stuttgart: Kreuz Verlag, 1968), xxi.

16. Ibid., 51.

17. Dorothee Soelle in conversation with the author, Boldern Evangelische Academie, near Zurich, September 1999.

18. See, for example, her critique of Bultmann in *Political Theology* (trans. John Shelley; Philadelphia: Fortress, 1974); trans. of *Politische Theologie, Auseinandersetzung mit Rudolf Bultmann* (Stuttgart: Kreuz Verlag, 1971).

19. This is the basis of Dorothee Soelle's and my theological kinship. See her introductions to the German edition of my book *Und Sie Ruhrte Ihr Kleid An* (Stuttgart: Kreuz Verlag, 1985); trans. of *The Redemption of God: A Theology of Mutual Relation* (Lanham, Md.: University Press of America, 1982), and to the forthcoming German publication of my more recent *Saving Jesus from Those Who Are Right: Rethinking What It Means to Be Christian* (Minneapolis: Fortress, 1999); also her essay "Mutuality," in *Against the Wind,* 96–97.

20. Whether or not such a God ever was is not clear in Soelle's early work; if he ever "was," he "died," victim of modernism. In her later work, especially as she is increasingly influenced by feminist and Latin American liberation theologies during the 1980s and 1990s, Soelle becomes clear and emphatic that an omnipotent (almighty) God *cannot* be also a loving God in relation to the world.

21. Soelle, *Suffering,* 3.

22. God only knows how Dorothee is responding to current events, in 2002, in Europe, the United States, and elsewhere, given the United States' superviolent reaction to September 11, 2001, and all that has followed.

23. This is, for example, how I interpret the "boundary" preoccupation among many Christian feminist pastors, theologians, and teachers—as a struggle not against suffering per se but against the complexity of human social relations that often cause or involve suffering. It has seemed to me that we cannot wage a successful struggle against human suffering as long we are fighting against the complexity of how our bonds are formed and sustained in the real world. I think this is an arena in which many Christian feminists have confused acceptance with resignation. I don't think we Christian feminists, or anyone else, are as likely to get bogged down in this confusion when we are dealing with the larger questions of, for example, how global capitalism is destroying life. Ironically, it is often when the stakes are

enormous that it is easier not to confuse acceptance with resignation. On the larger stage, especially during the 1990s (after the Berlin Wall came down) and now, at the outset of the 2000s (after September 11), we are increasingly compelled to accept the realities we are facing—capitalism, terrorisms of many kinds, violence, suffering indeed—and only then to begin to look for ways together of making a creative difference in our communities and world. These are the kinds of commendable efforts we're witnessing now among anti-globalization forces, environmentalists, and peace builders.

24. Soelle, *Suffering,* 9–32.

25. In her lectures and conversation, Christian feminist ethicist Beverly Wildung Harrison often discusses "capitalist spirituality." This is one of many points of passionate agreement between Harrison and Soelle.

26. Dorothee Soelle, *The Silent Cry: Mysticism and Resistance* (trans. Barbara and Martin Rumscheit; Minneapolis: Fortress, 2001); trans. of *Mystik und Widerstand: "Du stilles Geschrei"* (Hamburg: Hoffmann and Campe Verlag, 1967), 93.

27. Ibid., 88ff.

28. Ibid., 90.

29. A Christian feminist theologian who has written extensively on the connection between mysticism and justice, especially among women, is Grace M. Jantzen in *Power, Gender, and Christian Mysticism* (Cambridge: Cambridge University Press, 1995).

30. Soelle, *Silent Cry,* 92–93.

15. Dorothee Soelle as Pioneering Postmodernist

Beverly Wildung Harrison

Introduction: The Roots of Soelle's Political Theology

Nearly fifty years ago, H. Richard Niebuhr, probably the Christian theologian most admired by peers in the United States during his lifetime and in the decades that followed, assessed his work in the *Christian Century* series "How My Mind Has Changed."[1] Musing on what perhaps he could have done differently, he observed that he might well have chosen to travel more with the poets than with the philosophers. To my knowledge, no academic theologian has ever inquired as to what difference it might have made had Niebuhr, in fact, followed this intimation of an alternative path to a theological voice. Nor have I read any serious discussion of how such a methodological move might have affected the subsequent doing of theology within the confines of the American academy.

Ironically, since the era of the two Niebuhrs, it is difficult to name a Christian male academic theologian in this country who actually has joined the poets in actively reimaging the contemporary meaning of Christian faith. To some extent, the ever more insular character of male-generated Protestant and Catholic theology in the United States during the second half of the twentieth century is foreshadowed in the reluctance of male theologians to seriously engage the possibility of genres of theological speech that embrace the creative and re-creative dimensions of spiritual knowing. Since the late-1960s, the voices

239

of most established theologians have been directed at asking whether and for whom theological reflection can be done. In fact, it may be said that if the work of those holding theological professorships in divinity schools is taken as the measure, Christian theology in the United States could be said to be much talked about but little done by professionals!

Most theological tomes written by university-based theological professors in the latter half of the century addressed questions of what if any justifications for theological discourse exist, whether there really are legitimate forms of theological utterance or any discursive substance to Christian theology. Methodological preoccupations have been the center of university-based discourses, and some have claimed that constructive statements as to what the meaning of the Christian theological message in our time and place might be are possible. However, the truth is that in the corridors of institutions where professional theologians were being shaped, little reinterpretation emerged and practicing Christians ignored professional theology done in academy. By the last decades of the century, practitioners of Christian theology seemed even to abandon dialogues with the philosophers, and few teaching in university-based institutions hazarded fresh ways of speaking of faith or conjuring its practice. Slowly but surely, attention turned to reiterating teaching familiar and comforting to the already convicted and ecclesially loyal Christian, and interest in public impact of any sort was lost.

All of this took place at a historical moment when, for many within the academy, Christian faith claims were losing plausibility and becoming increasingly suspect on epistemic grounds. Frequently, the well educated, including those raised in liberal Christian traditions, ceased the practice of Christianity, and within the churches, denominational piety became increasingly cut off from public culture. As the churches became more privatized, the focus within that public world shifted toward a culture-wide preoccupation with enhancing human material existence. Ardor for constructing a post-World War II liberal society came to the center of political and economic life. H. Richard Niebuhr's musings notwithstanding, what Martin Rumscheidt describes in this volume as theo-poetics did not emerge among male academic theologians. That methodological development had to await the advent of the powerful theo-poetics of the woman whom Rumscheidt elegantly celebrates here.

It is not too much to say that Dorothee Soelle was the earliest and most distinctive reconstructive voice to emerge in an era in which European culture began to experience a profound sense of displacement and cultural decentering. As the twentieth century entered its sixth decade and debates over the "death of God" were taking shape in Europe and the North American context, Soelle emerged as the first of what would become a panoply of new liberationist voices. As a European voice, she acknowledged the huge cultural shift that these discussions about God talk signaled, but she used this cultural rupture to reimage and restate the meaning of Christ for our time, thereby proposing a fresh conception of the theological task in a world in which traditionalist theism had become problematic for some very legitimate reasons.

Few have recognized the significance of Soelle's work methodologically, especially her pioneering reconception of the way theology must now be done in this deeply changed world, one where no single cultural episteme can serve to ground truths that can be abstracted from specific histories and cultures. Making a profound theological shift, Soelle voiced Christian memory and hope in concrete and nonimperialistic terms. Christian theology in the present moment can profit by revisiting her theoretical assumptions because she found ways of affirming wisdom out of Christian tradition, not by treating tradition as fixed and established treasure, but rather as memory of origin and awareness of human vocation, on the one hand, and as source of an indestructible dream of possibilities not yet realized, on the other. What Soelle did parallels exactly what the Jewish lesbian feminist poet Adrienne Rich has described as the role spiritual tradition plays in orienting us to the source of our strength and the direction in which we elect to move into the future. The similarity between Soelle's moves and the manner specified by Rich for reclaiming her own religious tradition should not surprise us, for Rich, one of the greatest poets of the American cultural tradition, embraced the power of poetic imagination as a challenge to imperial and dominant modes of patriotism. In Rich's words, spiritual identity enables awareness of "from whence our strength comes" and "with whom our lot is cast."[2] But of course, for Soelle, to find her way to a form of liberative religious speech was far more difficult than for Rich, because for Soelle, the powerful history of the Christian-legitimated triumphalism of German Christianity had intervened. For her, any reclaiming of Christian ways of speaking could have integrity only after a blunt facing of ongoing Christian complicity in evil and a radical reorientation of one's current political practice as a clear evidence of genuine repentance. Among German political theologians, Soelle was singularly insistent in demanding a new form of ecclesial practice. The "political night prayer" movement, which she helped to found and continuously participated in, was testimony that a different practice was a nonnegotiable condition of truthful religious speech. Theology that conjures hope when there is no hope, positive aspiration when that is called for, and steely critique and resistance to "what is" when that is what is needed, is possible only as part of an active public practice of resistance.

Soelle was, then, the first of many to give voice to a genuinely praxis-oriented theology, what she called Christian "*Phantasie.*" But *Phantasie* for her is not merely an imaginative act but rather a fully political and publicly engaged way to live one's life. That what the latter affirmed turned out to be very much akin to the way Rich later reenvisaged the meaning of Jewish tradition as she reembraced it as her own living spirituality should not surprise us. Both of these superb poets place a biblical moral tradition of right relationship and "justice making" at the center of what any memory of origin requires. And both stand in adamant opposition to all established power that resists inclusive visions of justice.

The constructive Christian theology done in the late twentieth century by Soelle, other radical feminists, or other liberation theologians was authored by those whose spiritual concerns stand in deep variance to traditional ones, and whose interests are not focused on the justificatory preoccupations so central to theology done for the churches or within the academy. Soelle's books were sold not to professional peers but to an educated and politically concerned lay readership. Hers was a public theological voice, perhaps the first genuinely public theologian in the postmodern era.

My colleague at Union, Professor Christopher Morse, once remarked, after a research trip to Germany, that he had heard a young German graduate student say that he and his peers read Soelle for the same reason that earlier young Germans had read Martin Luther. Like Luther, this student remarked, Soelle was reshaping German language and culture even as she spoke. Her small books were found not only in academic bookstores but wherever a reading public shopped. How unlike her male theological contemporaries!

What is noteworthy is that the movement of Christian theology into this work of *Phantasie,* or what some others called utopic envisagement, would not have occurred without a deep discontent with the way the various Christian traditions had been articulating contemporary theological claims. It was their varied rejection of established theological norms that won a fresh hearing for liberative theologies, including the German movement of "political theology" with which Soelle is associated and in which she stands out in terms of cultural impact.[3] Within conventional theological institutions, the lack of excitement I have already alluded to was fed by the fact that those in charge were deeply aligned with the directions in which dominant social, political, and cultural life was moving. By contrast, Soelle's work was distinctive in the lucidity of its articulation of the dangers of the established religious landscape.

Soelle's Impact on My Own Work

I remember very clearly the impact of Soelle's early work on me. It may be difficult for contemporary readers to imagine the scene as the 1950s receded and to sense the despair that began to pervade professional theological faculties at the time. The immediate postwar period had been a time of heady optimism for liberal Protestantism, then widely celebrated as contributing wisdom to the public culture that had made the "good war" against fascism successful. Faced in the 1960s with sudden awareness that all was not well in Protestantism, and that something like a collective depression had descended, I picked up Soelle's work more out of curiosity than expectation. I was astonished at the fresh energy that reading her evoked. It is not too much to say that it rekindled anew my own intellectual pilgrimage. Having only recently committed to traveling the path of professional theology, I felt both relief and elation when I read, and then reread, both *Christ the Representative* and *Political Theology*.

Truth to tell, my decision two years earlier to concentrate my work in Christian ethics, rather than on what we at Union Seminary call systematic theology, had been made self-consciously out of a growing sense that the entire theological project was in crisis. By the end of my first year of graduate study, it had become clear to me that the theological guild I had expected to join was in very deep trouble indeed. Listening to ongoing discussions of a number of books on the "death of God" made me aware of the deep defensiveness, even resentment, toward critical challenge felt by academic theologians, including a number of my own teachers and their peers in sister institutions. Sensing the urgent need for new critical perspectives, I embraced social ethics and opted to give priority to ongoing social analysis, thereby shifting the focus of my work away from theology as such. My own interest in critical social analysis, I realized, would enable me to address living social ills in ways that would not depend on the persuasiveness of particular theological claims about God talk. It became ever more obvious to me that the need to address the tangible and growing social suffering and growing social problems deserved priority. My own vocation to the continuing moral formation of communities that called themselves Christian was work that had to be done, whatever happened within Christian theology.

It was reading Soelle, then, that restored my confidence that there was a constructive role for Christian God talk in the present. There was, I realized, a vital function for Christian theology in the deeply changing and shifting intellectual landscape of the 1960s. Even more important for my own agenda, I came to see that there was a *genuinely* critical role for Christian intellectuals to play, a role that no established male voice was proffering. These early years of my doctoral study had created a rather deeply felt distress in me about how often liberal theologians reiterated calls for "critical thinking," and yet how infrequently they actually said anything that really was critical of reigning social convention. By contrast, Soelle's work resonated in my hearing, with new insight about the spiritual malaise of the culture of which I was a part. As it subsequently turned out, it would be Dorothee Soelle and other "unnatural" speakers from the cultural worlds that constituted the "underside of history" who collectively moved the theological task onto a new path of reimaging a not yet realized *Phantasie* of hope and resistance, not out of a traditionalist certitude, but rather out of the fragments of faith remembered by those who had struggled for new possibilities in the past.[4] The work of theology, it became clear, was not primarily explanatory, the creation of justifications for the way things are, but rather an evocative task, a calling forth of energy and power to struggle against spiritual entrapment. This revisioning of the world aimed to equip us with the courage and passion to struggle toward what is not yet and resist what is death dealing. Such a reorientation to what is the proper work of the theologian was indeed good news to my ears!

For me, learning to actually participate in the fuller unfolding of this way of doing theology, of moving beyond theological reflection as a "mere" effort to uncover positive knowledge, took some time. When my own students asked me why I did not give more constructive attention to theology itself, I often said, with some truthfulness, that I was insufficiently the poet and left the invocations of hope to the Soelles, the Heywards, the Williamses, the Guiterrezes, and others whose poetic conjuring abilities exceeded my own.[5] Yet in time, my own theological voice was reshaped by the breaking open of imagination that these most impacting colleagues elicited. I am not speaking with hyperbole when I say that Soelle's voice was primal in my own recovery of theological hope and helped me understand that theological utterance is a form that courage takes in situations in which despair is the easier course.

The Importance of Reading Soelle through Postmodernist Eyes

I have reiterated my reasons for celebrating Soelle's place in contemporary theology to make clear her methodological discontinuity with the generation of Protestant theologians who preceded her. This seems important to me, in part, because for some, including some contemporary feminist theologians in the academy, Soelle's work is sometimes perceived as standing more in continuity with the cultural traditions of German male-generated theology than with postmodernist sensibilities. While many Roman Catholic feminists have engaged her work seriously, perhaps because of the impact of political theology in Catholic circles, too few Protestant feminists, with the exception of those included in this volume, have focused attention on her work. By contrast, I believe that it is essential to interpret Soelle's theological stance so that she can be seen clearly as a groundbreaker within the development of postmodernist theological discourses. She pioneered in finding a way to articulate Christian meaning concretely, in a climate in which there was no abstract, "scientific," or privileged epistemic standpoint. She should be credited as one who found her way by doing the work of faithful speaking when the very possibility of affirmative theological utterances was very much in doubt. As she herself has stressed, and as her earliest published works attested, Soelle understood and accepted from the outset that traditionalist transcendentalist epistemic claims were passé, and that any direct access to theistic transcendentalism was no longer intellectually tenable. For her, Christian integrity required surrendering noetically privileged claims to Truth. The contestability of theological ways of construing life is presumed and moral practice is the measure of the integrity of theological speech. It is the power of theological utterance to illumine the depth dimensions of life that commend it to listeners, not the power of Christian cultural tradition per se. For her, as I have already stressed, the cultural domination of Christianity is a problem to faithfulness, not an advantage to those who desire a living faith.

This, surely, was the import of her way of reformulating Christology. Her way of making sense of Jesus as Christ-bearer situates his significance in the fully human life-world, and in a way that is spiritually immanent in that world, a point that Carter Heyward's eloquent essay included in this volume makes clear.[6] Christ "the representative" is one who holds open a place in time and history that enables historical movement toward human fulfillment, especially of those who have not counted in the dominant historical scripts. What is essential to appreciate is Soelle's unqualified acceptance of the necessity of indirect address to transcendence through immanent spirituality. Hers is a transcendence found in radical humanism and in embrace of the concrete particularity of the created order of things. There is no pie-in-the-sky for Soelle. Faith is the ability to see divine presence with us in a way that deepens our communal struggles for life. Faith enables a godly, reverent humanism. At the same time, Soelle shaped a powerful critique of reigning theological liberalism, a critique hardly noticed by her contemporaries.

Soelle's Critique of Liberalism

In evaluating Soelle's theological contribution, it is also of particular importance not only to observe but especially to emphasize how distinctive this criticism is and how it differs from the endless accusations made against liberalism in the current academy. The current assault on liberalism bears the stamp of the present reactionary climate of neoliberalism. Liberalism is chastised ad nauseam for its failure to repeat Christian teaching in a sufficiently pristine traditionalist guise.

Soelle, by comparison, noted the privatizing and personalistic subjectivism in the way liberals specified the arena in which faith operated. Contrary to the endless charges that liberalism compromised dangerously with modernity, Soelle located the problem in acquiescence to power and privilege and capitulation to spiritual privatization. This limiting of the spheres of spirituality to inwardness was itself a massive form of acquiescence to domination. Locating theological meaning only in the psychological dimension was the form that obeisance to existing power took.

Her brilliant critique of her own teacher, Rudolph Bultmann, makes clear that the way forward for a progressive spirituality must avoid the subjectivism of interpreting Christian truth exclusively as a matter of personal transformation. To my mind, her analysis of the limits of Bultmann's psychologizing of theology deserves to stand as one of the most important constructive theological texts of the twentieth century.[7] And it must be conceded that just such spiritual subjectivism has continued to characterize mainline liberal theology over most of the intervening years. Political theology, in Soelle's rendering of it, must always be interpreted as a protest against personalistic reductionism and as a way of construing the irreducibly public meaning of faith.

As post-Second World War attention began to shift toward a radical interdependence of nation-states created by the political-economic hegemony of postwar capitalism, Soelle remained mindful of the dangers of these privatizing tendencies. She saw them as parallel to the failures of German Christianity under Nazism. Any embrace of a Statist authoritarian theology, she believed, extended anti-Judaism and what Soelle never ceased to name as "Christofascism," a reality she believed is alive and well in our present theological scene. She resisted more deeply than any of her contemporaries the strong tendencies of churchly Christianity to embrace the status quo in our current context.

An unapologetic leftist, she rejected the Cold War ideology that increasingly came to pervade Christian teaching, a tendency to conflate spirituality with matters deeper and higher than politics, a reading that made postwar theological liberalism congenial to and welcomed by cold warriors. At a time when personal piety rather than the address of public issues supported the reigning anti-communist stance, Soelle's work cut against the grain and began to offer a genuine alternative to the Eurocentrism of the dominant worldview.

No doubt it was her intense and searing awareness of German Christians' earlier complicity in Nazism, which sharpened her hermeneutical suspicions of any form of triumphalism in theology and also provided her with an especially clear and critical awareness of the role Christian intellectuals should play. No one should miss this point crucial to Soelle's political theology—any methodology that addresses personal well-being apart from the transformation of historically based communal well-being reinforces the dominant and dominating patterns of existing reality.

It is essential, then, to situate Soelle's work in the contestations that began in the Vietnam era and that continue until today. Vietnam represented the first occasion when the signs of resistance to Eurocentric cultural hegemony began to take definite political shape. Looked at in this light, it becomes clear that the "death of God" discussions emergent in Europe and in the United States were, in fact, initial cultural responses that foreshadow and manifest a response to this decentering of the western Eurocentric worldview.

Since the death of God discussions of the late 1950s and 1960s have been more caricatured than analyzed in the interim, it is important to revisit them, not as a symptom of "liberal theological superficiality," as they are often construed in today's "neoliberal theological climate," but rather as a sign that the wider social dislocations caused by Euro-American economic and political imperialisms were beginning to register.[8] Such resistance to these powerful imperializing changes has only increased, not ceased, in the meanwhile. As we assess developments in the interim, it is especially necessary to see the connection between such resistance and all that is specified by the virulent anti-Americanism that we now designate as "terrorism." Failure to see this point may make discerning and honest Christian reading of the current political scene not only difficult but actually impossible. I have long agreed with my former colleague, Tom Driver, that the 1960s must be remembered as a genuine cultural watershed, when the first signs of the blindness to other cultures that Euro-American intellectual hegemony was generating began to become visible on a global scale.[9] Since then, Euro-American cultures have shown many signs of internal struggle, and tensions between those who seek to reassert an uncritical western cultural supremacy and those willing to learn what it means to reimage European and North American traditions as but one strand of a far more complex and inclusive planetary cultural diversity.

It is this awareness, with its openness to discover and employ less imperialistic modes of communal self-understanding, that should be foremost in our minds when we ask what constitutes the best in those developments we term "postmodernism." The death of God conversations signaled the need to acknowledge this cultural shift, and those like Soelle who searched for more modest and more concrete forms of theological speech created a "testimonial voice" in which Christian theology called us to and evoked a deeper humanity and an ongoing solidarity with real suffering in our actual historical moment.

Keeping a Genuinely Critical Postmodernist Option Alive amid Reactionary Politics

The reason it is vitally important to situate alternative liberationist voices, including Soelle's, on the postmodernist side of the modern/postmodern continuum is precisely because of the growing reactionary trend already alluded to, within western and nonwestern cultures—that trend I have referred to here as neoliberalism. When references are made, as they frequently are these days, to growing political conservatism, it is really the triumph of neoliberalism to which people refer. But neoliberalism is neither conservatism in the concrete form that conservatism took in the western past, nor is it in any serious sense a reassertion of traditionalism, though a nostalgic embrace of traditionalism may make frightened religious folk feel safe in light of the deep and massive changes occurring. The triumph of neoliberalism is due to the massive and successful redefining of the terms of public debate accomplished in the Reagan/Bush/Bush2 era. Even the ethos of centrist and chastened liberalism that the Clinton political interim created must not be read as anything more than a temporary interlude, a slowing down rather than a reversal of the triumph of the new ideology.

Its intellectual trump card has been its success in convincing intellectual elites that the need for ideology is, in fact, dead. Ironically, the deadliest of western political ideologies has turned out to be the one that proclaims that ideology is no longer necessary, that we have transcended the vagaries of politics through the triumph of capitalist modes of production, unleashed from the interference of the contentious debates that political interests interject. What politicians cannot accomplish can be left to the wisdom of "free" market exchange, in which mechanisms of efficiency and rationality prevail. The new neoliberal reaction—proclaiming a triumph of markets over politics as the way forward in human problem solving—has mounted an extraordinarily successful reinterpretation of history in which the intrinsic good of capitalist political economy can now be seen by all who possess a responsible concern for human well-being. Even more astonishing is neoliberal success in dramatically reoriented public dialogue and debate so as to erase public awareness of the existence of any genuinely left dissent about the future of political-economy and public policy. Alternatives to capitalism have become truly unthinkable.

In addition, the new Right has launched a remarkably effective disinformation campaign against any remaining liberation movements, a campaign that depicts progressive political agendas for change as passé or even as misguided efforts at social engineering. A continuous assault is being made on groups that propose strategies for social justice. Those who want social change are characterized as self-righteous "do-gooders" who traffic in moralistic attempts to enforce "political correctness."[10] These attacks have worked well in silencing liberals. Neoliberals have succeeded, to a distressing degree, in creating a widespread contempt for pro-democratic politics, especially in academic contexts. An atmosphere of thinly veiled intolerance prevails in academy whenever the subject of politics is up, but most important, any criticism of capitalist political economy, as such, is taken as a symptom of an outdated worldview forged by the ideologies of the cold war era. The end of ideology, we should be aware, is really the elimination of discourses seriously critical of capitalism.

It is because of this intellectual climate, itself the result of the new conditions of "masked ideology," that we may well characterize the contemporary political scene as what, two decades ago, Bertram Gross termed "friendly fascism."[11] We must recover the capacity to read liberation theologies, including especially Soelle's political theology, as "first wave" postmodernist Christian theological reflection, which we must continue to hone and craft in ever new, constructive directions. To do so makes it obvious that the road ahead permits no abandonment of the concrete justice agendas that have engaged activist Christians in the immediate past. Any destabilizing of the agendas of anti-white racist work, sexual and gender justice, or resistance to poverty and class oppression is capitulation to neoliberalism. Refusal of these critical agendas is never the result of greater awareness of complexity and cultural sophistication. It is capitulation to the powers that are in place.

All of this is difficult to see, in part, because in the last decade of the twentieth century, the enthusiasm for being a postmodernist has gained standing in the various academic guilds while historical amnesia has eroded awareness of why postmodernism matters from a moral point of view. In short, the rhetoric about postmodernism has become thoroughly academized and far too fashionable for our own good. Those who can remember what historical amnesia is about should be deeply concerned about the losses of critical consciousness that all such amnesia entails.

As a result, in some contemporary literary hermeneutical circles, rhetorical cleverness has become a substitute for serious moral-political analysis. And a rather thin and clever, and largely apolitical, sort of "modernist"/postmodernism has appeared, generating its own highly technical style accessible only to academic in-groups. Because postmodernism presumes a social constructionist awareness that our history is created by us even as it is being named, the creative power of the activity of human speech has sometimes been embraced as though radical ways of speaking were themselves the heart of political change. The result is precisely the loss of the intrinsically social character of human species-being that radical social theory was shaped to protect.

The entire European radical social theoretical tradition, what is known as "critical theory," aimed to correct bourgeoisie misrepresentation of human species-being as possible apart from forms of political life and social cooperation. All of the movements of critical theory that arose in Europe in resistance to the earlier rise of fascism were born out of respect for the moral value of human political construction, but the conception of politics was fulsome, involving the creation of new alliances and forms of community. Today, among the new literati, the sense of the political has become attenuated. Human speech acts, important as an aspect of social change, now sometimes become the central metaphor for all historical action. It sometimes seems, in reading youthful postmodernism, that the authors actually believe that revolutions take place in classrooms and that acts of verbal violence are of the same moral magnitude as long-standing, institutionally embodied injustice.[12] Ironically, today, the most elegant postmodernist discourses can participate in the privatizing, subjectivizing, and depoliticizing of all truth claims in precisely the way Soelle's work specified one of the dangers of liberalism. Furthermore, the reduction of politics to verbal performance goes hand in hand with an increasing cynicism about morality itself, a cynicism that leads to a subjective rereading of and dismissal of the significance of morality. The result is a new quietism about political and economic reconstruction that exquisitely serves a triumphant neoliberalism.

Even so, for most spiritually engaged postmodernists, the fact that the social world is a human moral construction still continues to deepen the moral seriousness and carefulness of our actions and choices. Social constructionism enables us to see what is at stake in the way we enact our social morality because it is now clear historically that, over time, we will be stuck with the sort of world that we, in fact, embody or conjure. From this viewpoint, the morality we shape is the true measure of our spirituality. However, as noted, when creativity for its own sake displaces moral seriousness, enthusiasm for postmodernism can lead to the sort of moral relativism that sees morality merely as taste or arbitrary personal preference.[13] It has become fashionable among younger academics to pooh-pooh any moral seriousness or any attempt to ground morality in shared values. Among a few postmodernist cultural critics, any effort at reconstructive religious and moral discourse has come to be suspect simply as such.

It is this moral relativism, even moral myopia, which Soelle and her husband, Fulbert Steffensky, criticized in their recent discussion of postmodernism.[14] It would be a serious mistake, however, to read this essay as any sort of indication that Soelle is currently moving into a more traditionalist theological voice. Her recent concerns about an uncritical postmodernism must be situated not in a traditionalist voice but in her growing worries about the success of neoliberal cultural reformation and about the increasing power of the dominant political economy to erase concrete historical memories and to desensitize us both to the reality of social sin and to the need to actively resist social evil.

The Importance of Rereading Political Theology in the Concrete Context of German Critical Theory

What many young intellectuals on this side of the Atlantic seem to have forgotten, or perhaps, given the current cultural preferences for French intellectual guidance rather than German, have never fully grasped, is the continued relevance of the intellectual project that the critical theory tradition addressed.

Its efforts aimed at the failures of the political left itself and at the need to find more creative cultural strategies for change, and in particular to discern better, more humane ways to shape a genuinely democratic culture. The German experience of fascism exposed the terrible failures of processes of personal identity formation within that society. What sort of cultural life, the critical theorists asked, would sustain a community in the process of struggling toward genuine social equality? In particular, German critical thinkers searched for a social theory that not only illumined class formation through the workings of political economy—long the goal of Marxist and neo-Marxist work—but also sought to make greater sense of the political apathy and preferences for the status quo that characterized those who lived and labored in capitalist culture. It was chiefly the lack of political resistance to destructive practices within capitalist societies that needed to be better understood. Trying to account for the political and cultural complacency of Germans and their willingness to endure socially generated inequality was what led German critical thinkers to begin their reexamination of religion.

A few, including the younger Tillich and several Jewish philosophers, set out to develop a genuinely critical religion that addressed these concerns and that aimed at discernment of the spiritual depth of their culture and the unmasking of its social untruths. However, the first generation of German critical theorists survived, if they did so, only by going into exile in the United States.[15] Soelle was among a very few in the subsequent generation who survived the demise of Nazism to place her work on the path staked out by critical theory. It is remarkable that she resumed the path of struggle toward a newly critical religious perspective, given that those best known on this side of the Atlantic for extending critical theory were German social philosophers who not only remained hostile to religion but greatly reduced the explicit political commitments that had informed the earlier theory.[16]

Neither Soelle nor liberation theologians who emerged elsewhere have followed German or U.S. academics in abandoning the quest for a critical religion or spirituality that would play a role in unmasking social mystification and create culturally potent religious rituals and practices that would make truthful political consciousness possible. Today, in advanced capitalist societies, the same reluctance exists to refuse political leadership that disparages their interests, and political quietism abounds, making any struggle for alternatives seem futile. The same refusal to enhance conditions for their own personal and communal well-being that stunned the first generation of critical theorists in Germany prevails here as well. And the serious failures of political progressives to create spiritual enthusiasm for genuinely democratic changes continues among us as well.

It was the power of capitalist culture to mesmerize, to create uncritical loyalty, that German intellectuals observed through the rising power of Nazism.

Their entire intellectual project was shaped by a passion to effectually address the spiritual value of democracy. Their suspicions of the power of capitalism to disempower resistance and to mystify its anti-democratic directions during economic crisis are what led German critical theorists to make religious critical reflection central in the work of social reconstruction. Can a seriously postmodernist perspective, one that accepts the decentering of Eurocentric abstract rationalism, afford to abandon these concerns so central to critical theory?

Perhaps it was the utter crassness of the Nazi-generated Euro-centric fantasy of the so-called Aryan myth, a version of racial supremacy vulgar to the more highly educated gaze of U.S. intellectuals, that makes it hard to read the parallels between our situation and earlier German fascism. As the quest for a genuinely critical theory gave way to the more muted academic, and less politically urgent, voice of Jürgen Habermas, the urgency of the task of demystifying social reaction has receded.

The truth is that the present spiritual hegemony of what economic historians sometimes designate as Late/Transnational Capitalist Political Economy has actually been even more successful at obscuring growing social injustice than earlier German critical social theory feared that capitalism would be. We live today in a situation in which we can readily observe the social construction of apolitical human identity, and the spiritual malaise of social forgetfulness manifests itself all around us. The death of politics is proclaimed as the advent of harmony and the automatic progress of market wealth production, a wealth production that assures the triumph of cultural harmony and the nearly inevitable improvement of the human condition. Never mind that many voices warn of impending catastrophe in environmental degradation, that the scope and scale of human suffering created by the way the political economy itself functions is documented daily. There probably has never been a time in U.S. history when dissent from loyalty to existing political order would be met with more violent, or at least vituperative, reaction.

Dorothee Soelle's life work eloquently attests that participation in and collusion with any form of social amnesia is a most devastating form of evil. She has lived her life in adamant refusal of any triumphalist rereading of Christian doctrinal supremacy, letting no one who bears the self-designation "Christian" forget the genocidal consequences of the self-satisfied and self-assured theological voice. But it is not only the rereading of Soelle's personal work that is at stake in the way we position her legacy. Even more importantly, all of the ongoing work of constructive Christian theology will suffer if we fail to see the concrete shape that her work and that of others have laid out as the proper direction of authentic postmodernism. We need urgently to interpret all of the recent theological labor done in the service of suffering and silenced communities as the best exemplifications of postmodernist Christian discourses. Black, Latin American, African, and Asian male theologians; feminist and womanist voices from every community; gay, lesbian, and transgendered truth tellers of every culture; and indigenous voices everywhere must be counted as important expressions of Christian postmodernist theological speech.

Whatever criticisms can be made of liberation theologies of the first wave—and in my view, much needs criticism—all are engaged thinkers for whom theological discourse is unapologetically a species of contestable and contextual language. And all such speech aims not chiefly at understanding that world but at reshaping that world spiritually.

Though old habits of definitive authoritative voice die hard, especially among male liberation theology speakers, liberation vocalizations have aimed not at positive knowledges legitimated through Eurocentric cultural hegemony but at the critical knowledge of understanding the "lies, secrets, and silences" that keep power in place. This can enable us to imagine a future, to avoid being locked into the "naturalized scripts" contained in the dominant prescriptions of what our futures must be. The point is important precisely because among far too many academics in major theological centers, liberation theologies have been treated with something bordering on contempt, as fads, or more recently, as "overly ideological" perspectives lacking in appropriate intellectual elegance and creativity. Far too many contemporary U.S. theologians seem unaware of the maldistribution of intellectual tools and resources that support the "elegance" of the work that we are able to do at the center of the global system as opposed to those working in poverty, without those resources.

While liberation theologies have deeply reshaped some seminary programs and a few other arenas of pastoral education, university-based discourses have become increasingly oriented to critique or deconstruction of ecclesial claims. In many religious studies contexts, theology itself has come to be viewed exclusively as a form of ideological mystification, and the role of the intellectual who studies religion has been cast, more and more, merely as deconstructive. There is no problem, per se, with deconstructive work, but the political currents outlined here make such fixations on critique dangerous to our public spiritual health, although deconstructive critique is a safe course in universities and colleges being pressured to move in a neoliberal direction. The directions of the theological work that we are called to do in the future requires that we continue to walk the road of justice makers who are also truth tellers. Like Dorothee, we must be unapologetically in love with life and angry at all that inhibits creatures from experiencing the joys and pleasures of abundant life, or living as godly lovers who know the ecstasy of being with the Divine Companion.

Notes

1. H. Richard Niebuhr, "How My Mind Has Changed," in Harold Fey, ed., *How My Mind Has Changed* (New York: Vantage Books, 1962), 69–80.

2. Adrienne Rich, *Your Native Land, Your Life: Poems* (New York: W. W. Norton, 1986), 3–6; see also Rich, *On Lies, Secrets and Silence: Selected Prose, 1966–1978* (New York: W. W. Norton, 1979).

3. Dorothee Soelle, *Christ the Representative: An Essay in Theology after the 'Death of God'* (Philadelphia: Fortress, 1967); see also her *Political Theology* (Philadelphia: Fortress, 1974).

4. The phrase is widely used in liberation theologies rooted in Latin America. It originated first in the writing of extraordinary Peruvian theologian Gustavo Gutierrez, *A Theology of Liberation* (Maryknoll, N.Y.: Orbis, 1971).

5. I cite those theological writers whose work has been most influential in helping me understand the importance of the methodological shift I am celebrating here: Dorothee Soelle, Carter Heyward, Delores Williams, Gustavo Gutierrez, and others.

6. See the article in this volume by Carter Heyward, "Crossing Over: Dorothee Soelle and the Transcendence of God."

7. Dorothee Soelle, *Political Theology,* 83–98.

8. The term *neoliberal* here denotes social theorists who endorse the claim that "free markets" actually exist and constitute the "essence" of capitalism. Furthermore, they contend that government interference and state intervention in "the economy" should be avoided. It is a post-Keynsian version of laissez faire theory, which claims a positivist status as the only true "objectivist social science."

9. My former colleague Tom Faw Driver, Paul Tillich Professor Emeritus at Union Theological Seminary in New York, was the first Christian theologian in the United States to identify the importance of this cultural decentering. It is also relevant to notice that Professor Soelle was perhaps the first theologian to regularly do her theological work cross-culturally, writing in two languages and working and teaching not only in Europe and North America but from time to time in Central and Latin America.

10. See the important study by Richard Feldstein, *Political Correctness: A Response to the Cultural Left* (Minneapolis: University of Minnesota Press, 1997).

11. Bertram Gross, *Friendly Fascism: The New Face of Power in America* (New York: M. Evans, 1980).

12. I detect a tendency toward such depoliticizing in the recent work of feminist philosopher Judith Butler. She sometimes seems to me to reduce human activity to creative speech acts. She also seems to me to distinguish insufficiently between personal violence in the form of hostile and demeaning speech acts and violence of a collective and institutionalized sort. Bombs and weapons are, morally, even more heinous than verbal abuse. See Judith Butler, *Excitable Speech* (New York: Routledge, 1997).

13. Notions about the social construction of morality do not necessarily lead to the conclusion that morality is capricious and lacking in any intersubjective objectivity. Cultural relativism, while requiring us to develop more sophisticated ways of legitimating moral claims, does not vitiate the validity of well-formed moral claims. Moral relativism is not the same as scientific or cultural relativity.

14. Dorothee Soelle and Fulbert Steffensky, *Zwietracht in Eintracht: ein Religionsgespräch* (Zurich: Pendo Verlag, 1996).

15. Tillich's collaboration with other critical theorists is reflected in his earliest work; see Paul Tillich, *The Socialist Decision* (trans. Franklin Sherman; New York: Harper and Row, 1977). It is important to remember that Tillich became more reluctant to engage political and economic issues directly after he emigrated to this country. It should be noted that Soelle's encounter with critical theory came through the influence of Ernst Bloch and Hannah Arendt. See the preface of Soelle's *Against the Wind: A Memoir of a Radical Christian* (Minneapolis: Fortress, 1999), xi.

16. In the United States, German critical theory is understood through the contemporary work of Jürgen Habermas. To some extent, reading critical theory through Habermas also results in a depoliticizing of that tradition. Habermas became far less focused on praxis and more oriented to reconstructing theory after the 1960s. He also is far less interested in religion and cultural change than some of the earlier critical theorists. For a reliable account of critical theory, see Trent Schroyer, *The Critique of Domination: The Origins and Development of Critical Theory* (New York: George Braziller, 1973). A further reliable source on the implications of critical theory in relation to feminist theology is Marsha Hewitt, *Critical Theory of Religion* (Minneapolis: Fortress, 1995).

Contributors

ANNE LLEWELLYN BARSTOW is a retired professor of history at SUNY College at Old Westbury. Some of her recent publications are *Witchcraze: A New History of the European Witch Hunts* (San Francisco: Pandora, 1994); *War's Dirty Secret: Rape, Prostitution, and Other Crimes against Women* (Cleveland: Pilgrim, 2000); "Violence and Memory: The Politics of Denial," *JAAR* 68, no. 3 (September 2000): 591–602; and "Rape," *Encyclopedia Britannica* (forthcoming). Currently she is developing a critique of how just war theory is being used to justify recent U.S. wars. She has been a friend of Dorothee Soelle since her years at Union Theological Seminary and a coworker for human rights in Latin America.

ANDREA BIELER received her doctorate in 1993 at the University of Kassel. She served as assistant professor for practical theology at the Divinity School of the Georg-August-Universität Göttingen in Germany. Since 2000, she has been associate professor of Christian worship at Pacific School of Religion/Graduate Theological Union in Berkeley. Her new book, *Die Sehnsucht nach dem verlorenen Himmel. Jüdische und christliche Reflexionen zu Gottesdienstreform und Predigtkultur im 19. Jahrhundert (Yearning for the Lost Heaven: Jewish and Christian Reflections on Liturgical Reform and Preaching Culture in the Nineteenth Century)*, was published by Kohlhammer Verlag in 2003. Research interests and publications include feminist and multicultural perspectives on liturgy, liturgical theology, ritual studies, and Bible drama. She became acquainted with Dorothee Soelle in Hamburg many years ago and organized with others an international symposium on the occasion of her seventieth birthday. She is also an admirer of Dorothee's husband, Fulbert Steffensky, and of his work in the field of worship.

CHRISTINE E. GUDORF is professor of religious studies at Florida International University in Miami. She met Soelle in 1976, when she was Soelle's teaching assistant at Union Theological Seminary in New York. After receiving her doctorate from Columbia University's joint program with Union, Gudorf taught ethics at Xavier University in Cincinnati from 1978 to 1993, before moving to FIU. She has published books and articles in feminist ethics, liberation theologies, women and development, environmental ethics, and case method in ethics. Her most recent articles include "Resymbolizing Life: Religion on Population and Development" and "The Erosion of Sexual Dimorphism: Challenge to Religions and Religious Ethics"; and her newest book, *Boundaries: Cases and Analysis in Environmental Ethics,* coauthored with James Huchingson, was published by Georgetown University Press in 2003.

BEVERLY WILDUNG HARRISON is Carolyn Williams Beaird Professor Emeritus of Christian Ethics at the Union Theological Seminary in New York. She was privileged to have Dorothee Soelle as a colleague and friend at Union for a span of fifteen years. She now lives at Redbud Springs, a small residential collective of women who do educational work and offer hospitality to justice workers and writers. She is currently working on a follow-up volume to her earlier work, *Making the Connections* (Boston: Beacon, 1985). The new work also contains contributions by a group of her former students who teach in the field of Christian ethics to enhance its usefulness in teaching feminist ethics.

NANCY HAWKINS is assistant professor of systematic theology at St. Bernard's Graduate School of Theology and Ministry in Rochester, New York. Her interest in the theology of Dorothee Soelle began at Fordham University where she completed her doctoral studies. Her dissertation focuses on Dorothee Soelle's political theology and how Soelle's theology of God impacts the areas of suffering, feminism, and mysticism. She is a member of the Sisters, Servants of the Immaculate Heart of Mary, located in Scranton, Pennsylvania. She has been an educator for over twenty years and is greatly interested in the theological question of suffering and how it impacts the life of faith.

CARTER HEYWARD is Howard Chandler Robbins Professor of Theology at the Episcopal Divinity School in Cambridge, Massachusetts. Along with Beverly Harrison, she is a founding member of Redbud Springs, a small intentional justice and peace-building community in the mountains of western North Carolina. She is also the founder of "Free Rein," a therapeutic horseback-riding center in Brevard, North Carolina. She was a student of Dorothee Soelle's and, over the years, has become a close friend. The two have led a number of retreats together in the United States, Germany, and Switzerland. They were also together in a Witness for Peace delegation to Nicaragua in 1990.

Heyward is author or editor of more than a dozen books, including *Saving Jesus from Those Who Are Right: Rethinking What It Means to Be Christian* (Minneapolis: Fortress, 1999); and *God in the Balance: Christian Spirituality in Times of Terror* (Cleveland: Pilgrim, 2002).

FLORA A. KESHGEGIAN is assistant professor of systematic theology at the Episcopal Theological Seminary of the Southwest in Austin, Texas. She is the author of *Redeeming Memories: A Theology of Healing and Transformation* (Nashville: Abingdon, 2000), and numerous articles, including the entries "Memory" and "Suffering" in *Dictionary of Feminist Theologies,* (ed. Letty M. Russell and Shannon Clarkson; Louisville: Westminster/John Knox, 1996). Among her research interests are theologies of power, redemption, and history. Interdisciplinary in her approach, she explores the challenges posed by suffering, the dynamics of remembrance, and the nature of hope in history. She has found rich resources for her work in Dorothee Soelle's theology, especially Soelle's early work on suffering.

DIANNE L. OLIVER is assistant professor of religion at the University of Evansville in Evansville, Indiana, and was previously Program Director at the Wabash Center for Teaching and Learning in Theology and Religion in Crawfordsville, Indiana. Her research interests are in the intersection of theology, ethics, and spirituality, which frequently focus on liberation and feminist theologies and pedagogies. Currently she is exploring the understanding of community in ecological theology and the concept of dissent as a paradigm in education. Her interest and background in Soelle's theology is evident in her doctoral dissertation, "'Bound into the Web of Life': The Theological Vision of Dorothee Soelle," completed at Vanderbilt University in 2001, which explores the revisioning of transcendence as key to Soelle's theology. During the writing process, she had the opportunity to interview Soelle about her work both in the United States and at her home in Hamburg.

SARAH K. PINNOCK is assistant professor of contemporary religious thought at Trinity University in San Antonio, Texas. Her research deals with post-Holocaust Jewish and Christian thought, the problem of evil, moral objections to theodicy, and existentialist and Marxian philosophy. In 1997–98 on a German Academic Exchange (DAAD) Fellowship at the University of Hamburg, she interviewed Dorothee Soelle and attended many of her public talks, including a fall semester seminar entitled "Theologie und Poesie." Her dissertation, completed at Yale University in 1999, was recently published as *Beyond Theodicy: Jewish and Christian Continental Thinkers Respond to the Holocaust* (Albany, N.Y.: SUNY, 2002).

ROSEMARY RADFORD RUETHER is the Carpenter Professor of Feminist Theology at the Graduate Theological Union in Berkeley, California. For the past twenty-seven years she was the Georgia Harkness Professor of Applied Theology at the Garrett Theological Seminary and Northwestern University in Evanston, Illinois. She is the author or editor of thirty-six books on feminist, liberation, and ecological theologies and the history of Christian thought related to these fields. Some of her recent titles are *Religious Feminism and the Future of the Planet: A Buddhist-Christian Conversation* (New York: Continuum, 2001); *Christianity and the Making of the Modern Family: Ruling Ideologies, Diverse Realities* (Boston: Beacon, 2000); and *Women and Redemption: A Theological History* (Minneapolis: Fortress, 1998). She is a long-term friend of Dorothee Soelle.

MARTIN RUMSCHEIDT is a native German; his education took place in Germany, Switzerland, and Canada, with postgraduate and postdoctoral studies in Germany, Switzerland, the United States, and the Czech Republic. He is an ordained minister in the United Church of Canada and taught since 1970 in religious studies and theology at the University of Windsor and Atlantic School of Theology until he retired in 2002. His areas of research and publication are the work of Karl Barth, Dietrich Bonhoeffer, and Helmut Gollwitzer, as well as the Holocaust, Christian-Jewish relations, and the Protestant church's witness in East Germany from 1945 to 1989. He and his partner Barbara Rumscheidt have translated many German theological texts into English, including works by Luise Schottroff, Dorothee Soelle, and Dietrich Bonhoeffer. Not long after finishing the translations for this volume, Barbara lost her battle with cancer and died on January 20, 2003. Barbara, Martin, and Dorothee had been friends and mentors to each other for many years.

Born in Berlin in 1934, LUISE SCHOTTROFF studied Protestant theology at the Universities of Bonn, Mainz, and Göttingen. She taught New Testament studies at the Universities of Mainz and Kassel; at the latter, she inaugurated an interdisciplinary doctoral program in feminist exegesis and feminist theology. Since 2001, she has been Visiting Professor of New Testament at Pacific School of Religion and the Graduate Theological Union in Berkeley. Her areas of specialization are New Testament exegesis, feminist social history of early Christianity, and feminist liberation theology. She has published widely in German and English such books as *Feminist Interpretation: The Bible in Women's Perspective* (coauthored with Sylvia Schroer and Marie-Theres Wacker; trans. Barbara and Martin Rumscheidt; Minneapolis: Fortress, 1998); *Lydia's Impatient Sisters: A Feminist Social History of Early Christianity* (trans. Barbara and Martin Rumscheidt; Louisville: Westminster/John Knox, 1995); and *Let the Oppressed Go Free: Feminist Perspectives on the New Testament* (trans. Annemarie S. Kidder; Louisville: Westminster/John Knox, 1993).